THE NEW AVENGERS

REVOLUTION

Writer: **Brian Michael Bendis**
Art, Issue #26: **Alex Maleev**
Art, Issues #27-31: **Leinil Yu**
Color Art, Issues #27-31: **Dave McCaig**
Letters: **RS & Comicraft's Albert Deschesne**
Assistant Editors: **Molly Lazer & Aubrey Sitterson**
Editor: **Tom Brevoort**

Collection Editor: **Jennifer Grünwald**
Assistant Editors: **Cory Levine & Michael Short**
Associate Editor: **Mark D. Beazley**
Senior Editor, Special Projects: **Jeff Youngquist**
Senior Vice President of Sales: **David Gabriel**
Production: **Jerron Quality Color & Jerry Kalinowski**
Vice President of Creative: **Tom Marvelli**

Editor in Chief: **Joe Quesada**
Publisher: **Dan Buckley**

PREVIOUSLY:

It was the worst day in Avengers history. Wanda Maximoff, the Scarlet Witch, suffered a total nervous breakdown after losing control of her reality-altering powers. In the chaos created around the breakdown, beloved Avengers Hawkeye, Ant-Man and the Vision lost their lives. Many of the other Avengers were hurt, both emotionally and physically.

Then, the X-Men and the New Avengers found themselves allied against the growing threat of the Scarlet Witch's out-of-control powers. Afterwards, most of the mutants on Earth woke up to find themselves human — without their mutant gene. Only a few hundred mutants remain, when once there were millions. The truth about what happened and the Scarlet Witch's involvement remains a secret to the general population in order to keep the remaining mutants safe from a growing anti-mutant hysteria.

Those who remember the world that Wanda created refer to it as the "House of M." Clint Barton — Hawkeye — was reborn in the House of M, and then brutally killed a second time. He reappeared a second time as the world returned to the way it had been. He hasn't been seen since.

NEW AVENGERS VOL. 6: REVOLUTION. Contains material originally published in magazine form as NEW AVENGERS #26-31. First printing 2007. Hardcover ISBN# 0-7851-2445-4. Softcover ISBN# 978-0-7851-2468-9. Published by MARVEL PUBLISHING, INC., a subsidiary of MARVEL ENTERTAINMENT, INC. OFFICE OF PUBLICATION: 417 5th Avenue, New York, NY 10016. Copyright © 2006 and 2007 Marvel Characters, Inc. All rights reserved. Hardcover: $19.99 per copy in the U.S. and $32.00 in Canada (GST #R127032852). Softcover: $14.99 per copy in the U.S. and $24.00 in Canada (GST #R127032852). Canadian Agreement #40668537. All characters featured in this issue and the distinctive names and likenesses thereof, and all related indicia are trademarks of Marvel Characters, Inc. No similarity between any of the names, characters, persons, and/or institutions in this magazine with those of any living or dead person or institution is intended, and any such similarity which may exist is purely coincidental. **Printed in the U.S.A.** ALAN FINE, CEO Marvel Toys & Publishing Divisions and CMO Marvel Entertainment, Inc.; DAVID GABRIEL, Senior VP of Publishing Sales & Circulation; DAVID BOGART, VP of Business Affairs & Editorial Operations; MICHAEL PASCIULLO, VP Merchandising & Communications; JIM BOYLE, VP of Publishing Operations; DAN CARR, Executive Director of Publishing Technology; JUSTIN F. GABRIE, Managing Editor; SUSAN CRESPI, Production Manager; STAN LEE, Chairman Emeritus. For information regarding advertising in Marvel Comics or on Marvel.com, please contact Joe Maimone, Advertising Director, at jmaimone@marvel.com or 212-576-8534.

10 9 8 7 6 5 4 3 2 1

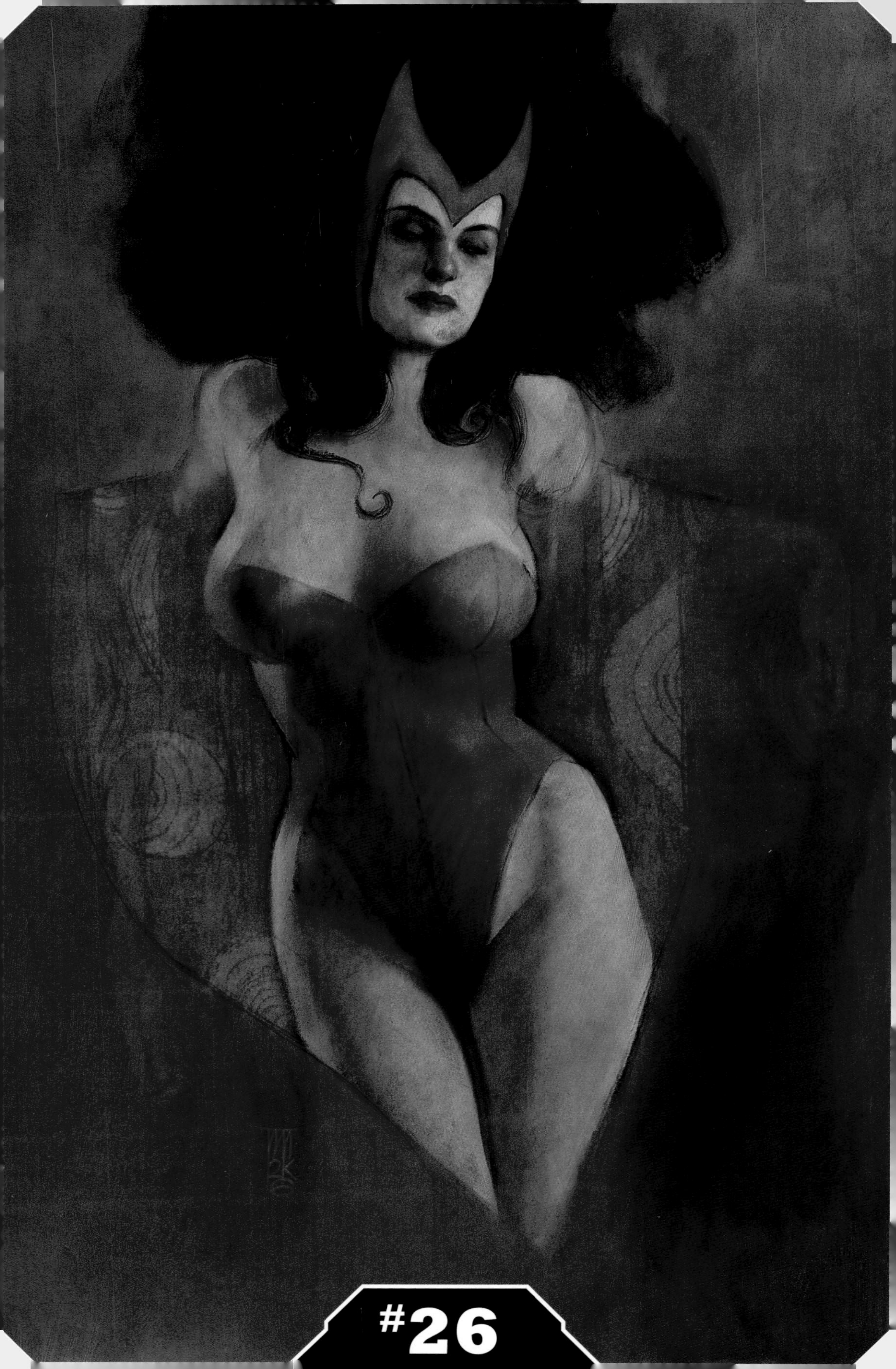
#26

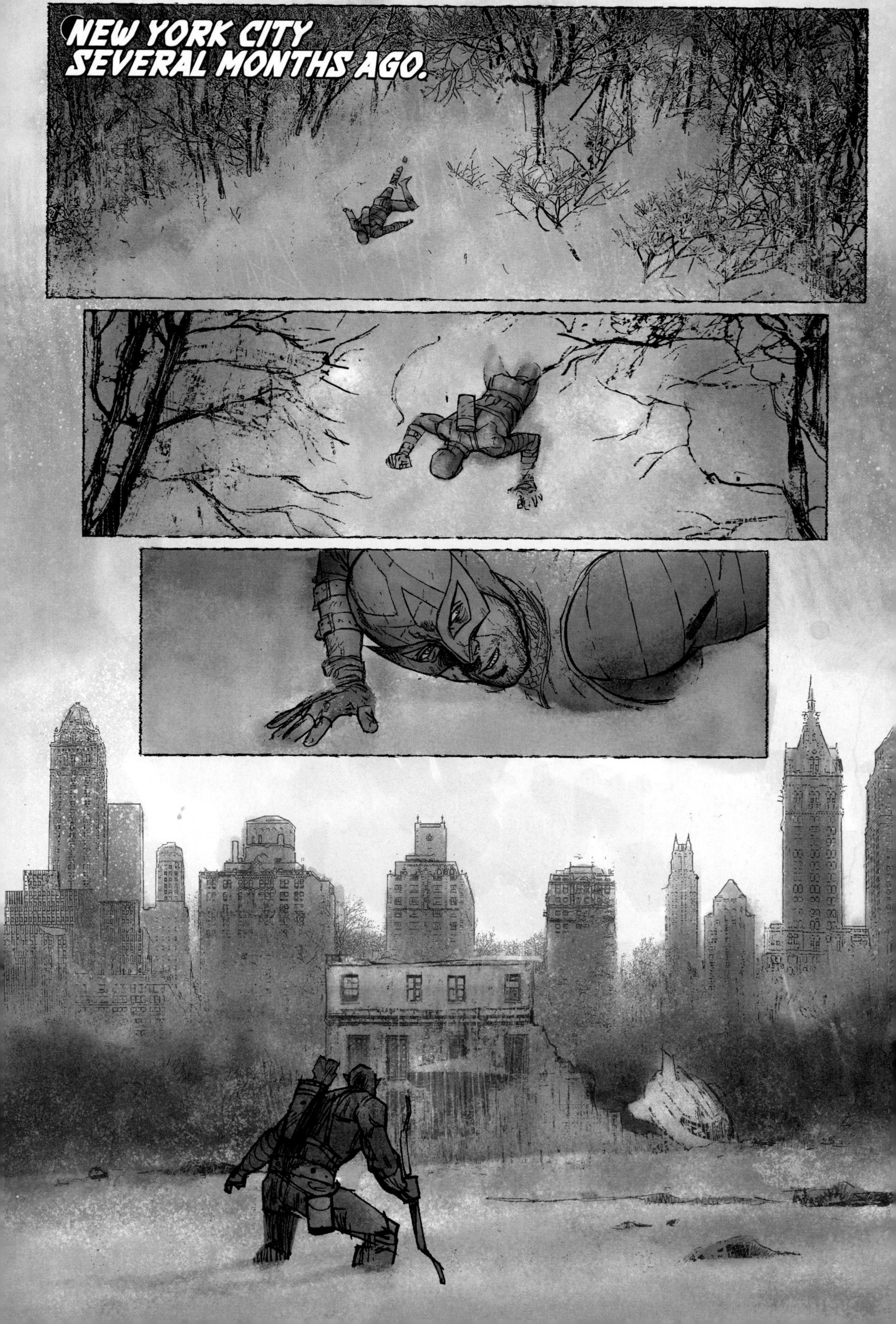
NEW YORK CITY
SEVERAL MONTHS AGO.

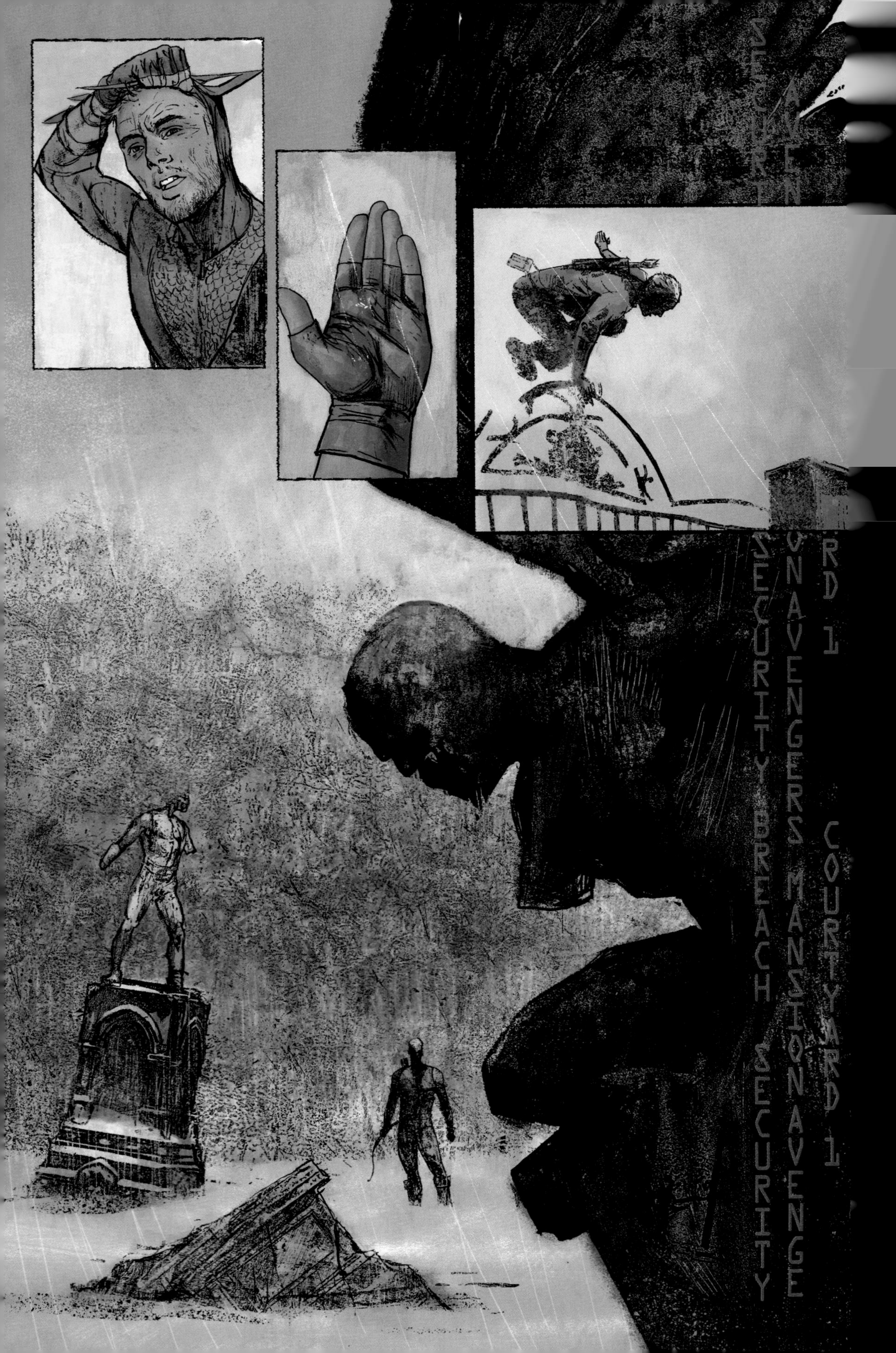
SECURI
AVEN
SECURITY BREACH SECURITY
NAVENGERS MANSION AVENGE
RD 1 COURTYARD 1

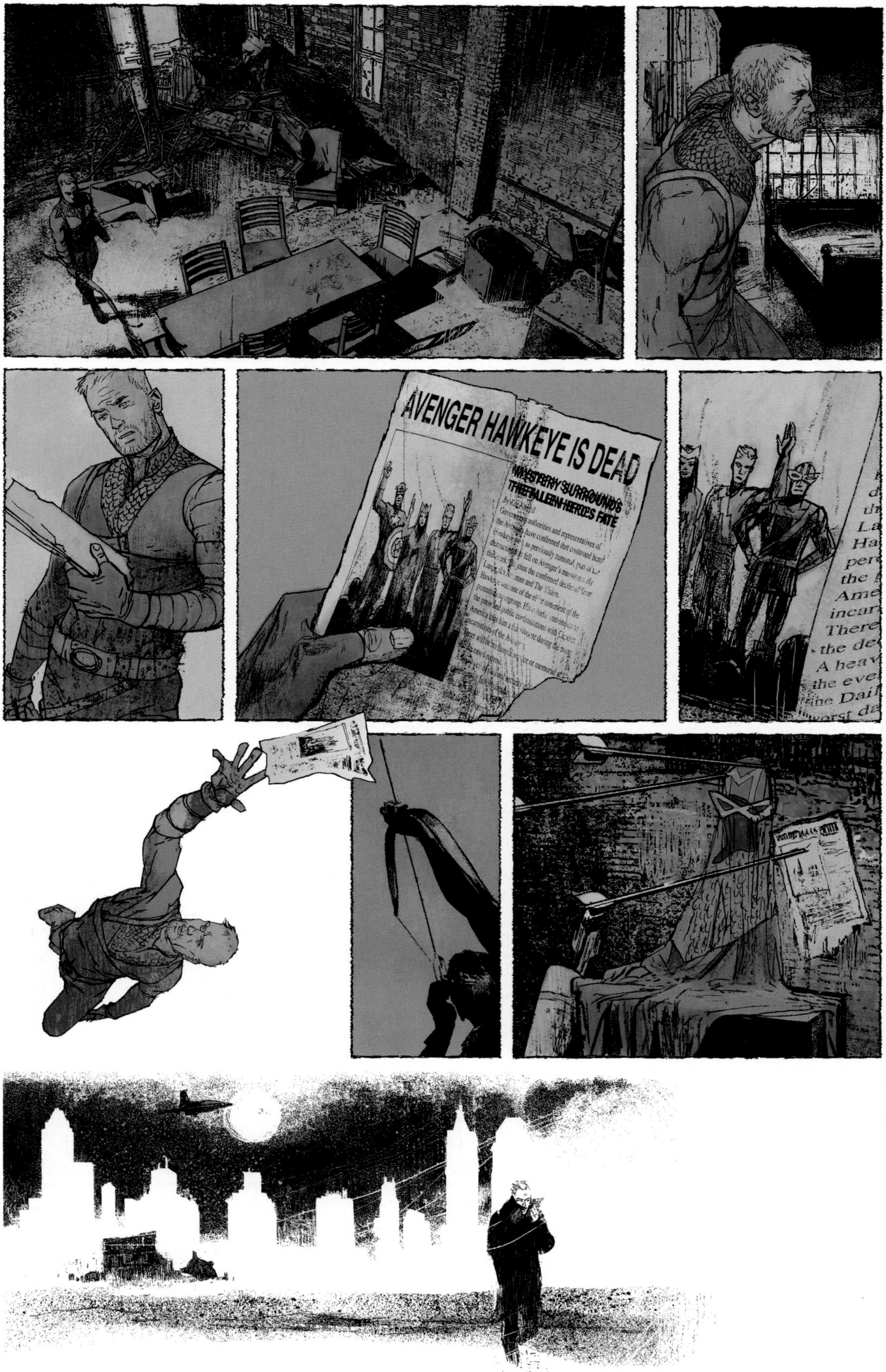
AVENGER HAWKEYE IS DEAD
MYSTERY SURROUNDS
THE FALLEN HEROES FATE

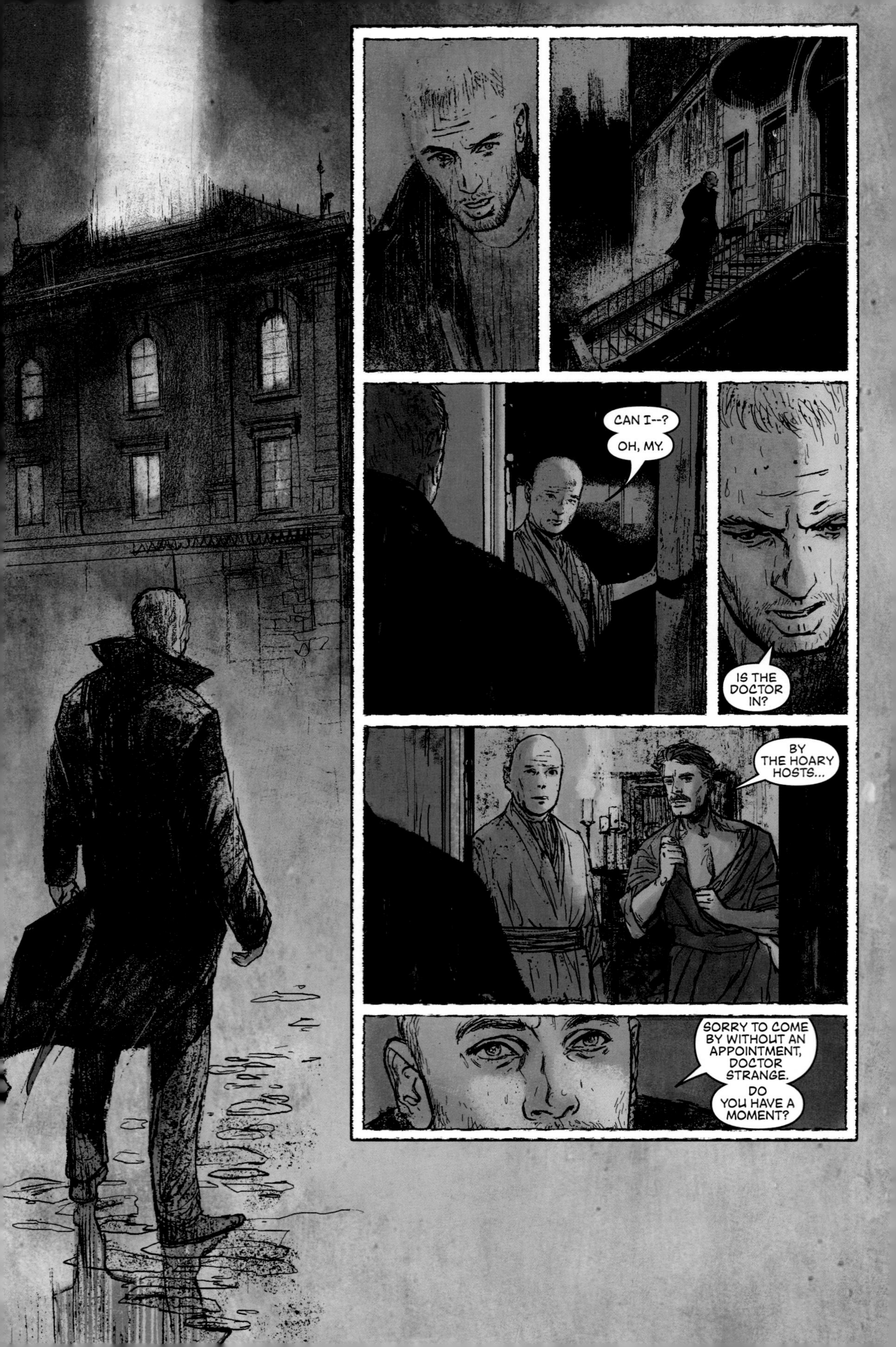
CAN I--?
OH, MY.
IS THE DOCTOR IN?
BY THE HOARY HOSTS...
SORRY TO COME BY WITHOUT AN APPOINTMENT, DOCTOR STRANGE.
DO YOU HAVE A MOMENT?

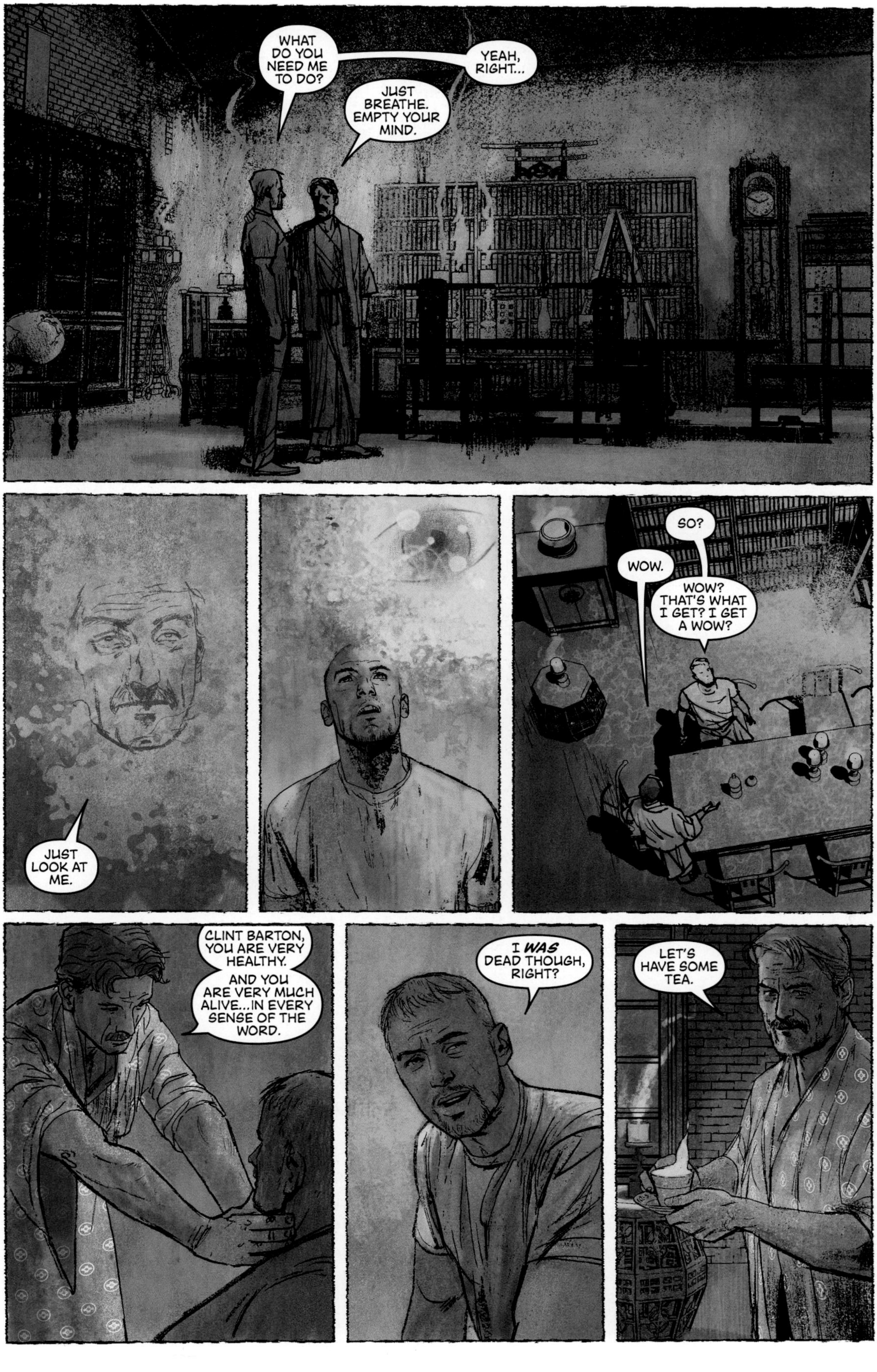
WHAT DO YOU NEED ME TO DO?
YEAH, RIGHT...
JUST BREATHE. EMPTY YOUR MIND.
JUST LOOK AT ME.
SO?
WOW.
WOW? THAT'S WHAT I GET? I GET A WOW?
CLINT BARTON, YOU ARE VERY HEALTHY.
AND YOU ARE VERY MUCH ALIVE...IN EVERY SENSE OF THE WORD.
I WAS DEAD THOUGH, RIGHT?
LET'S HAVE SOME TEA.

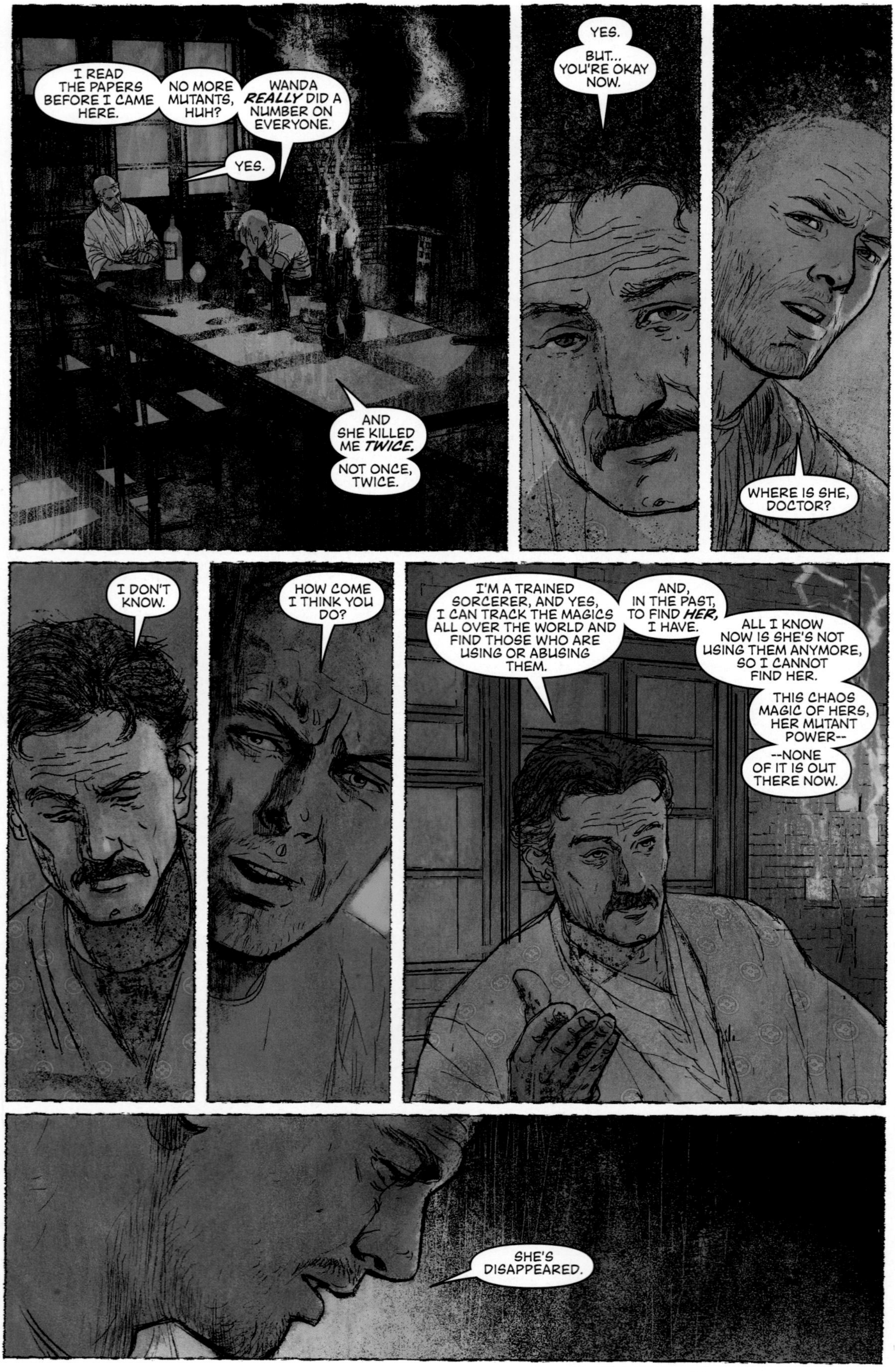
I READ THE PAPERS BEFORE I CAME HERE.
NO MORE MUTANTS, HUH?
WANDA *REALLY* DID A NUMBER ON EVERYONE.
YES.
AND SHE KILLED ME *TWICE.*
NOT ONCE, TWICE.
YES.
BUT... YOU'RE OKAY NOW.
WHERE IS SHE, DOCTOR?
I DON'T KNOW.
HOW COME I THINK YOU DO?
I'M A TRAINED SORCERER, AND YES, I CAN TRACK THE MAGICS ALL OVER THE WORLD AND FIND THOSE WHO ARE USING OR ABUSING THEM.
AND, IN THE PAST, TO FIND *HER,* I HAVE.
ALL I KNOW NOW IS SHE'S NOT USING THEM ANYMORE, SO I CANNOT FIND HER.
THIS CHAOS MAGIC OF HERS, HER MUTANT POWER--
--NONE OF IT IS OUT THERE NOW.
SHE'S DISAPPEARED.

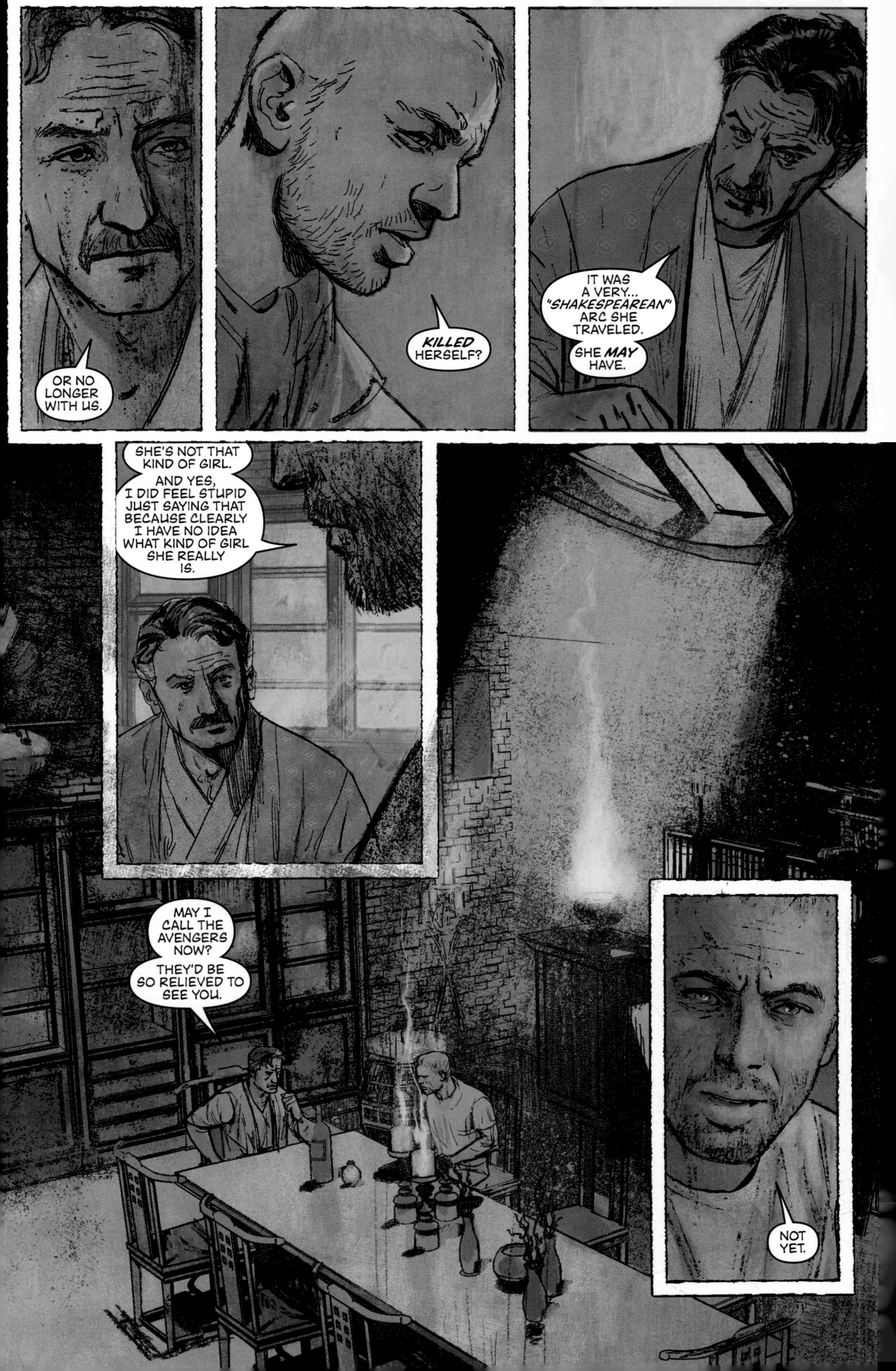
OR NO LONGER WITH US.
KILLED HERSELF?
IT WAS A VERY... "SHAKESPEAREAN" ARC SHE TRAVELED.
SHE MAY HAVE.
SHE'S NOT THAT KIND OF GIRL.
AND YES, I DID FEEL STUPID JUST SAYING THAT BECAUSE CLEARLY I HAVE NO IDEA WHAT KIND OF GIRL SHE REALLY IS.
MAY I CALL THE AVENGERS NOW?
THEY'D BE SO RELIEVED TO SEE YOU.
NOT YET.

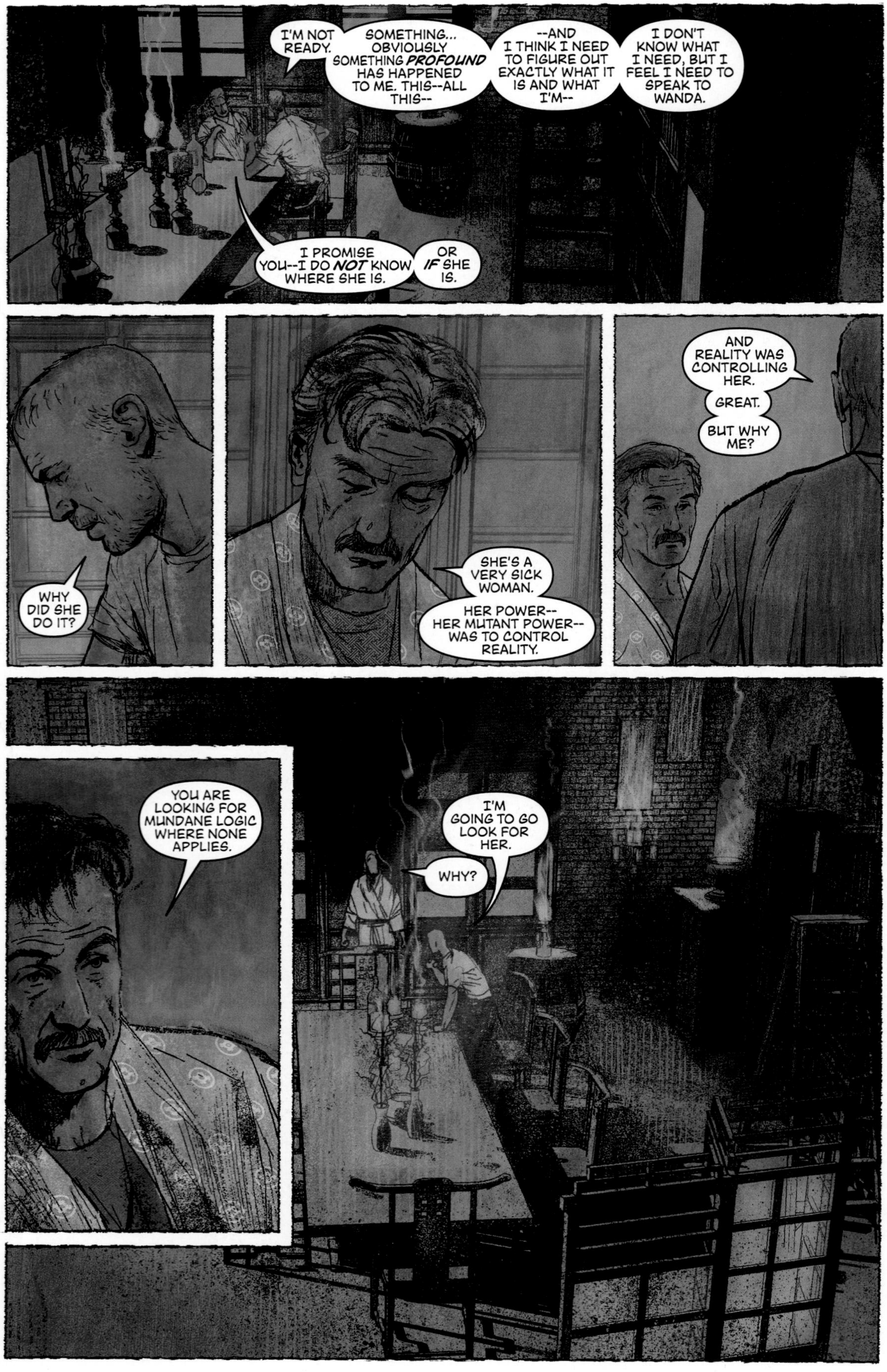
I'M NOT READY.
SOMETHING... OBVIOUSLY SOMETHING *PROFOUND* HAS HAPPENED TO ME. THIS--ALL THIS--
--AND I THINK I NEED TO FIGURE OUT EXACTLY WHAT IT IS AND WHAT I'M--
I DON'T KNOW WHAT I NEED, BUT I FEEL I NEED TO SPEAK TO WANDA.
I PROMISE YOU--I DO **NOT** KNOW WHERE SHE IS.
OR **IF** SHE IS.
WHY DID SHE DO IT?
SHE'S A VERY SICK WOMAN.
HER POWER--HER MUTANT POWER--WAS TO CONTROL REALITY.
AND REALITY WAS CONTROLLING HER.
GREAT.
BUT WHY ME?
YOU ARE LOOKING FOR MUNDANE LOGIC WHERE NONE APPLIES.
I'M GOING TO GO LOOK FOR HER.
WHY?

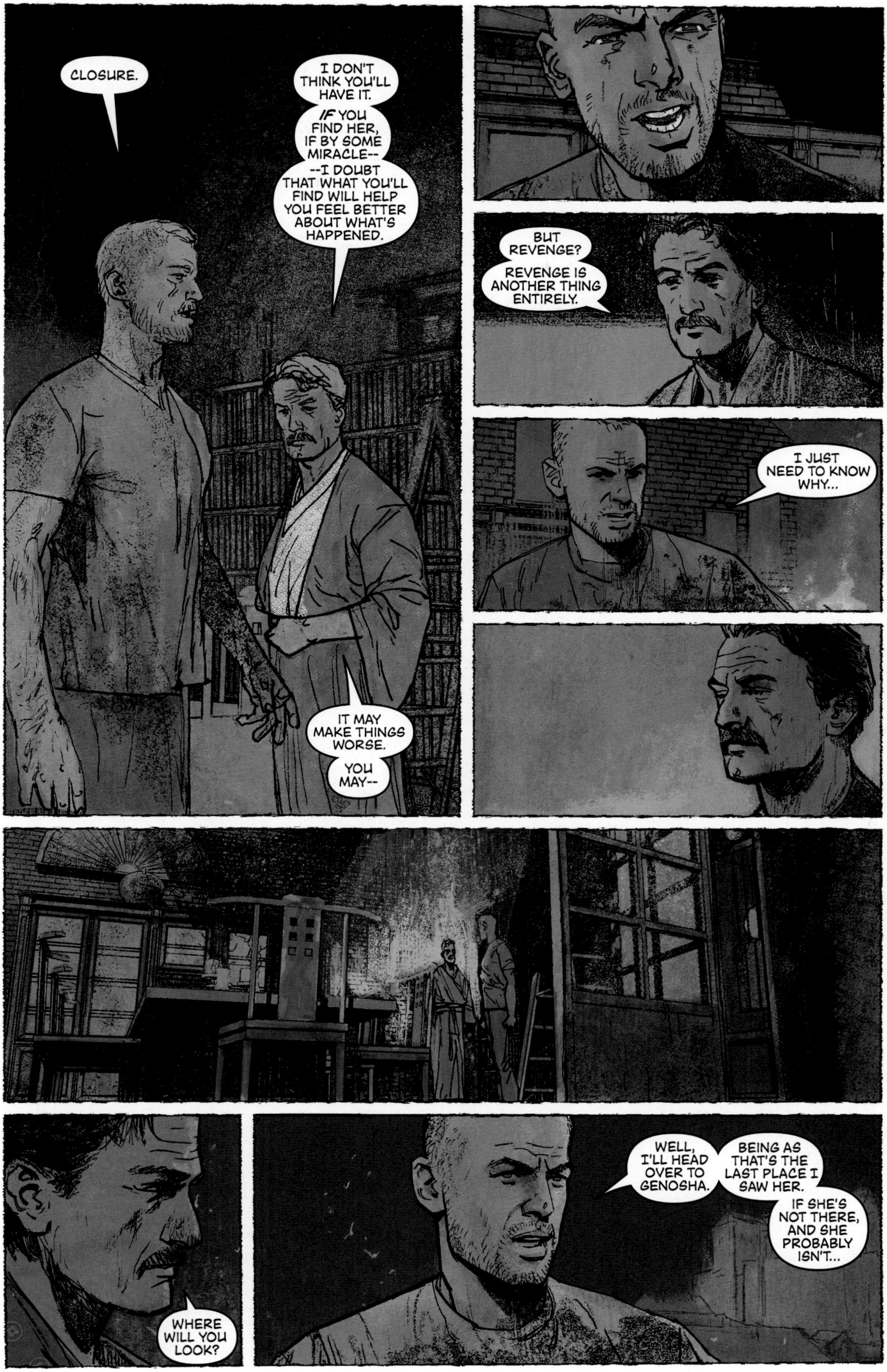
CLOSURE.
I DON'T THINK YOU'LL HAVE IT.
IF YOU FIND HER, IF BY SOME MIRACLE--
--I DOUBT THAT WHAT YOU'LL FIND WILL HELP YOU FEEL BETTER ABOUT WHAT'S HAPPENED.
IT MAY MAKE THINGS WORSE.
YOU MAY--
BUT REVENGE?
REVENGE IS ANOTHER THING ENTIRELY.
I JUST NEED TO KNOW WHY...
WHERE WILL YOU LOOK?
WELL, I'LL HEAD OVER TO GENOSHA.
BEING AS THAT'S THE LAST PLACE I SAW HER.
IF SHE'S NOT THERE, AND SHE PROBABLY ISN'T...

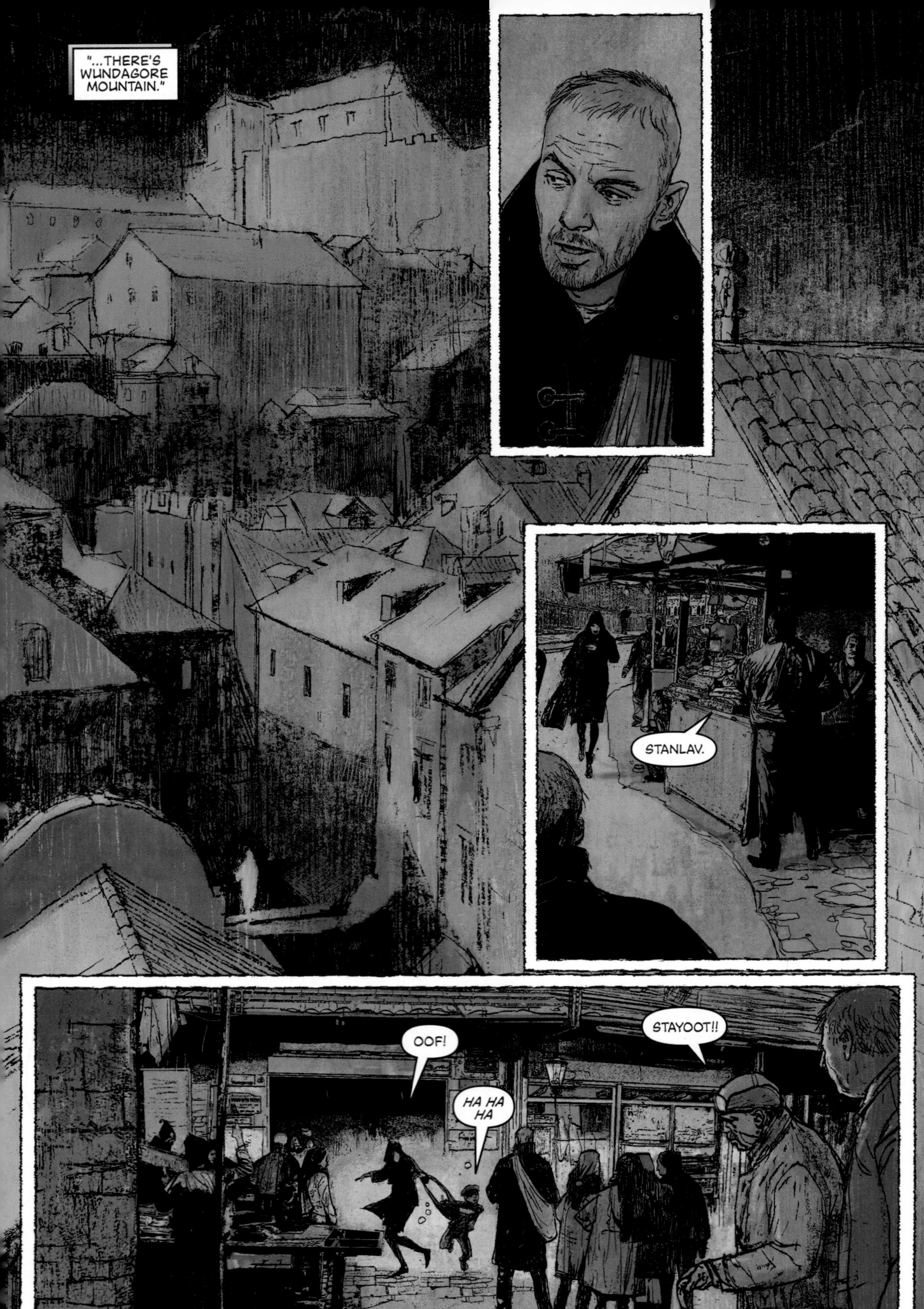
"...THERE'S WUNDAGORE MOUNTAIN."
STANLAV.
OOF!
HA HA HA
STAYOOT!!

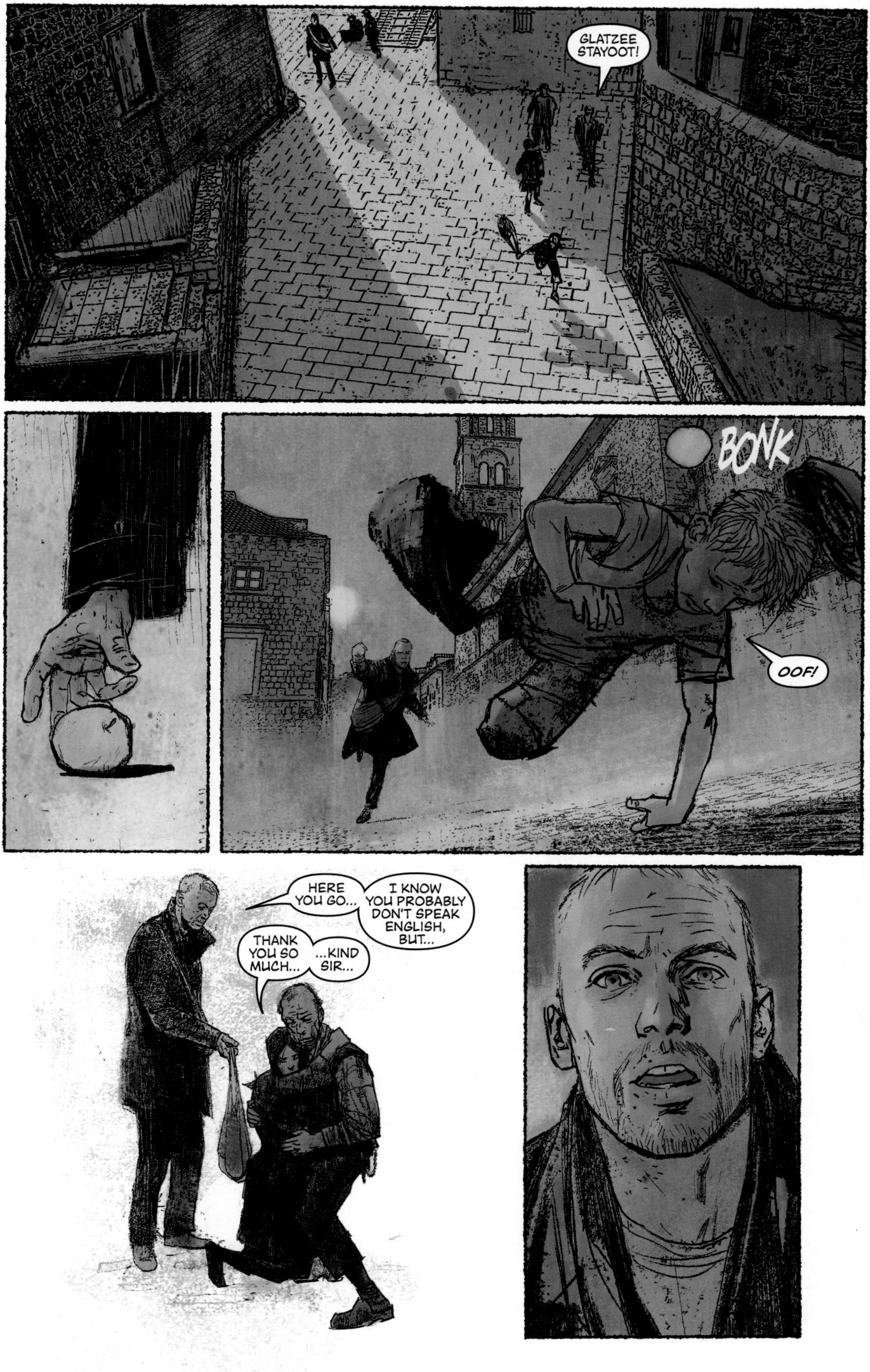
GLATZEE STAYOOT!
BONK
OOF!
HERE YOU GO...
I KNOW YOU PROBABLY DON'T SPEAK ENGLISH, BUT...
THANK YOU SO MUCH...
...KIND SIR...

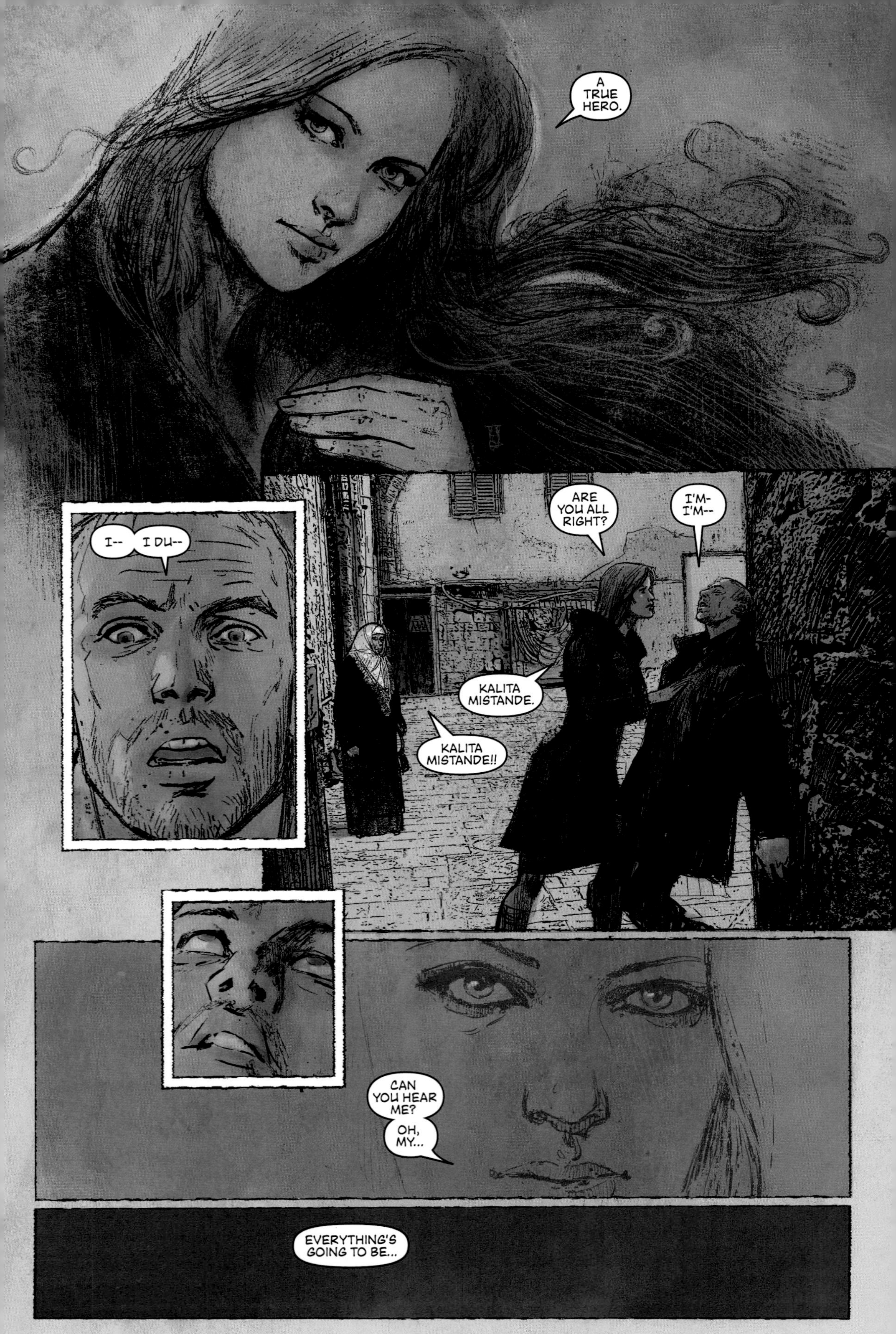
A TRUE HERO.
I--
I DU--
ARE YOU ALL RIGHT?
I'M-I'M--
KALITA MISTANDE.
KALITA MISTANDE!!
CAN YOU HEAR ME?
OH, MY...
EVERYTHING'S GOING TO BE...

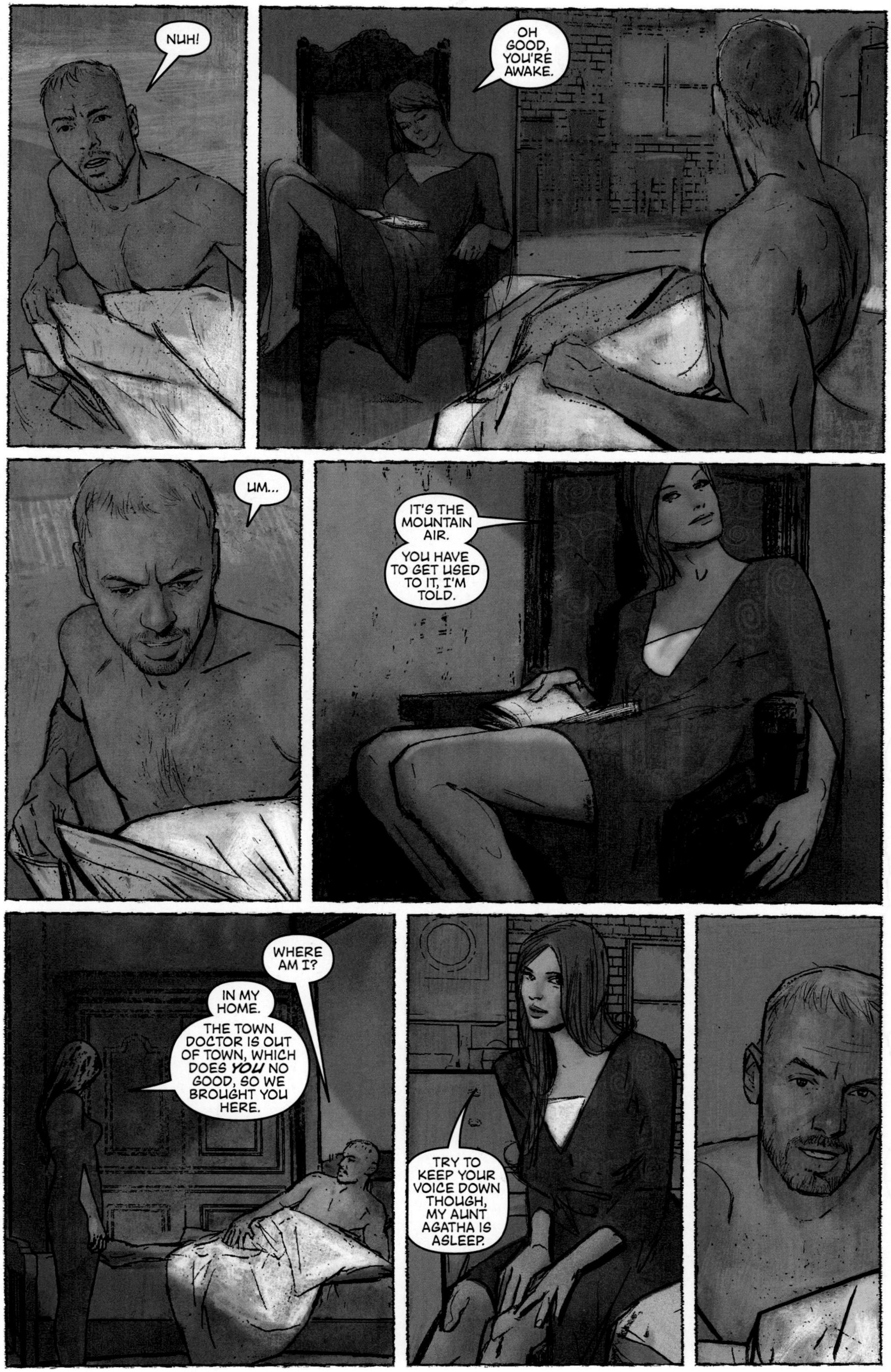
NUH!
OH GOOD, YOU'RE AWAKE.
UM...
IT'S THE MOUNTAIN AIR.
YOU HAVE TO GET USED TO IT, I'M TOLD.
WHERE AM I?
IN MY HOME.
THE TOWN DOCTOR IS OUT OF TOWN, WHICH DOES *YOU* NO GOOD, SO WE BROUGHT YOU HERE.
TRY TO KEEP YOUR VOICE DOWN THOUGH, MY AUNT AGATHA IS ASLEEP.

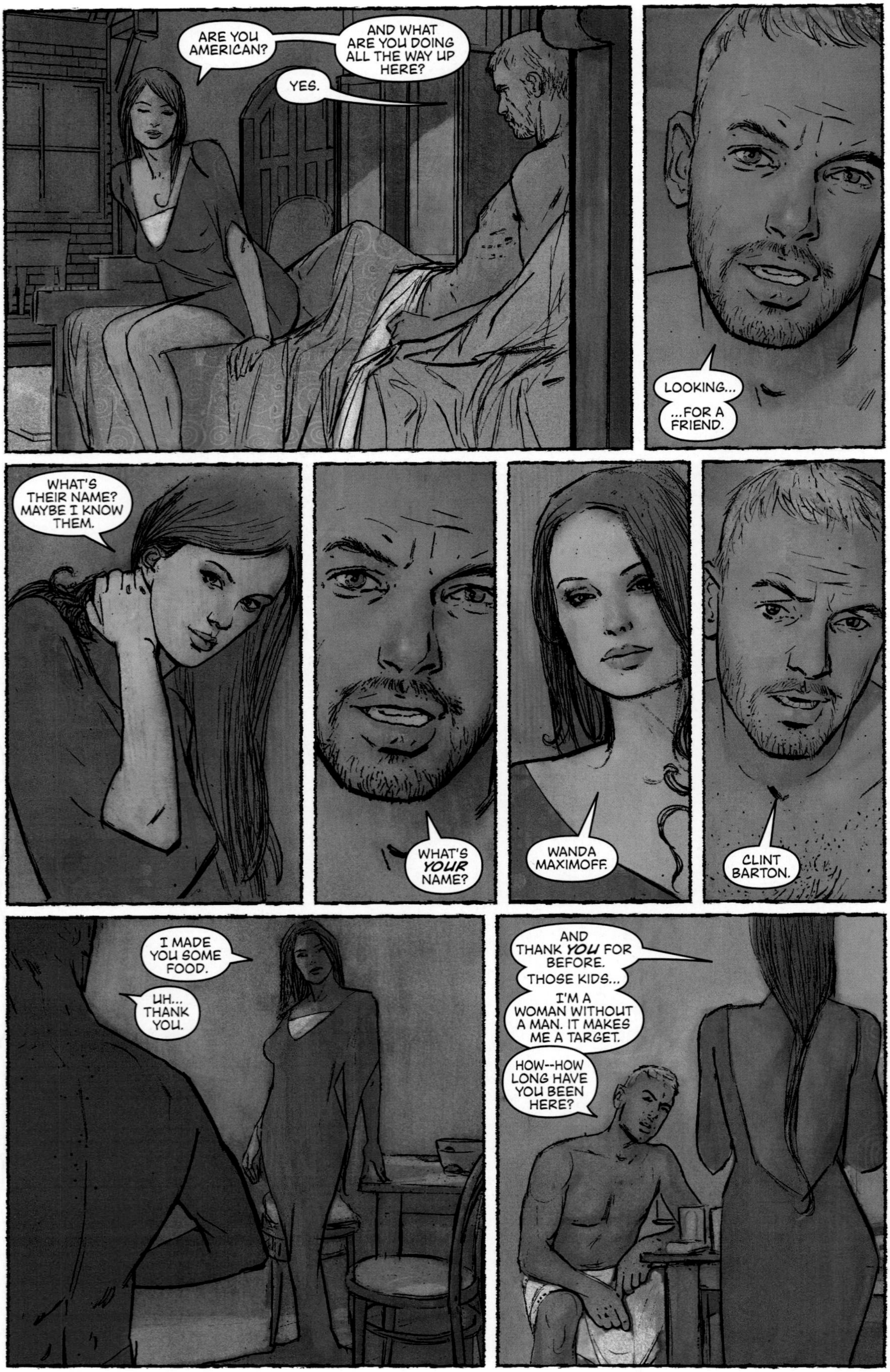
ARE YOU AMERICAN?
AND WHAT ARE YOU DOING ALL THE WAY UP HERE?
YES.
LOOKING...
...FOR A FRIEND.
WHAT'S THEIR NAME? MAYBE I KNOW THEM.
WHAT'S *YOUR* NAME?
WANDA MAXIMOFF.
CLINT BARTON.
I MADE YOU SOME FOOD.
UH... THANK YOU.
AND THANK *YOU* FOR BEFORE.
THOSE KIDS...
I'M A WOMAN WITHOUT A MAN. IT MAKES ME A TARGET.
HOW--HOW LONG HAVE YOU BEEN HERE?

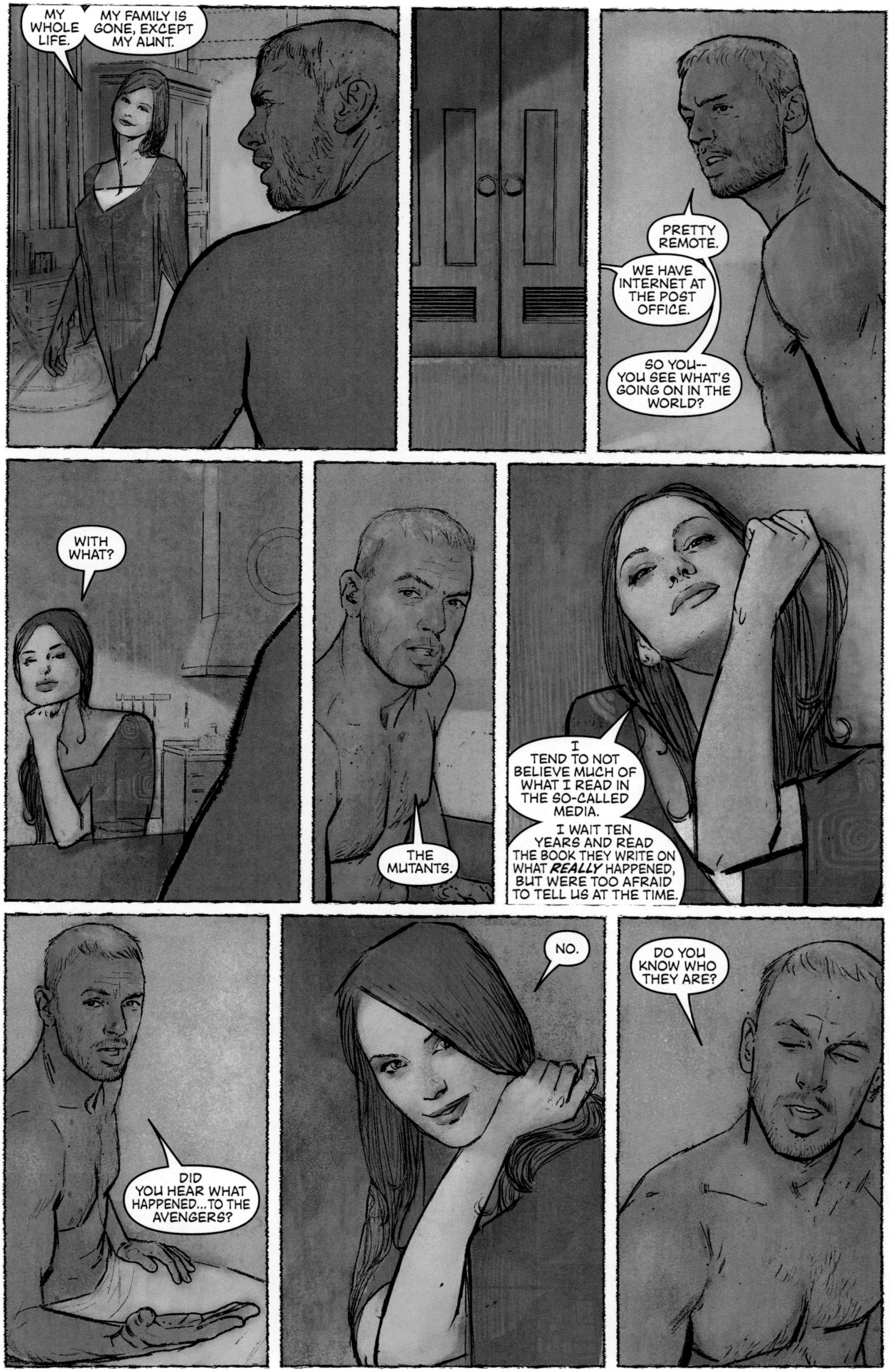
MY WHOLE LIFE.
MY FAMILY IS GONE, EXCEPT MY AUNT.
PRETTY REMOTE.
WE HAVE INTERNET AT THE POST OFFICE.
SO YOU-- YOU SEE WHAT'S GOING ON IN THE WORLD?
WITH WHAT?
THE MUTANTS.
I TEND TO NOT BELIEVE MUCH OF WHAT I READ IN THE SO-CALLED MEDIA.
I WAIT TEN YEARS AND READ THE BOOK THEY WRITE ON WHAT *REALLY* HAPPENED, BUT WERE TOO AFRAID TO TELL US AT THE TIME.
DID YOU HEAR WHAT HAPPENED...TO THE AVENGERS?
NO.
DO YOU KNOW WHO THEY ARE?

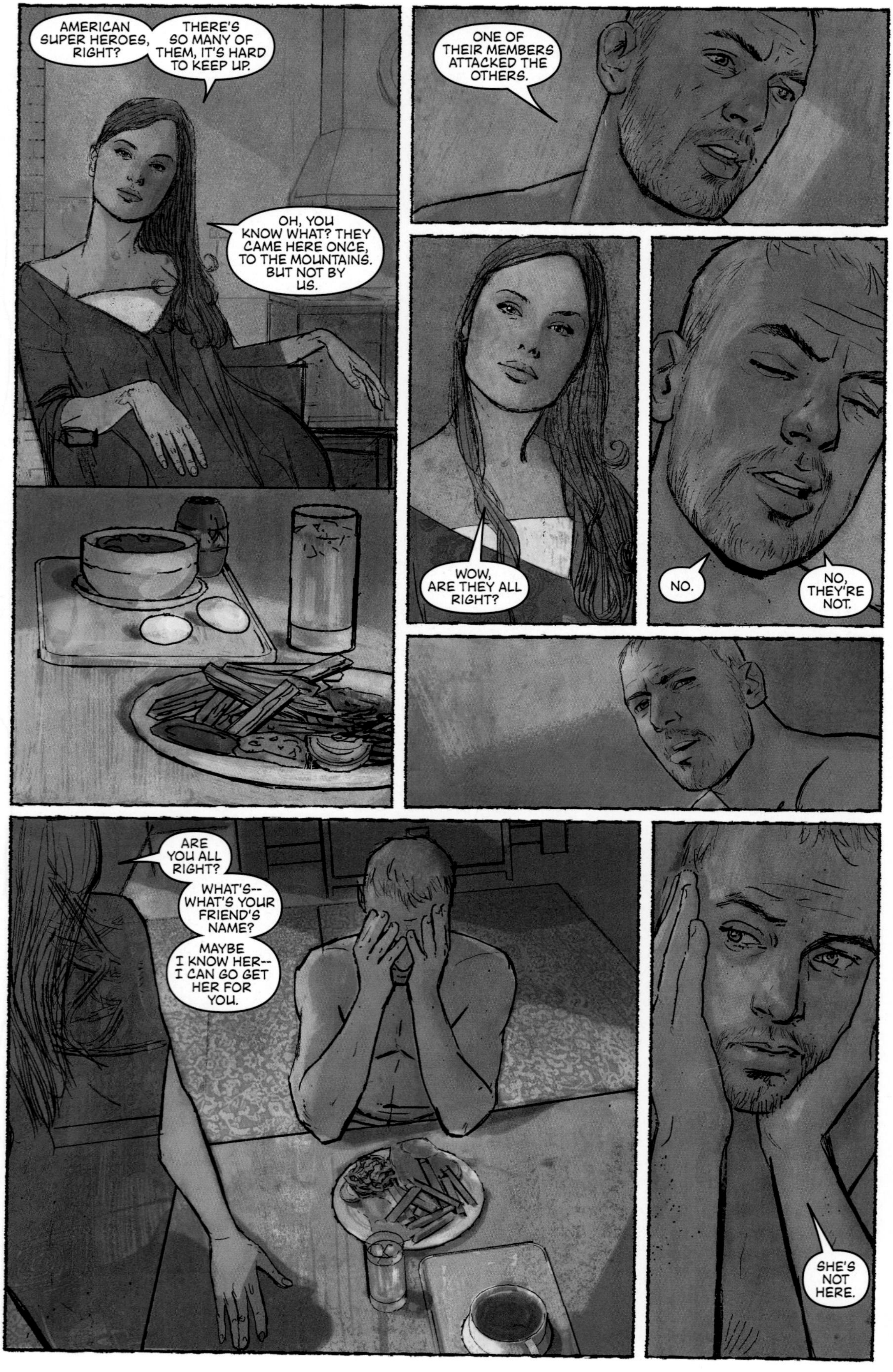
AMERICAN SUPER HEROES, RIGHT?
THERE'S SO MANY OF THEM, IT'S HARD TO KEEP UP.
OH, YOU KNOW WHAT? THEY CAME HERE ONCE, TO THE MOUNTAINS. BUT NOT BY US.
ONE OF THEIR MEMBERS ATTACKED THE OTHERS.
WOW, ARE THEY ALL RIGHT?
NO.
NO, THEY'RE NOT.
ARE YOU ALL RIGHT?
WHAT'S-- WHAT'S YOUR FRIEND'S NAME?
MAYBE I KNOW HER-- I CAN GO GET HER FOR YOU.
SHE'S NOT HERE.

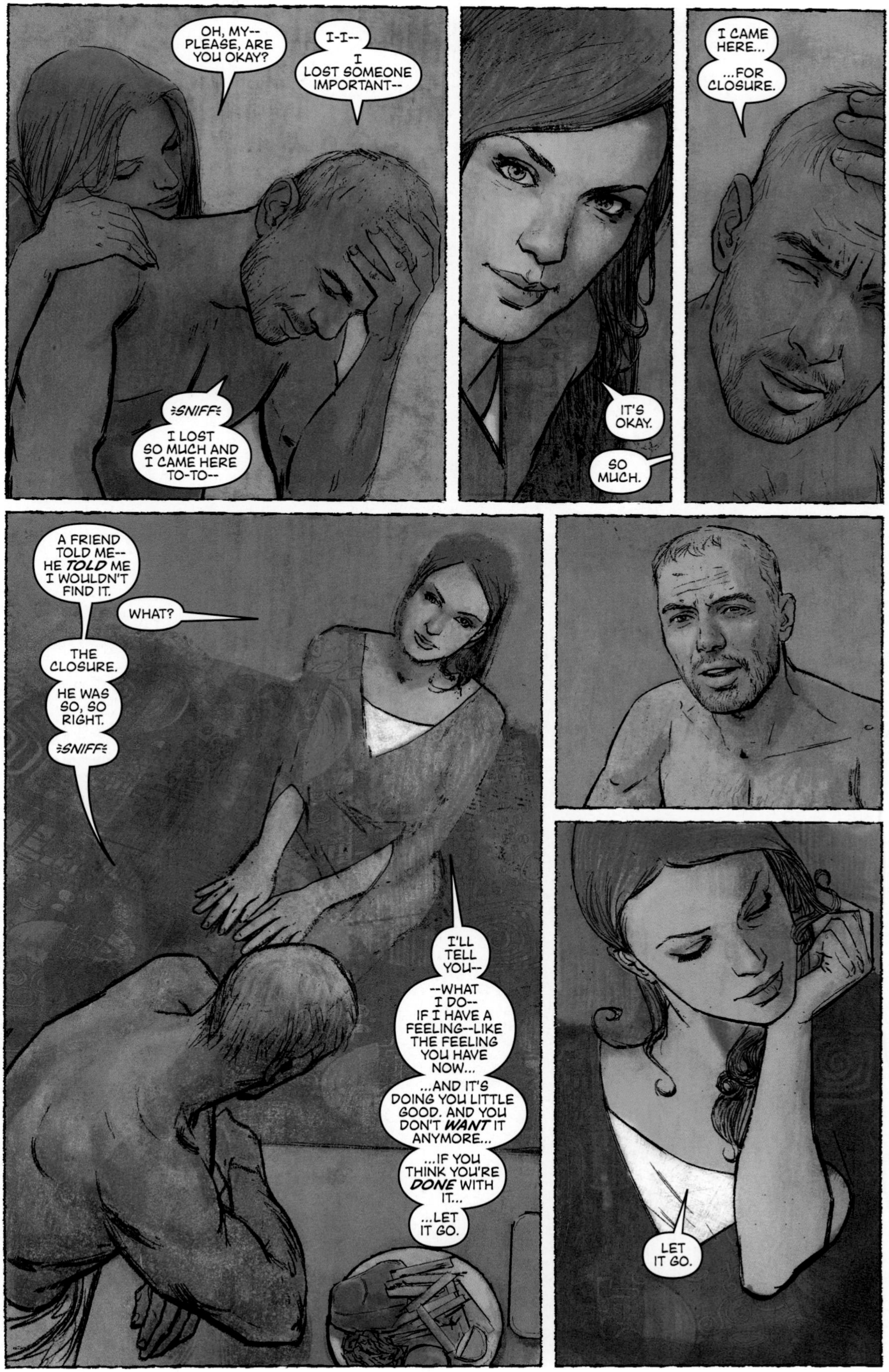
OH, MY-- PLEASE, ARE YOU OKAY?
I-I--
I LOST SOMEONE IMPORTANT--
≈SNIFF≈
I LOST SO MUCH AND I CAME HERE TO-TO--
IT'S OKAY.
SO MUCH.
I CAME HERE...
...FOR CLOSURE.
A FRIEND TOLD ME-- HE *TOLD* ME I WOULDN'T FIND IT.
WHAT?
THE CLOSURE.
HE WAS SO, SO RIGHT.
≈SNIFF≈
I'LL TELL YOU--
--WHAT I DO-- IF I HAVE A FEELING--LIKE THE FEELING YOU HAVE NOW...
...AND IT'S DOING YOU LITTLE GOOD. AND YOU DON'T *WANT* IT ANYMORE...
...IF YOU THINK YOU'RE *DONE* WITH IT...
...LET IT GO.
LET IT GO.

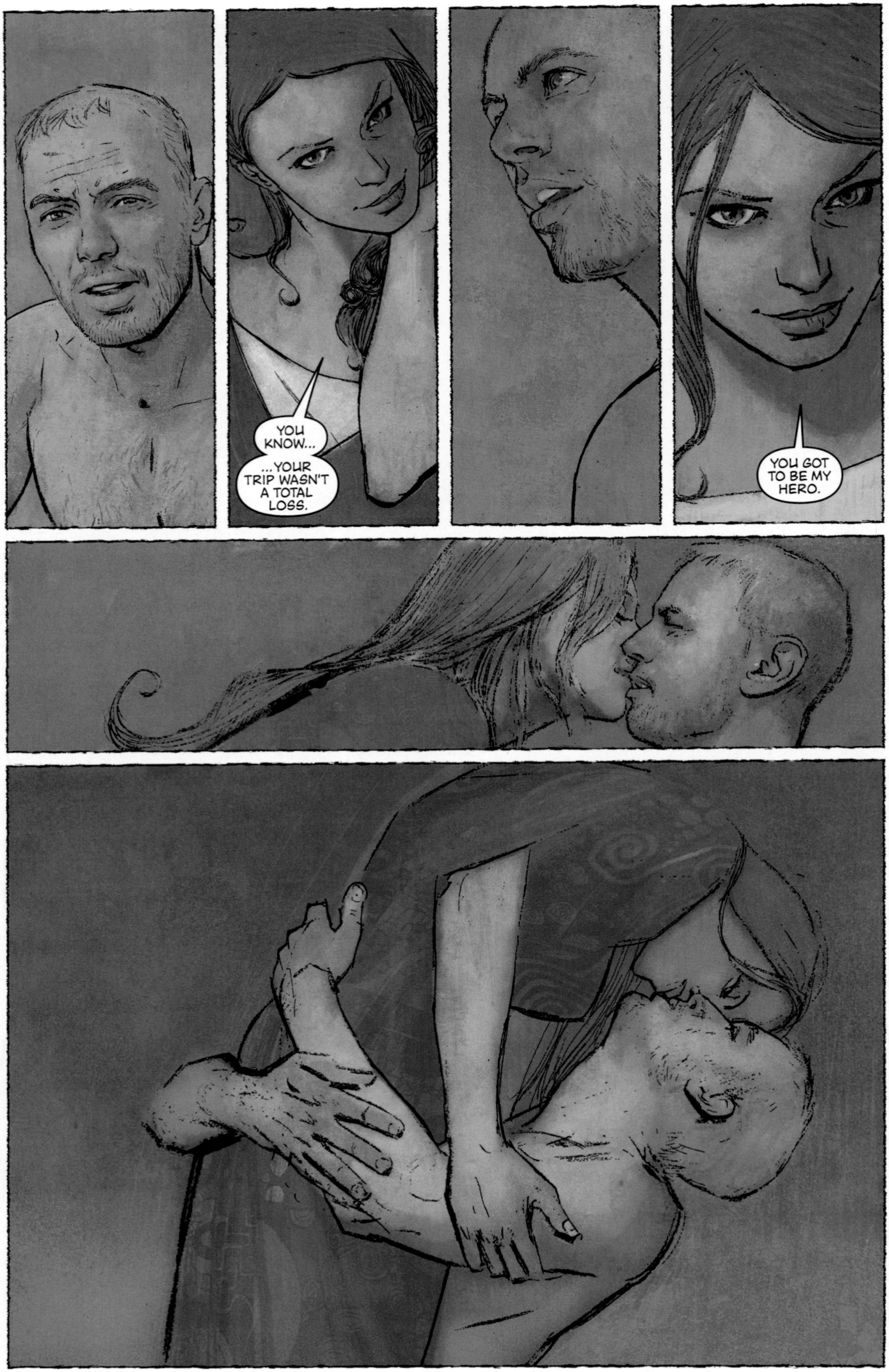
YOU KNOW...
...YOUR TRIP WASN'T A TOTAL LOSS.
YOU GOT TO BE MY HERO.

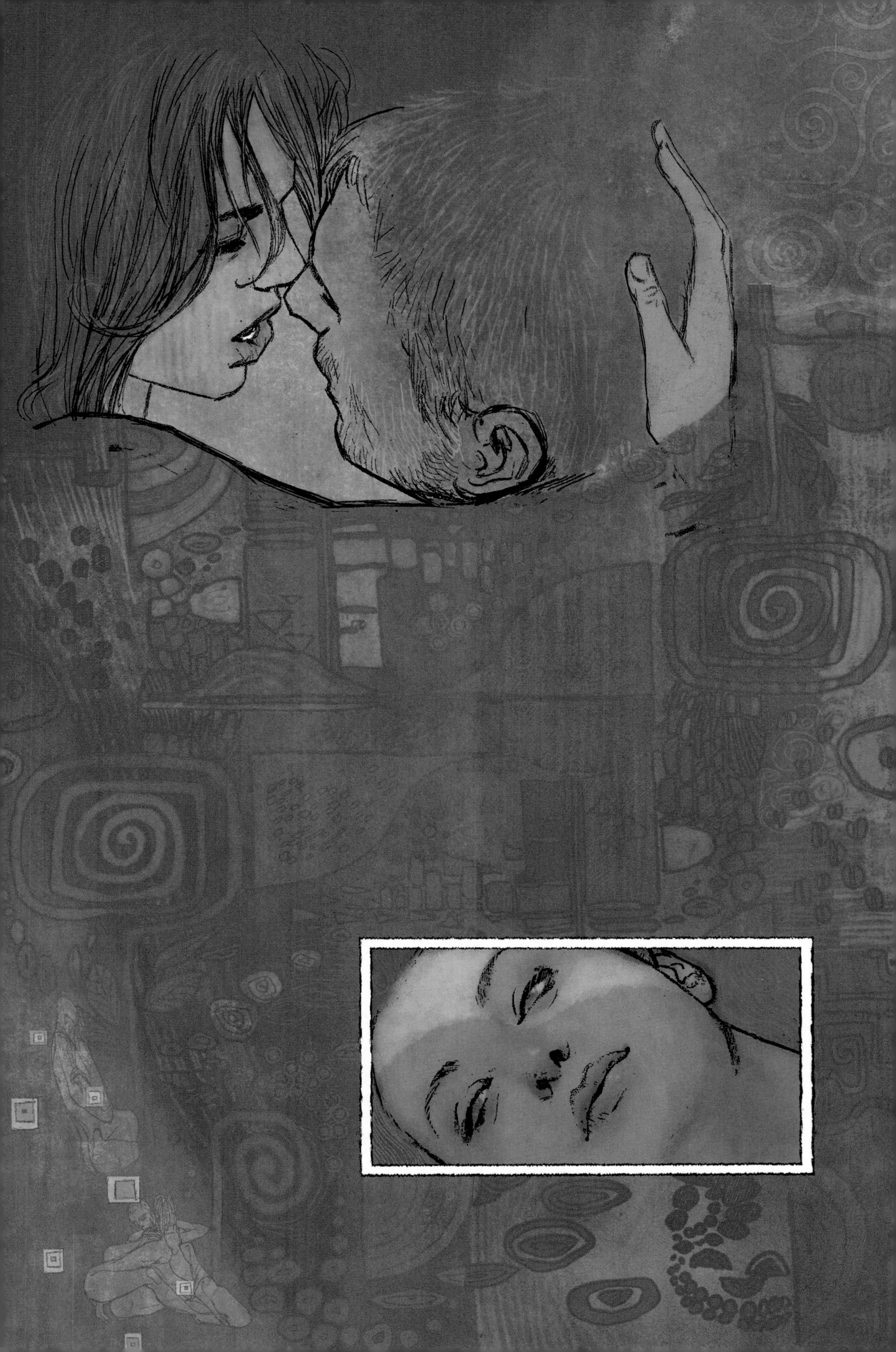

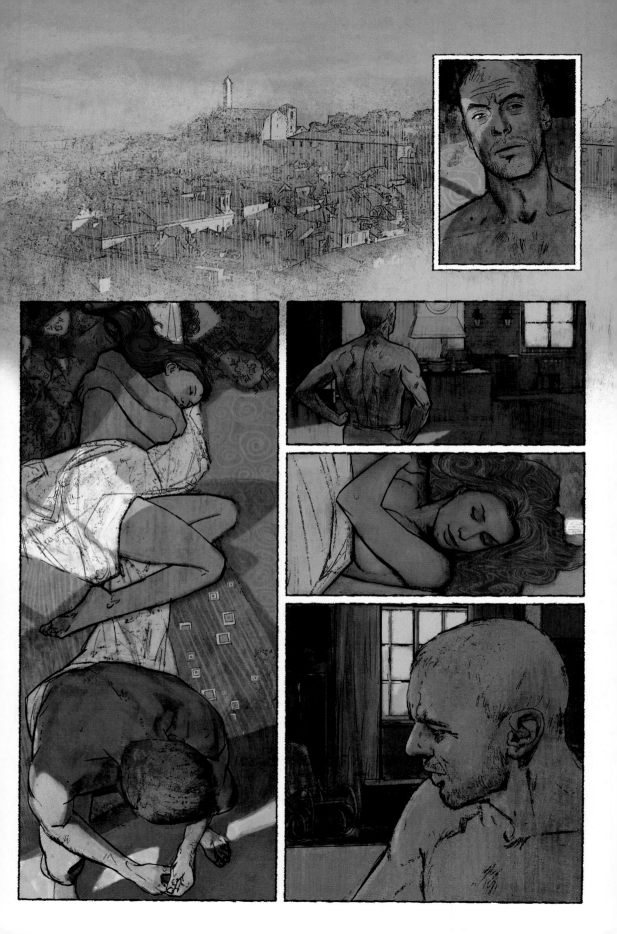

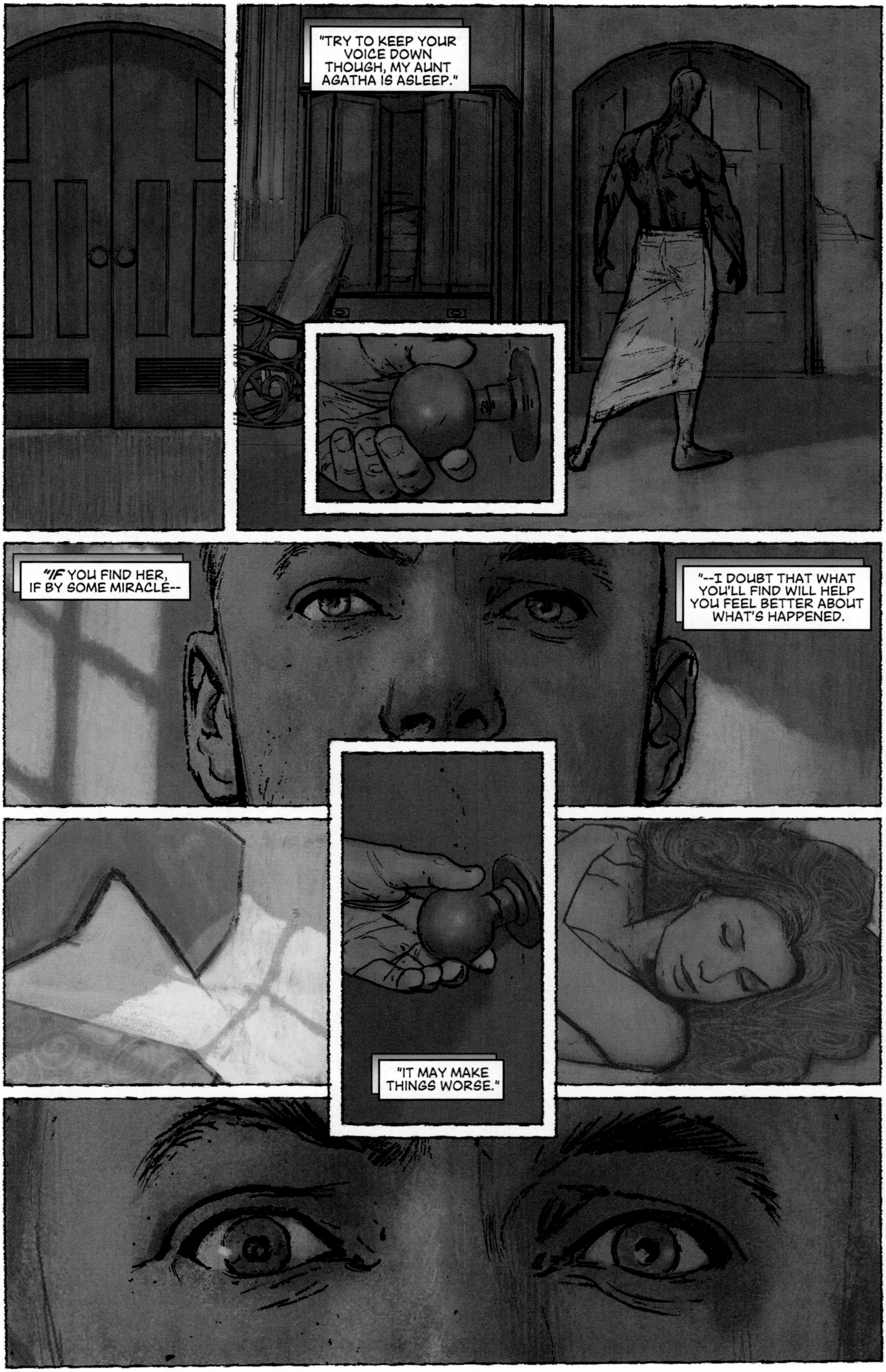
"TRY TO KEEP YOUR VOICE DOWN THOUGH, MY AUNT AGATHA IS ASLEEP."
"IF YOU FIND HER, IF BY SOME MIRACLE--
"--I DOUBT THAT WHAT YOU'LL FIND WILL HELP YOU FEEL BETTER ABOUT WHAT'S HAPPENED.
"IT MAY MAKE THINGS WORSE."

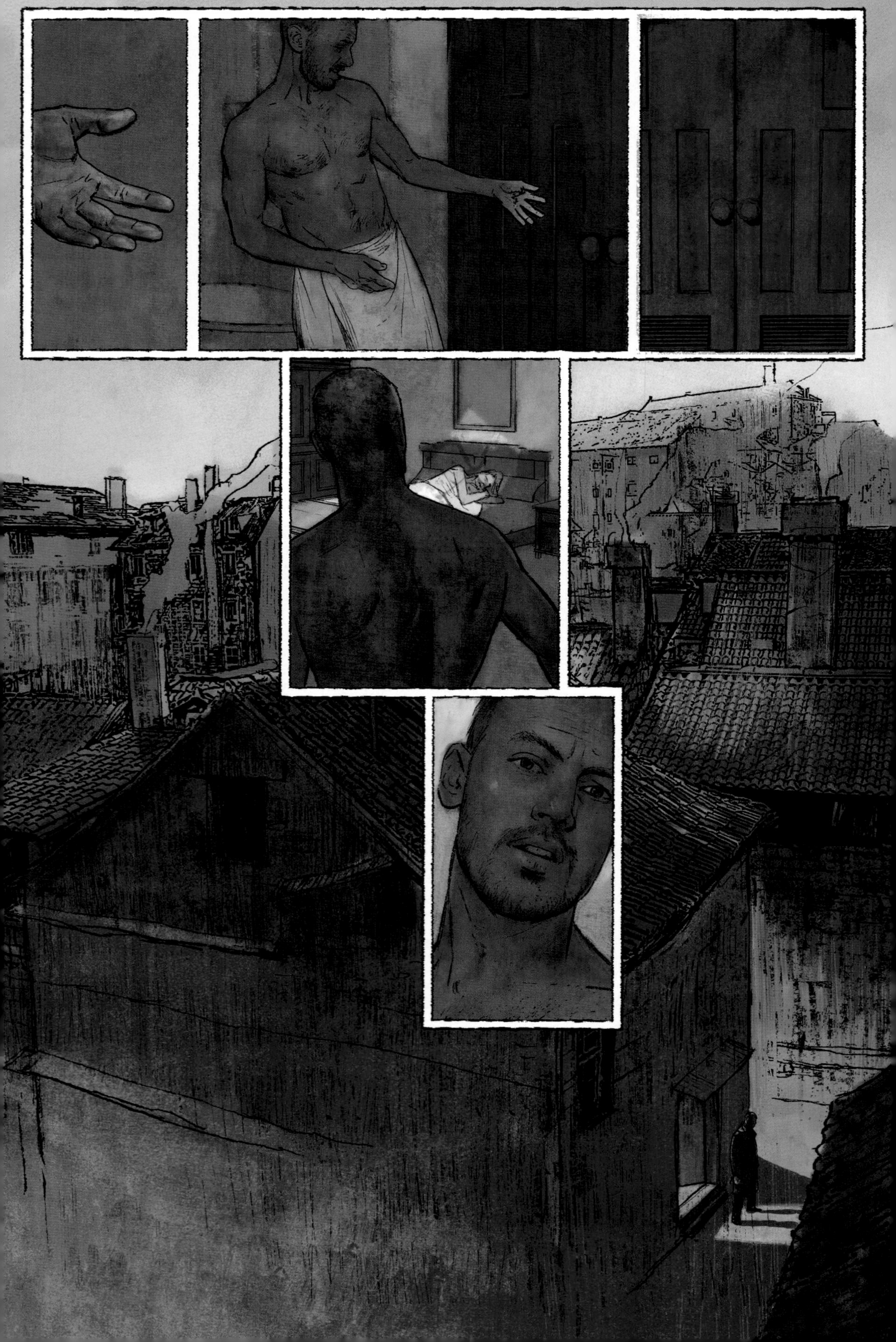

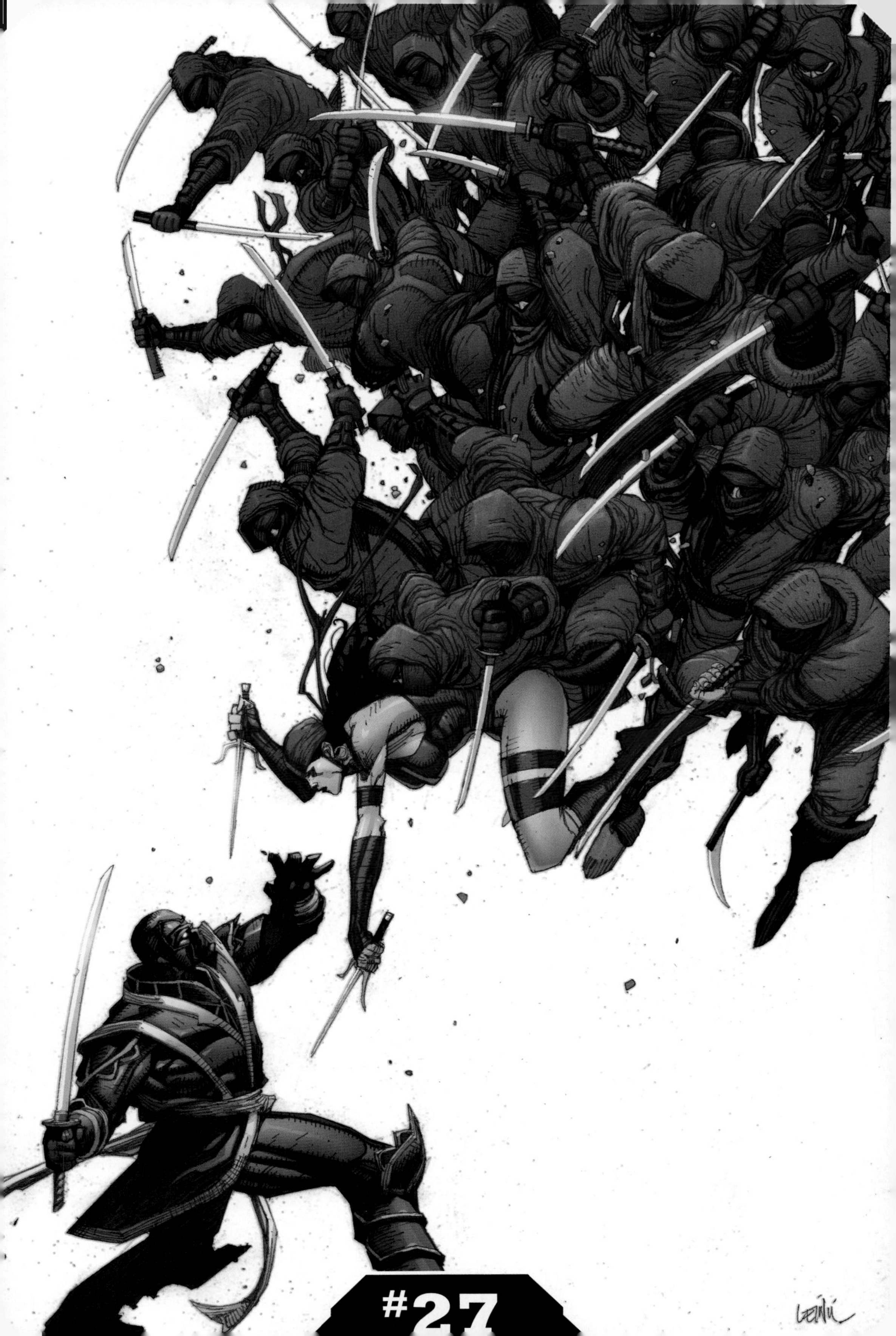
#27

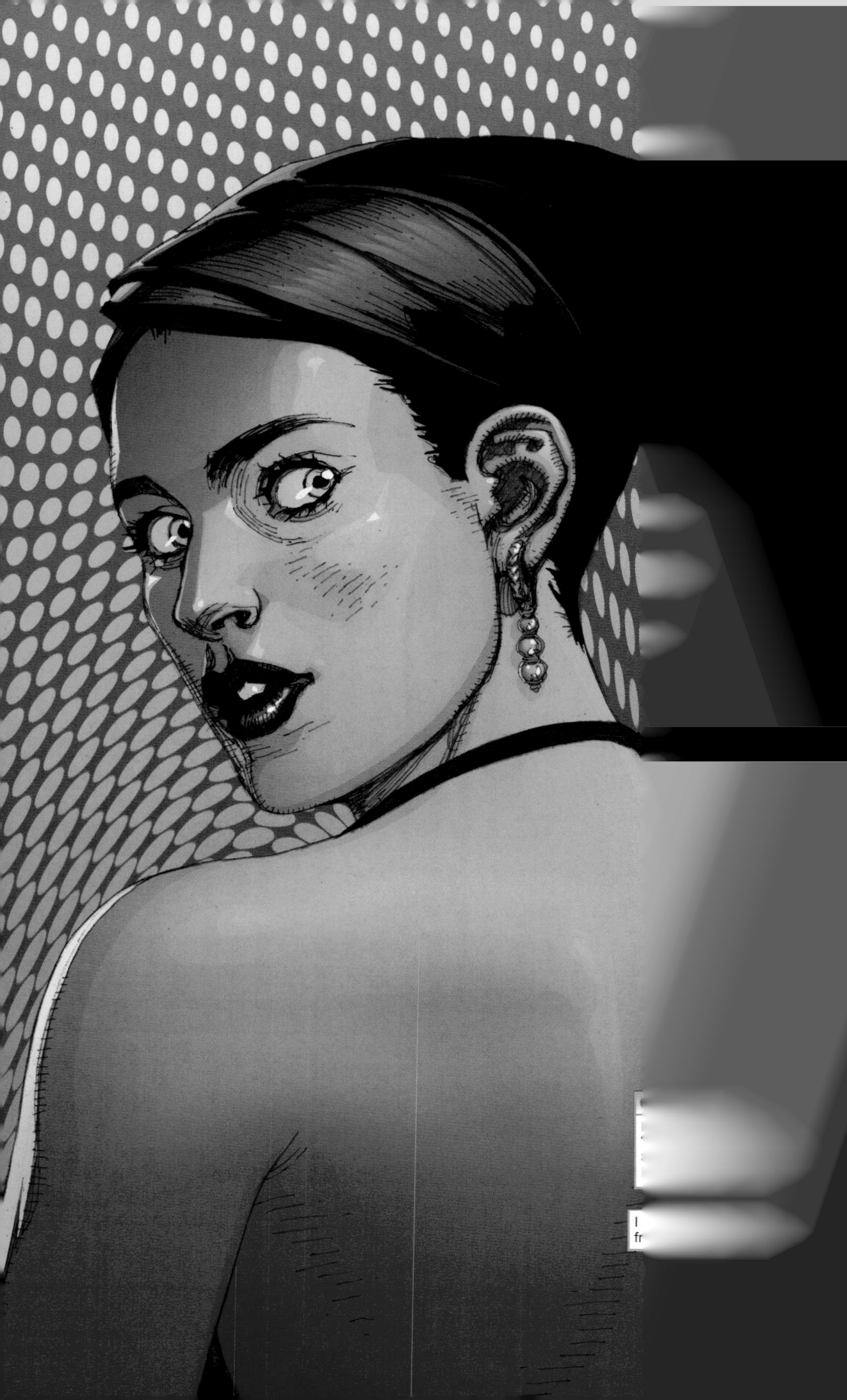

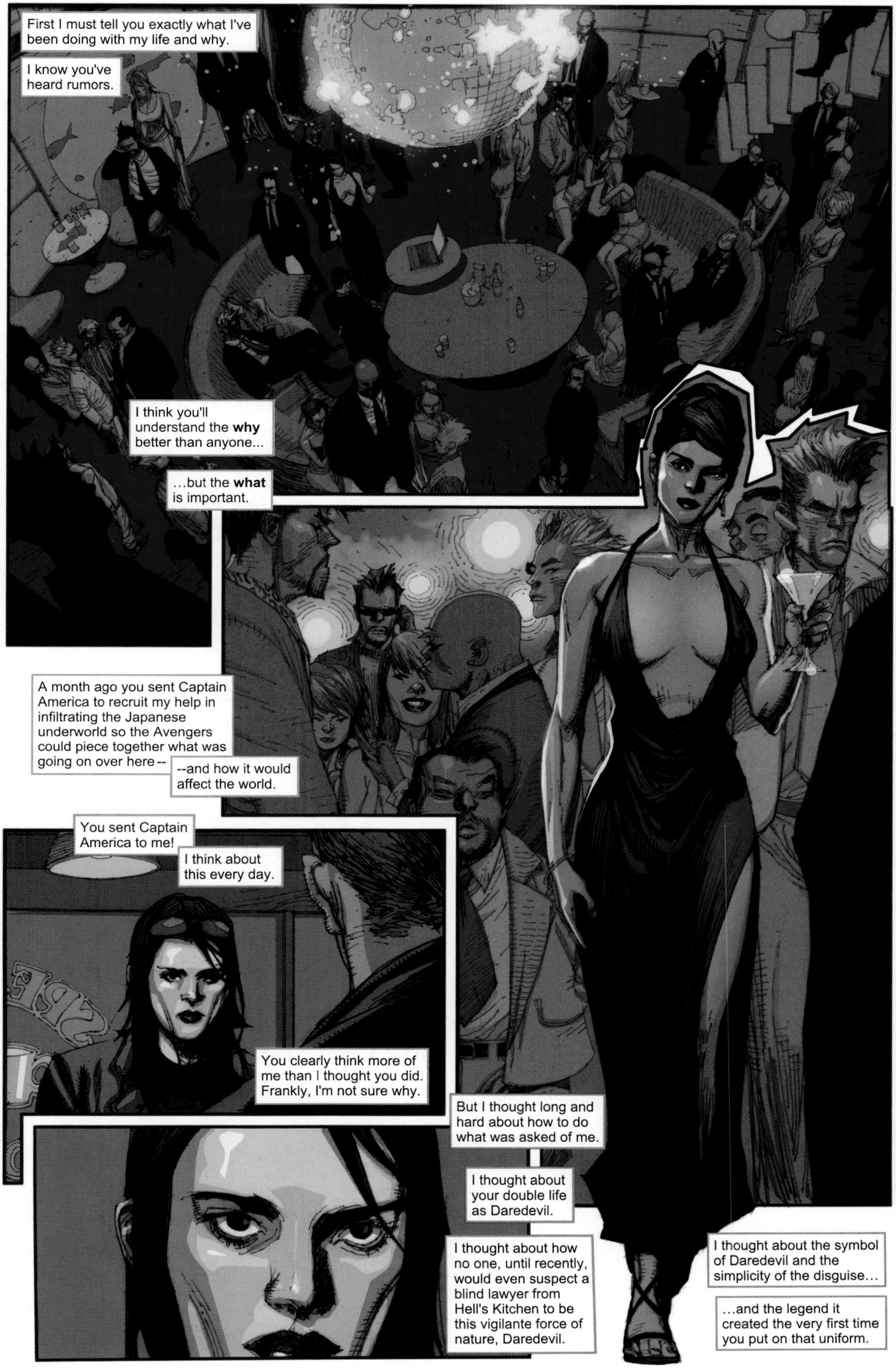
First I must tell you exactly what I've been doing with my life and why.
I know you've heard rumors.
I think you'll understand the **why** better than anyone...
...but the **what** is important.
A month ago you sent Captain America to recruit my help in infiltrating the Japanese underworld so the Avengers could piece together what was going on over here--
--and how it would affect the world.
You sent Captain America to me!
I think about this every day.
You clearly think more of me than I thought you did. Frankly, I'm not sure why.
But I thought long and hard about how to do what was asked of me.
I thought about your double life as Daredevil.
I thought about how no one, until recently, would even suspect a blind lawyer from Hell's Kitchen to be this vigilante force of nature, Daredevil.
I thought about the symbol of Daredevil and the simplicity of the disguise...
...and the legend it created the very first time you put on that uniform.

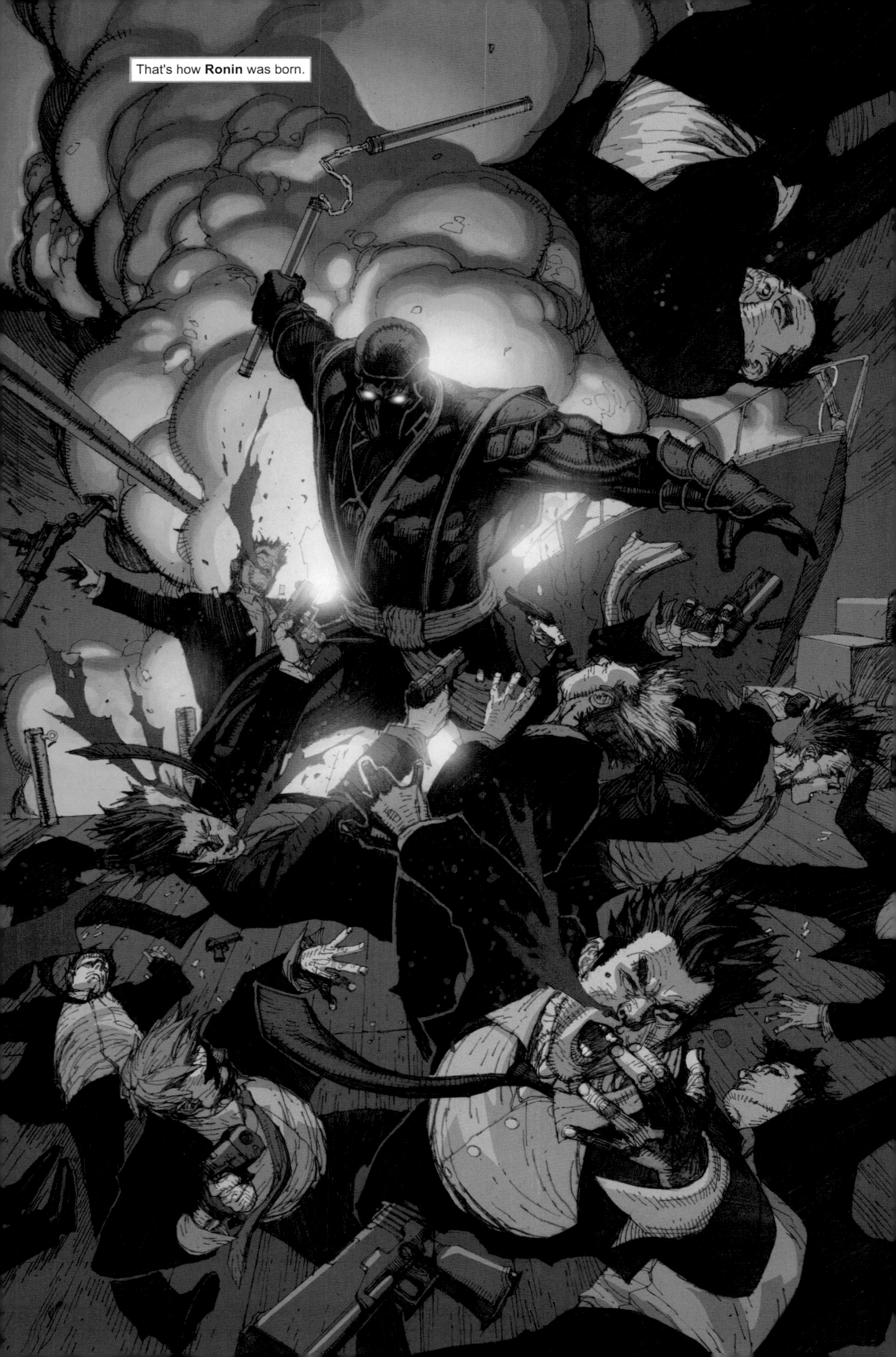
That's how **Ronin** was born.

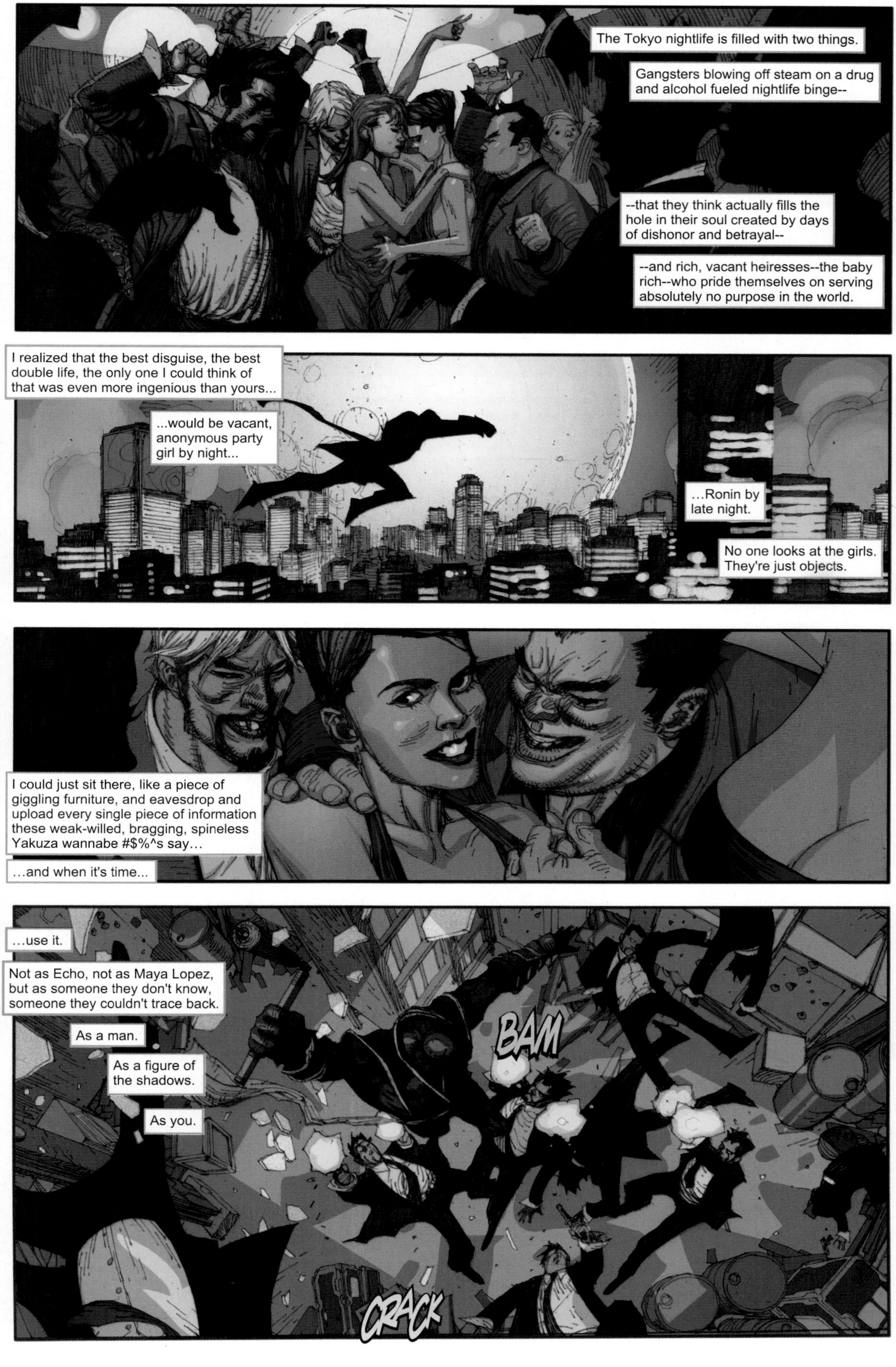
The Tokyo nightlife is filled with two things.
Gangsters blowing off steam on a drug and alcohol fueled nightlife binge--
--that they think actually fills the hole in their soul created by days of dishonor and betrayal--
--and rich, vacant heiresses--the baby rich--who pride themselves on serving absolutely no purpose in the world.
I realized that the best disguise, the best double life, the only one I could think of that was even more ingenious than yours...
...would be vacant, anonymous party girl by night...
...Ronin by late night.
No one looks at the girls. They're just objects.
I could just sit there, like a piece of giggling furniture, and eavesdrop and upload every single piece of information these weak-willed, bragging, spineless Yakuza wannabe #$%^s say...
...and when it's time...
...use it.
Not as Echo, not as Maya Lopez, but as someone they don't know, someone they couldn't trace back.
As a man.
As a figure of the shadows.
As you.
BAM
CRACK

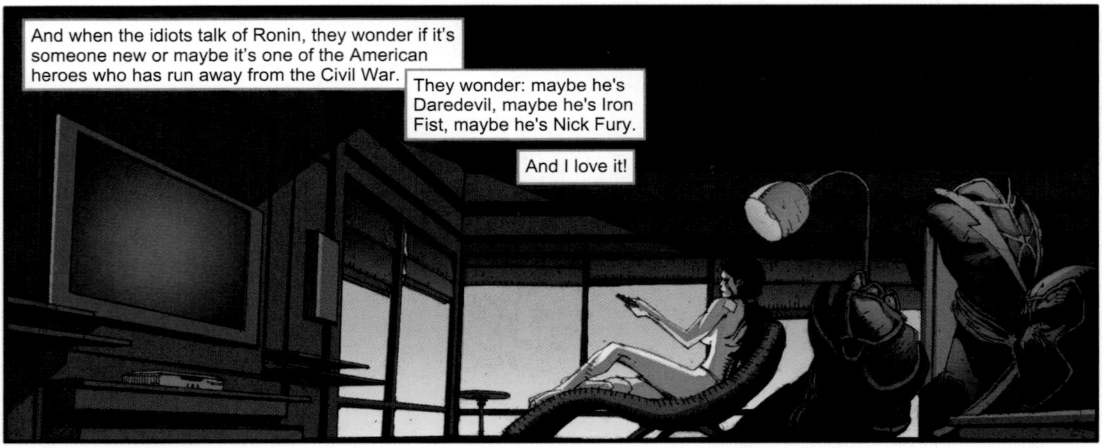
And when the idiots talk of Ronin, they wonder if it's someone new or maybe it's one of the American heroes who has run away from the Civil War.
They wonder: maybe he's Daredevil, maybe he's Iron Fist, maybe he's Nick Fury.
And I love it!

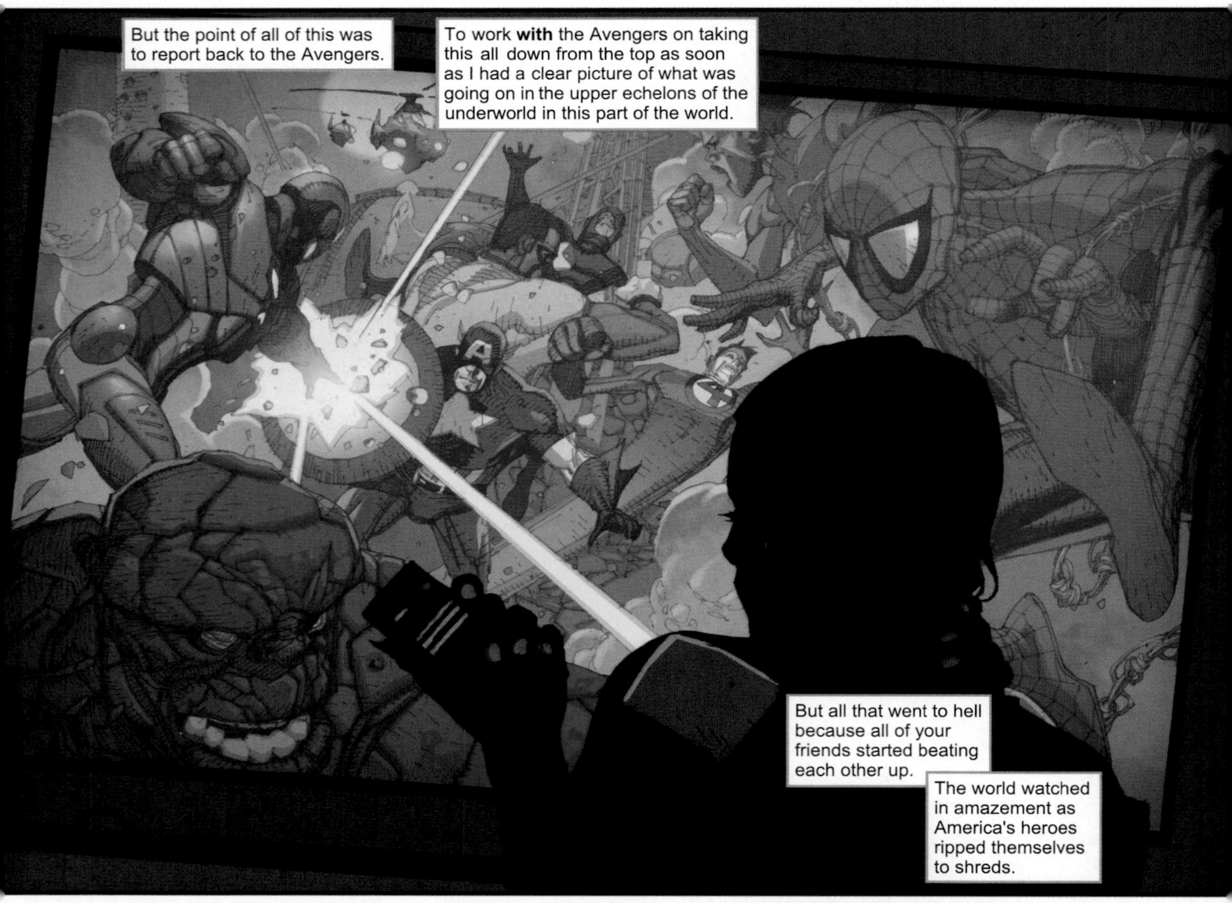
But the point of all of this was to report back to the Avengers.
To work **with** the Avengers on taking this all down from the top as soon as I had a clear picture of what was going on in the upper echelons of the underworld in this part of the world.
But all that went to hell because all of your friends started beating each other up.
The world watched in amazement as America's heroes ripped themselves to shreds.

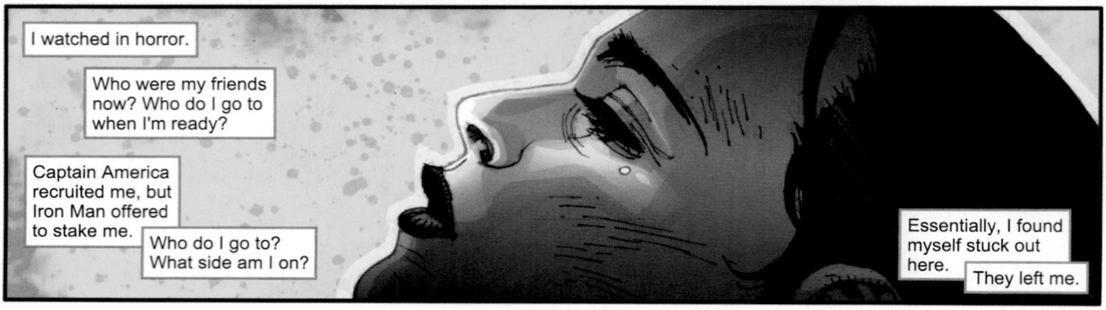
I watched in horror.
Who were my friends now? Who do I go to when I'm ready?
Captain America recruited me, but Iron Man offered to stake me.
Who do I go to? What side am I on?
Essentially, I found myself stuck out here.
They left me.

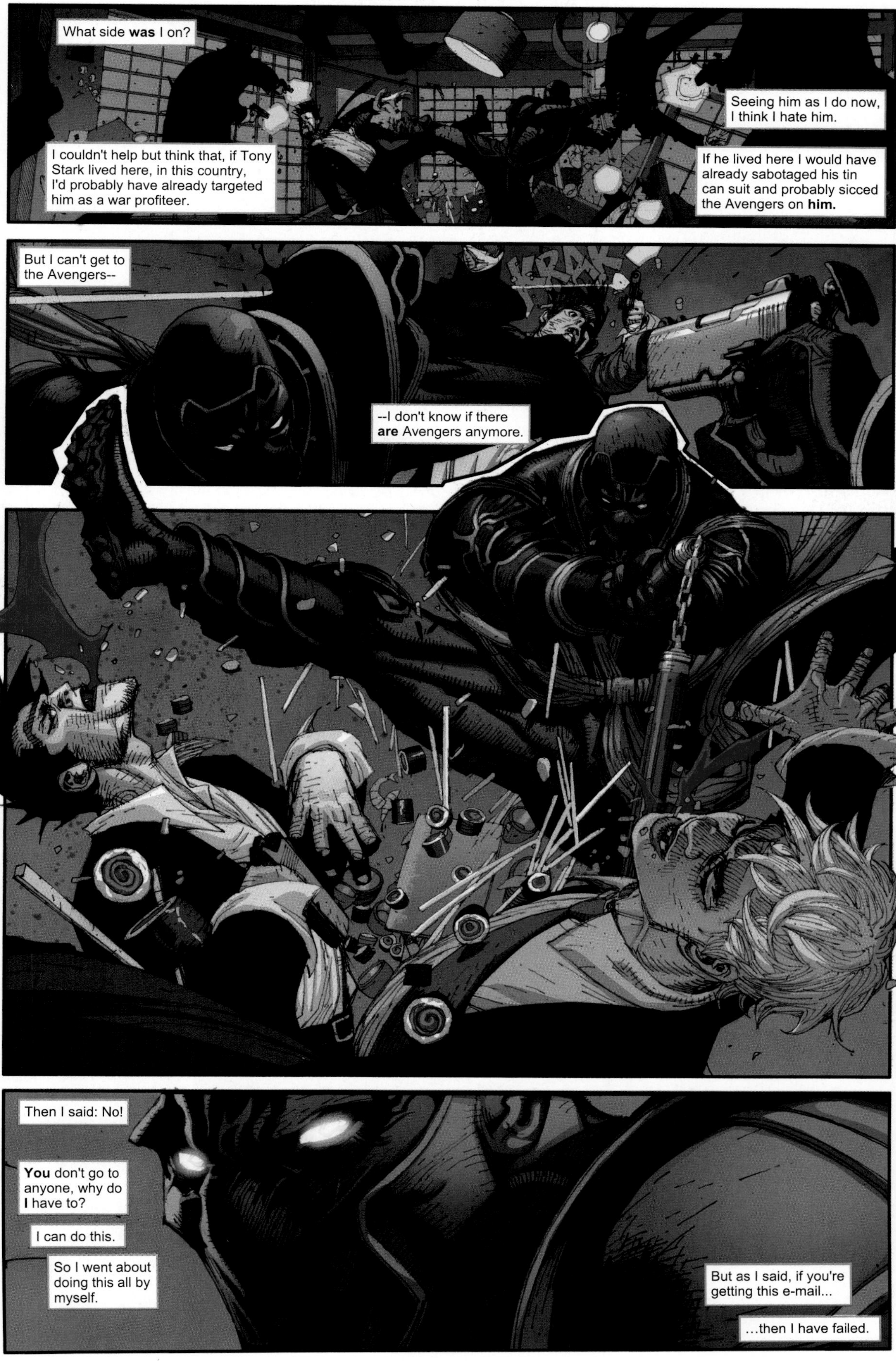
What side **was** I on?
Seeing him as I do now, I think I hate him.
I couldn't help but think that, if Tony Stark lived here, in this country, I'd probably have already targeted him as a war profiteer.
If he lived here I would have already sabotaged his tin can suit and probably sicced the Avengers on **him.**
But I can't get to the Avengers--
--I don't know if there **are** Avengers anymore.
Then I said: No!
You don't go to anyone, why do **I** have to?
I can do this.
So I went about doing this all by myself.
But as I said, if you're getting this e-mail...
...then I have failed.

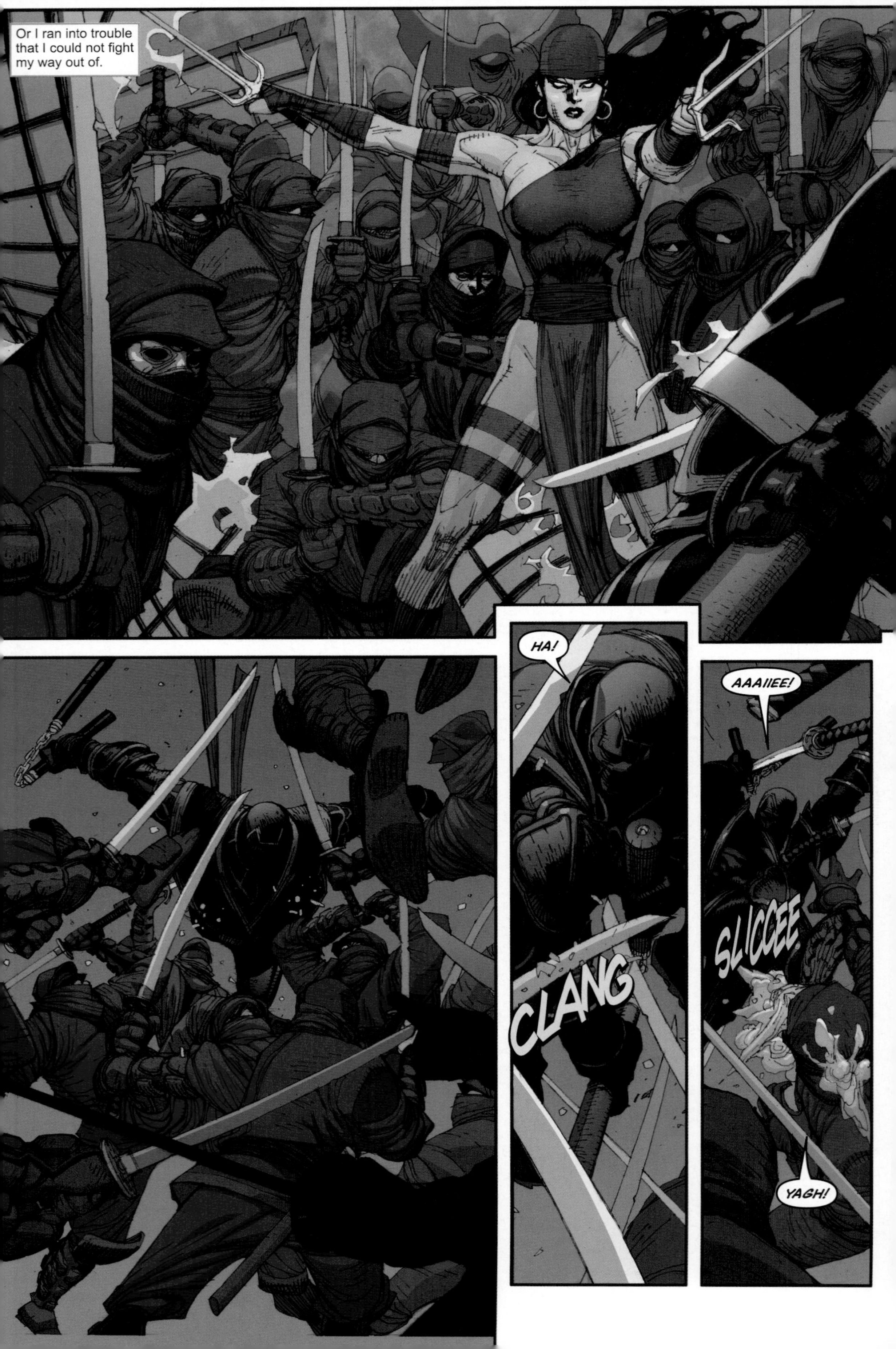
Or I ran into trouble that I could not fight my way out of.
HA!
CLANG
AAAIIEE!
SLICCEE
YAGH!

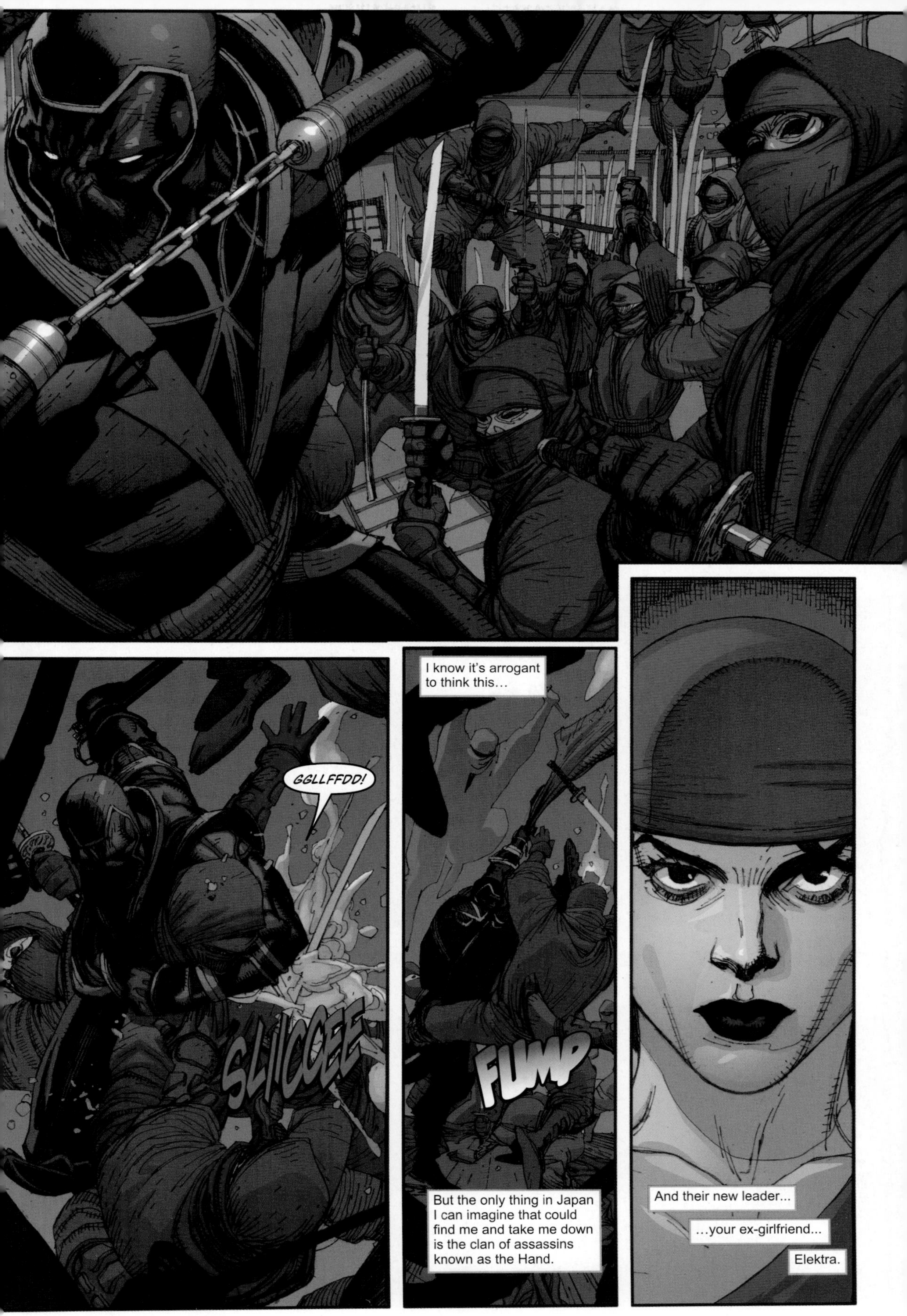
GGLLFFDD!
SLIICCEE
I know it's arrogant to think this…
FUMP
But the only thing in Japan I can imagine that could find me and take me down is the clan of assassins known as the Hand.
And their new leader...
…your ex-girlfriend...
Elektra.

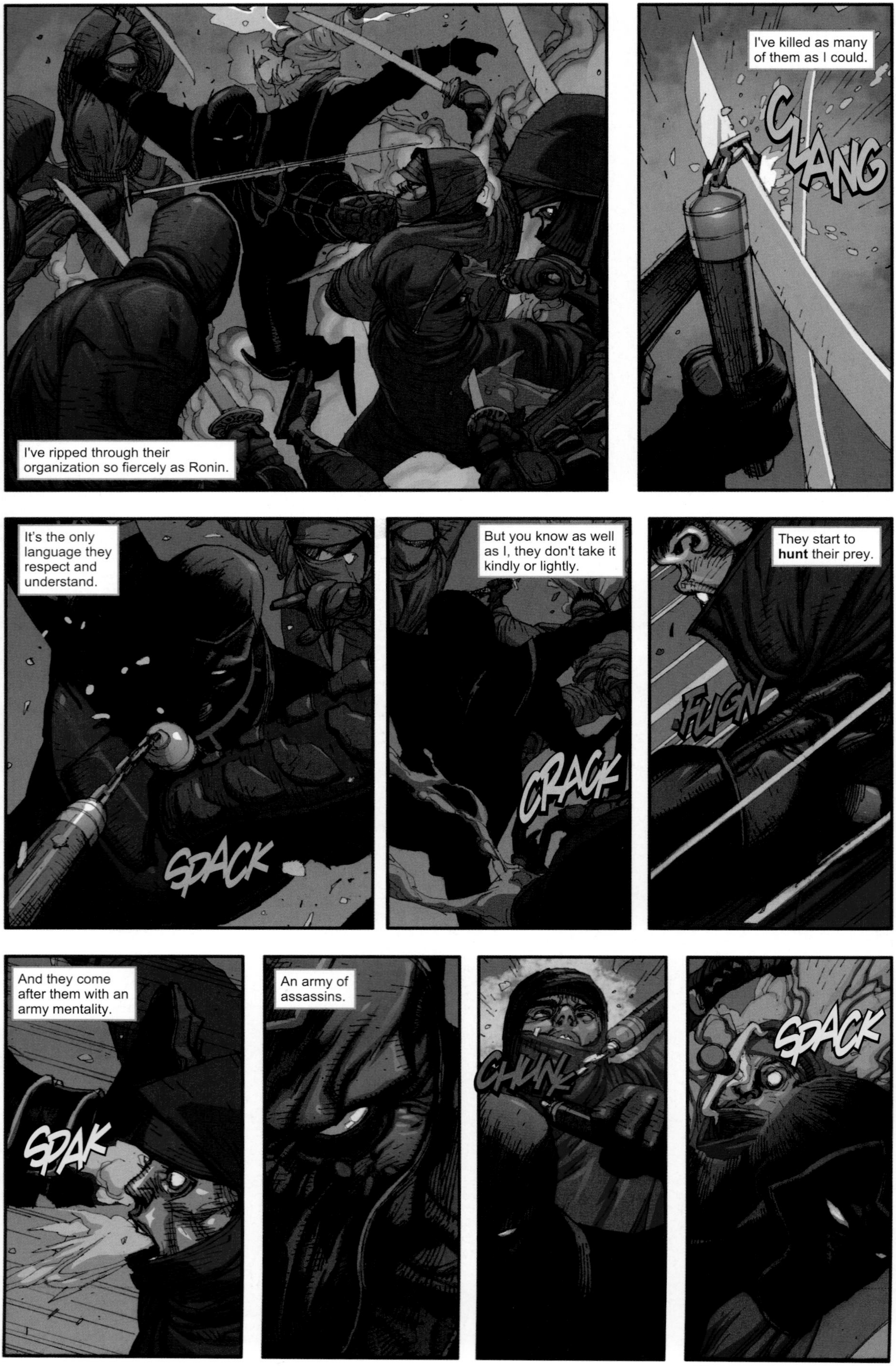
I've ripped through their organization so fiercely as Ronin.
I've killed as many of them as I could.
CLANG
It's the only language they respect and understand.
SPACK
But you know as well as I, they don't take it kindly or lightly.
CRACK
They start to **hunt** their prey.
FUGN
And they come after them with an army mentality.
SPAK
An army of assassins.
CHUNK
SPACK

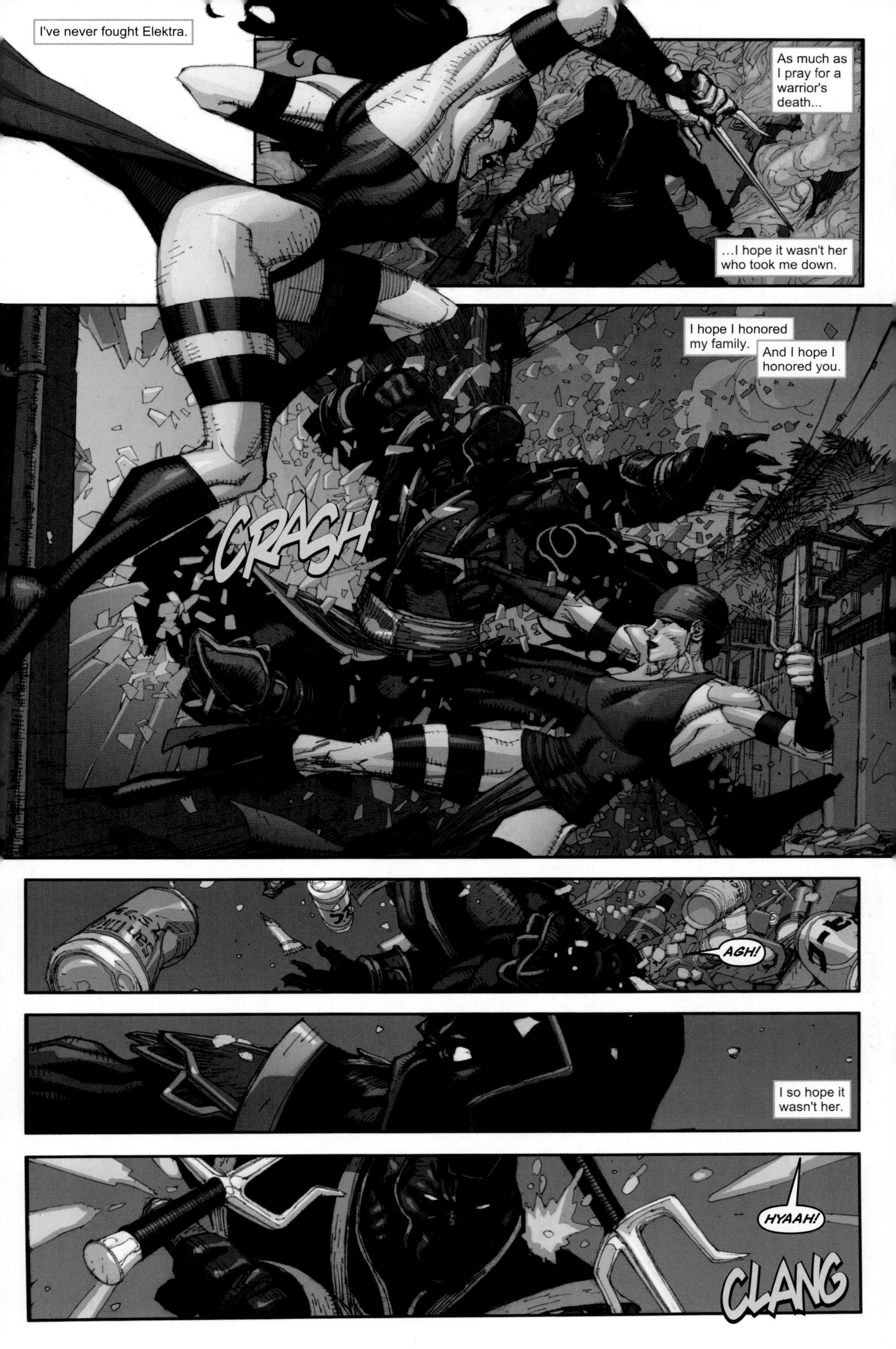

I've never fought Elektra.
As much as I pray for a warrior's death...
...I hope it wasn't her who took me down.
I hope I honored my family.
And I hope I honored you.
CRASH
AGH!
I so hope it wasn't her.
HYAAH!
CLANG

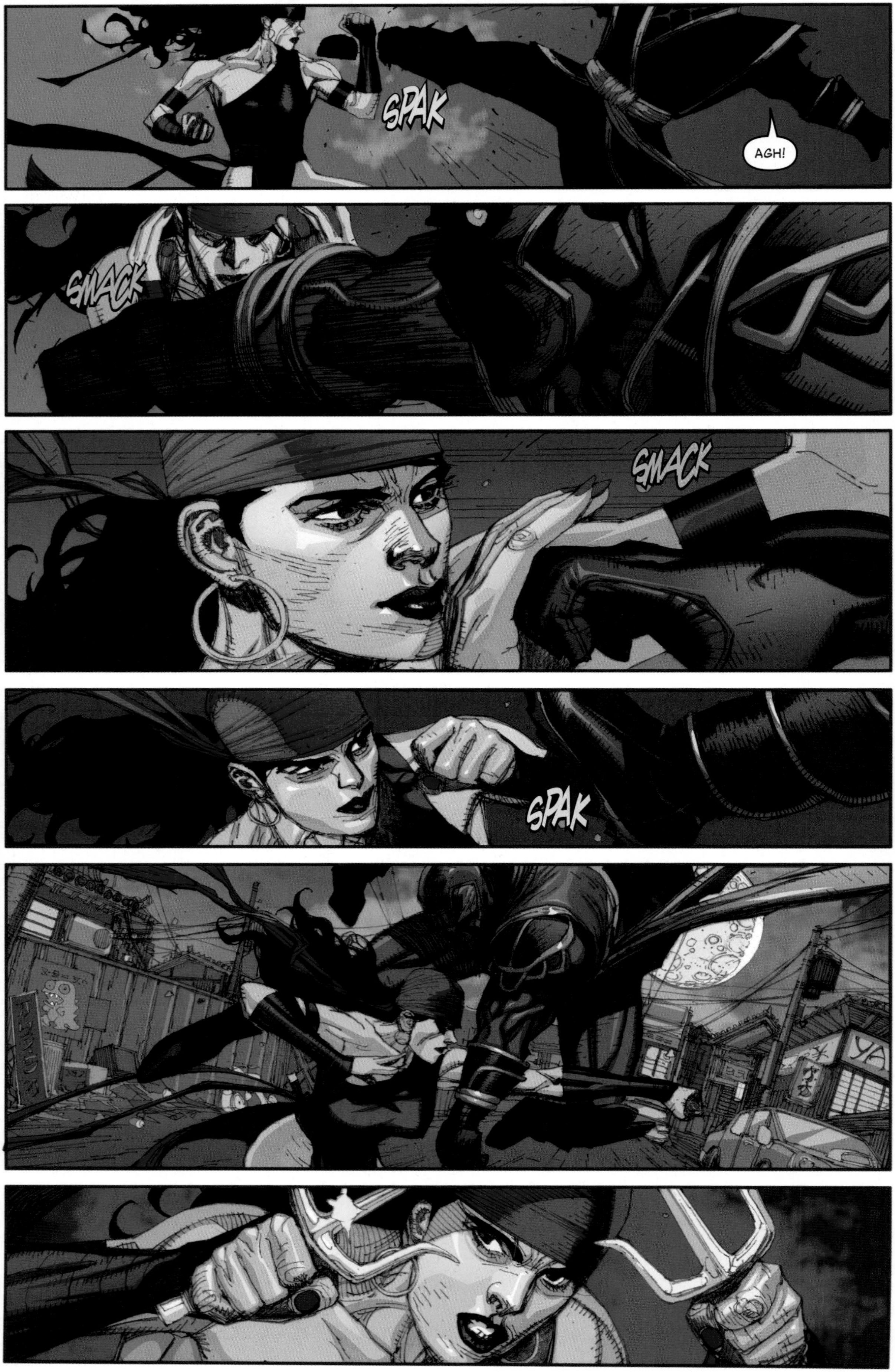
SPAK
AGH!
SMACK
SMACK
SPAK
YA

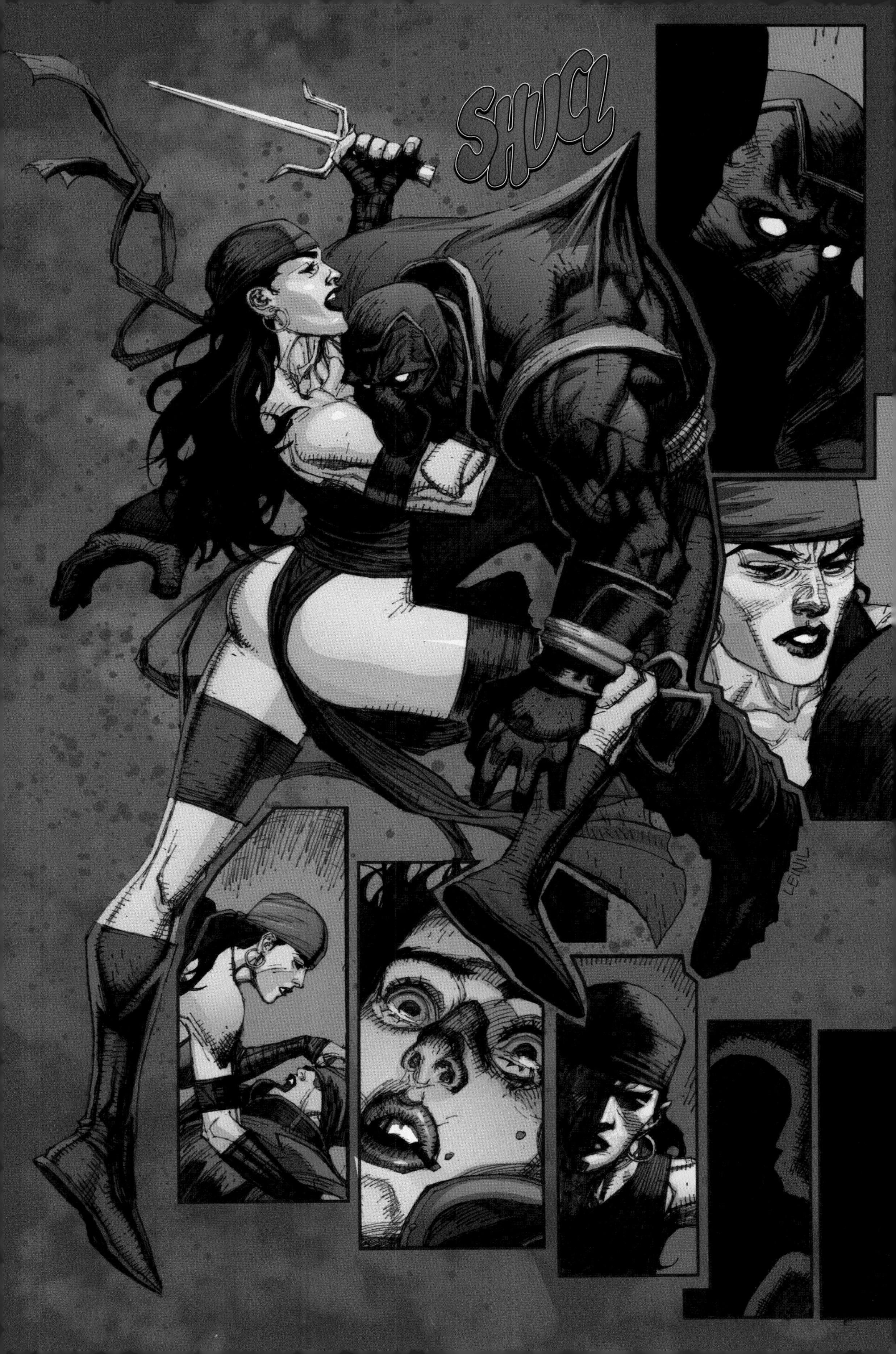
SHUCL
LEINIL

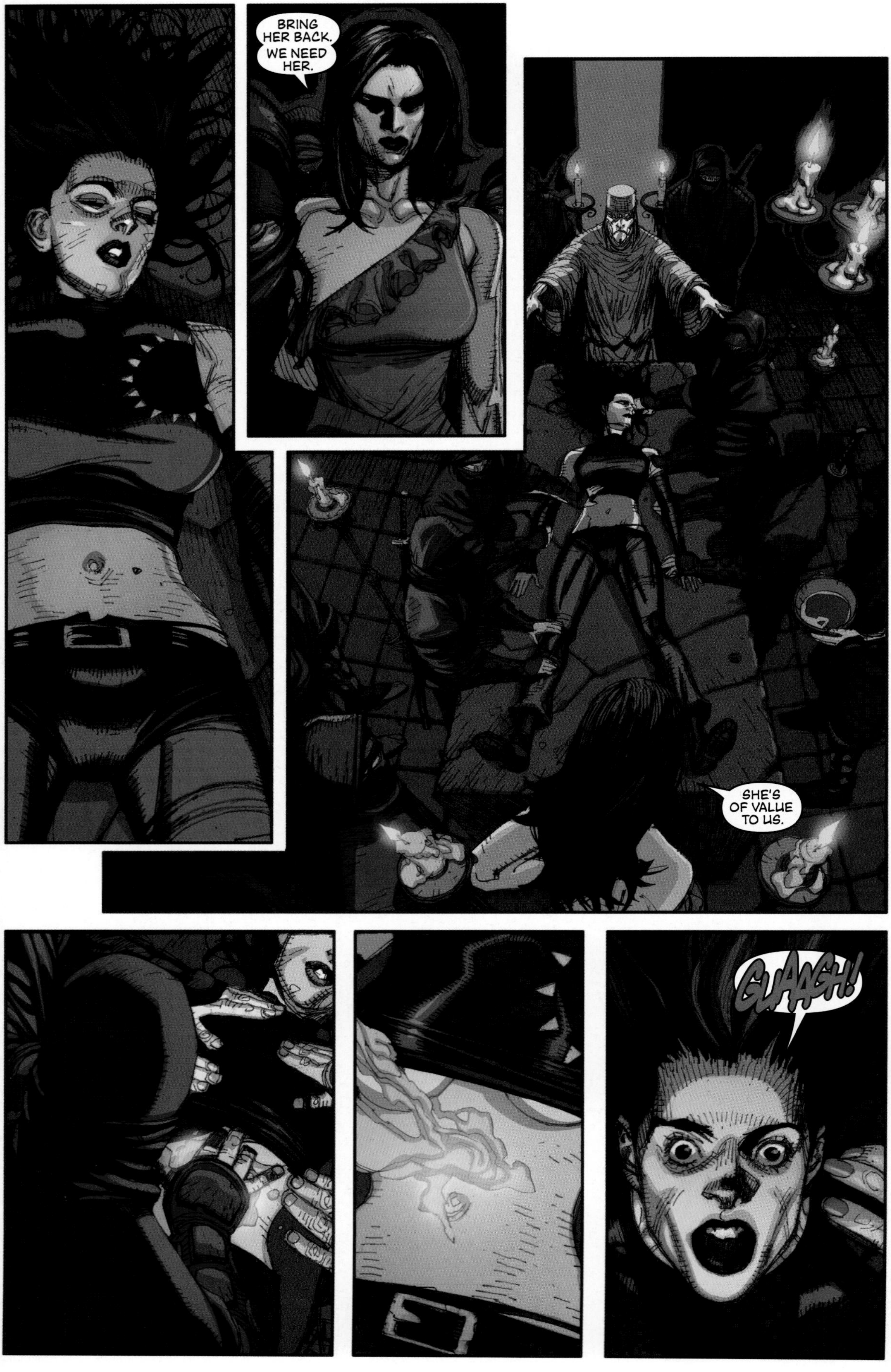
BRING HER BACK. WE NEED HER.
SHE'S OF VALUE TO US.
GUAAGH!

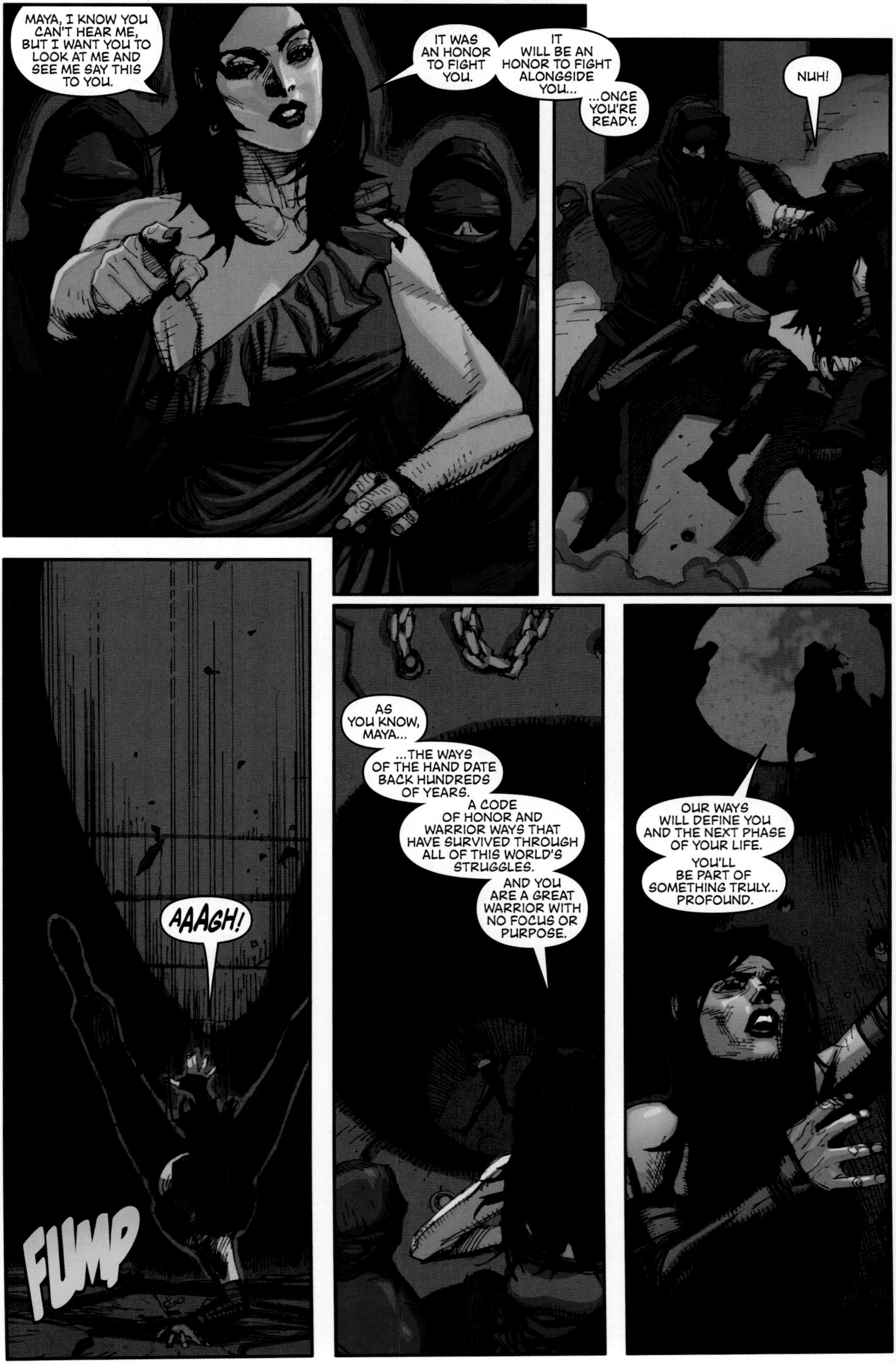

MAYA, I KNOW YOU CAN'T HEAR ME, BUT I WANT YOU TO LOOK AT ME AND SEE ME SAY THIS TO YOU.
IT WAS AN HONOR TO FIGHT YOU.
IT WILL BE AN HONOR TO FIGHT ALONGSIDE YOU...
...ONCE YOU'RE READY.
NUH!
AAAGH!
FUMP
AS YOU KNOW, MAYA...
...THE WAYS OF THE HAND DATE BACK HUNDREDS OF YEARS.
A CODE OF HONOR AND WARRIOR WAYS THAT HAVE SURVIVED THROUGH ALL OF THIS WORLD'S STRUGGLES.
AND YOU ARE A GREAT WARRIOR WITH NO FOCUS OR PURPOSE.
OUR WAYS WILL DEFINE YOU AND THE NEXT PHASE OF YOUR LIFE.
YOU'LL BE PART OF SOMETHING TRULY... PROFOUND.

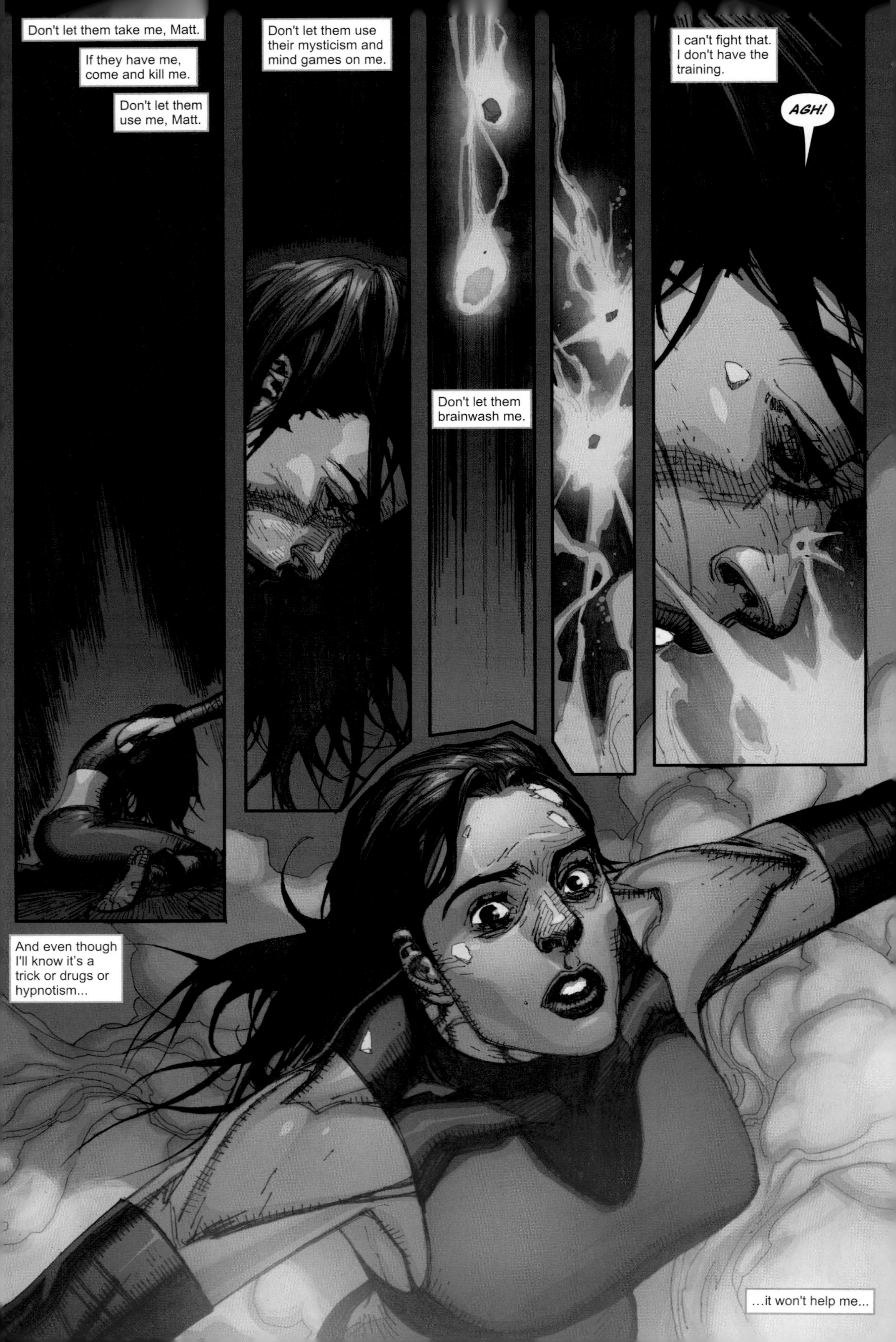
Don't let them take me, Matt.
If they have me, come and kill me.
Don't let them use me, Matt.
Don't let them use their mysticism and mind games on me.
Don't let them brainwash me.
I can't fight that. I don't have the training.
AGH!
And even though I'll know it's a trick or drugs or hypnotism...
...it won't help me...

...it'll only make it worse.

Don't let them crush me!

I mean it, Matt. I'm begging you.

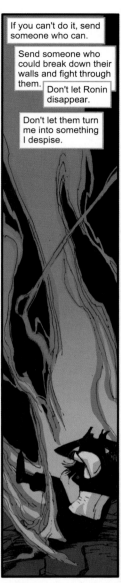

If you can't do it, send someone who can.

Send someone who could break down their walls and fight through them.

Don't let Ronin disappear.

Don't let them turn me into something I despise.

IF THE SCROLLS SAY THREE DAYS THEN THREE DAYS SHOULD BE--

And if they've killed me...

...avenge me.

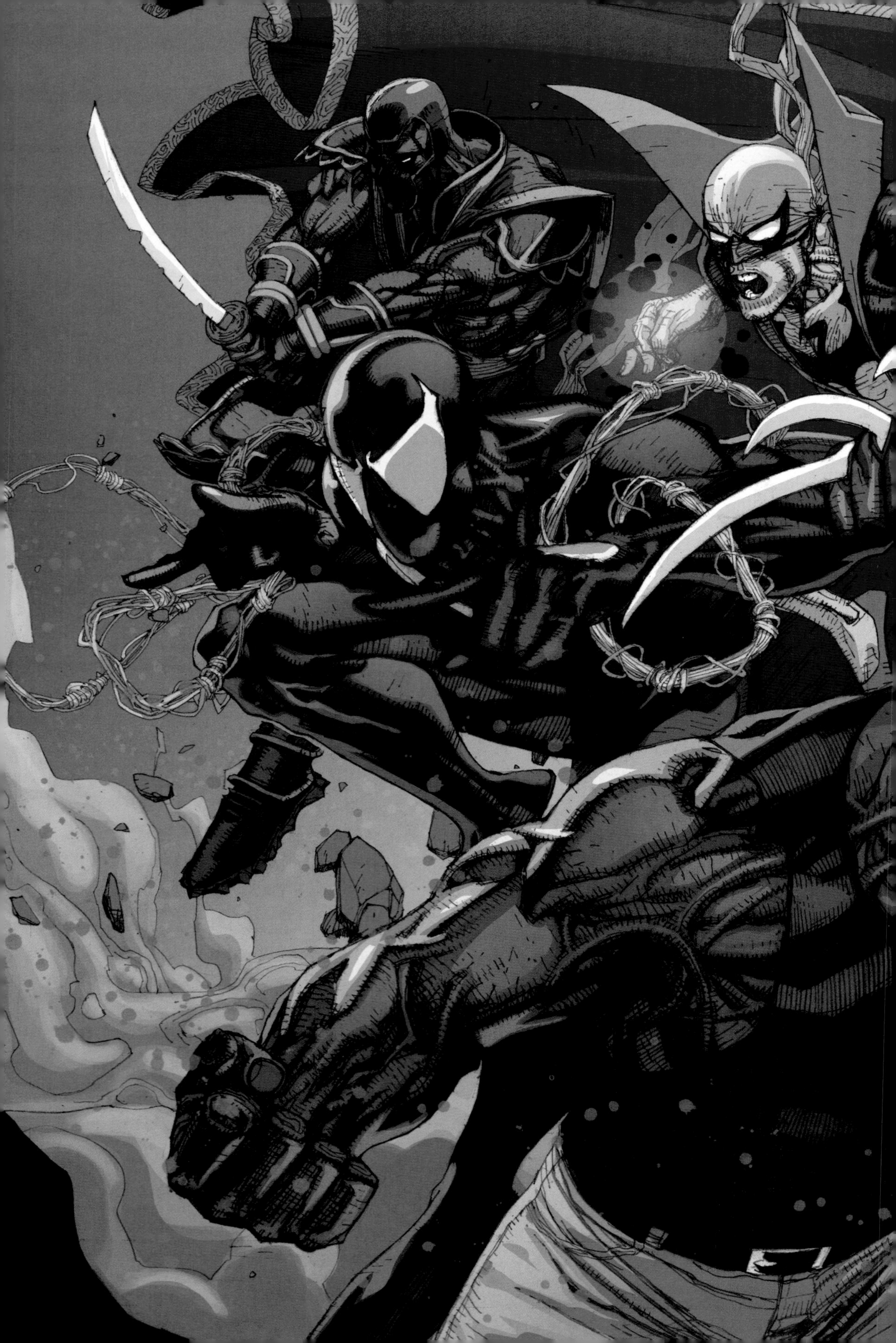

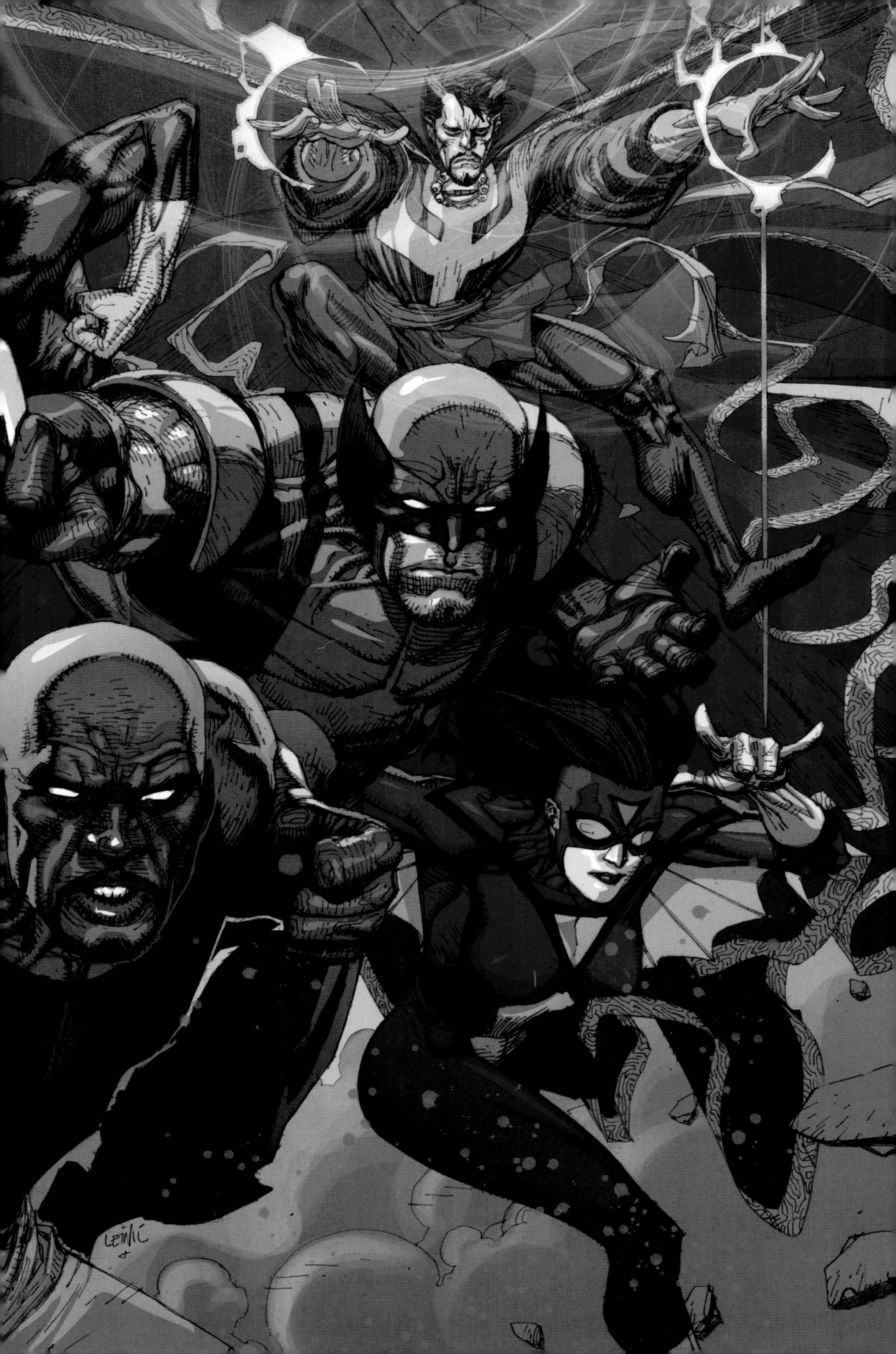

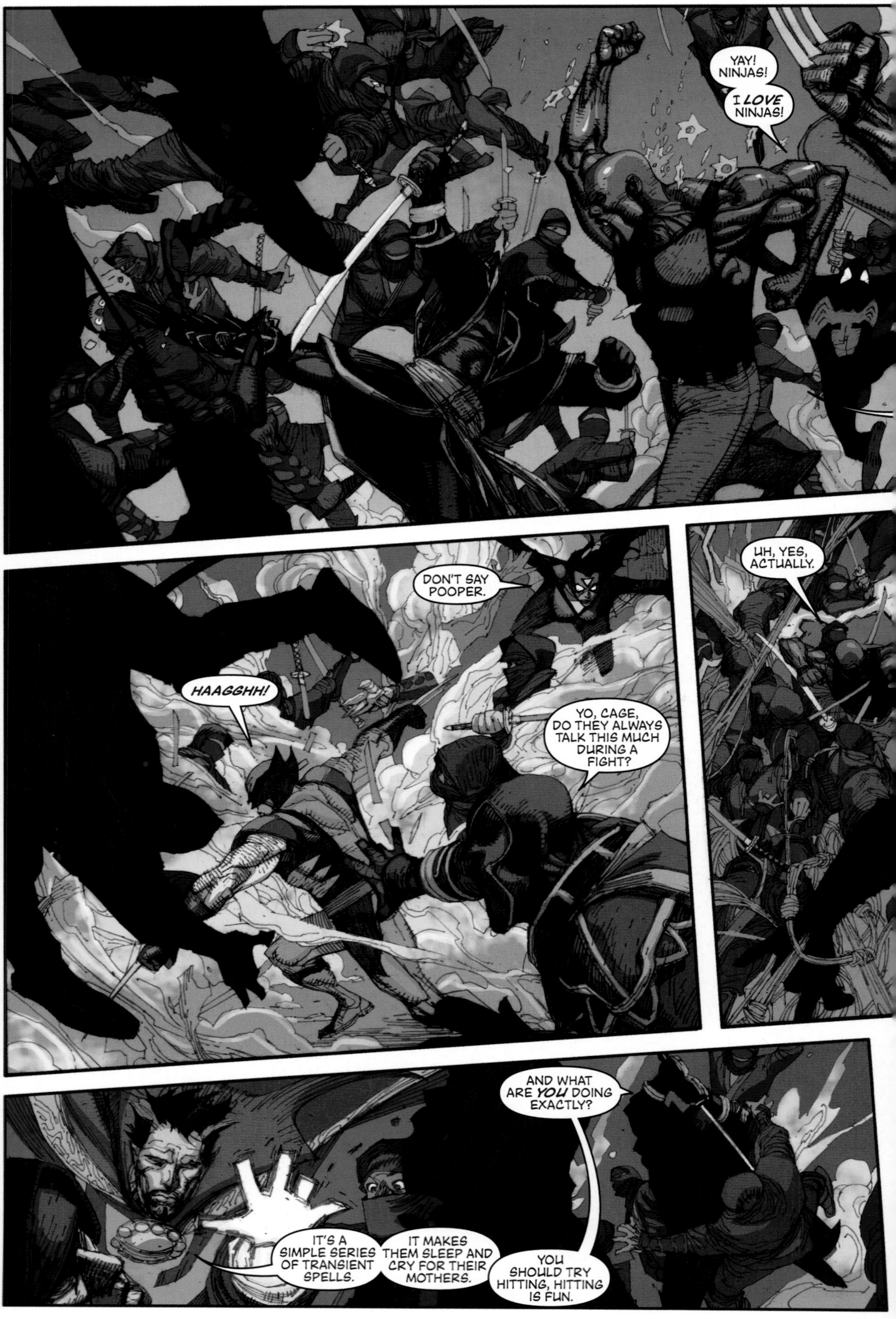
YAY! NINJAS!
I LOVE NINJAS!
DON'T SAY POOPER.
UH, YES, ACTUALLY.
HAAGGHH!
YO, CAGE, DO THEY ALWAYS TALK THIS MUCH DURING A FIGHT?
AND WHAT ARE YOU DOING EXACTLY?
IT'S A SIMPLE SERIES OF TRANSIENT SPELLS.
IT MAKES THEM SLEEP AND CRY FOR THEIR MOTHERS.
YOU SHOULD TRY HITTING, HITTING IS FUN.

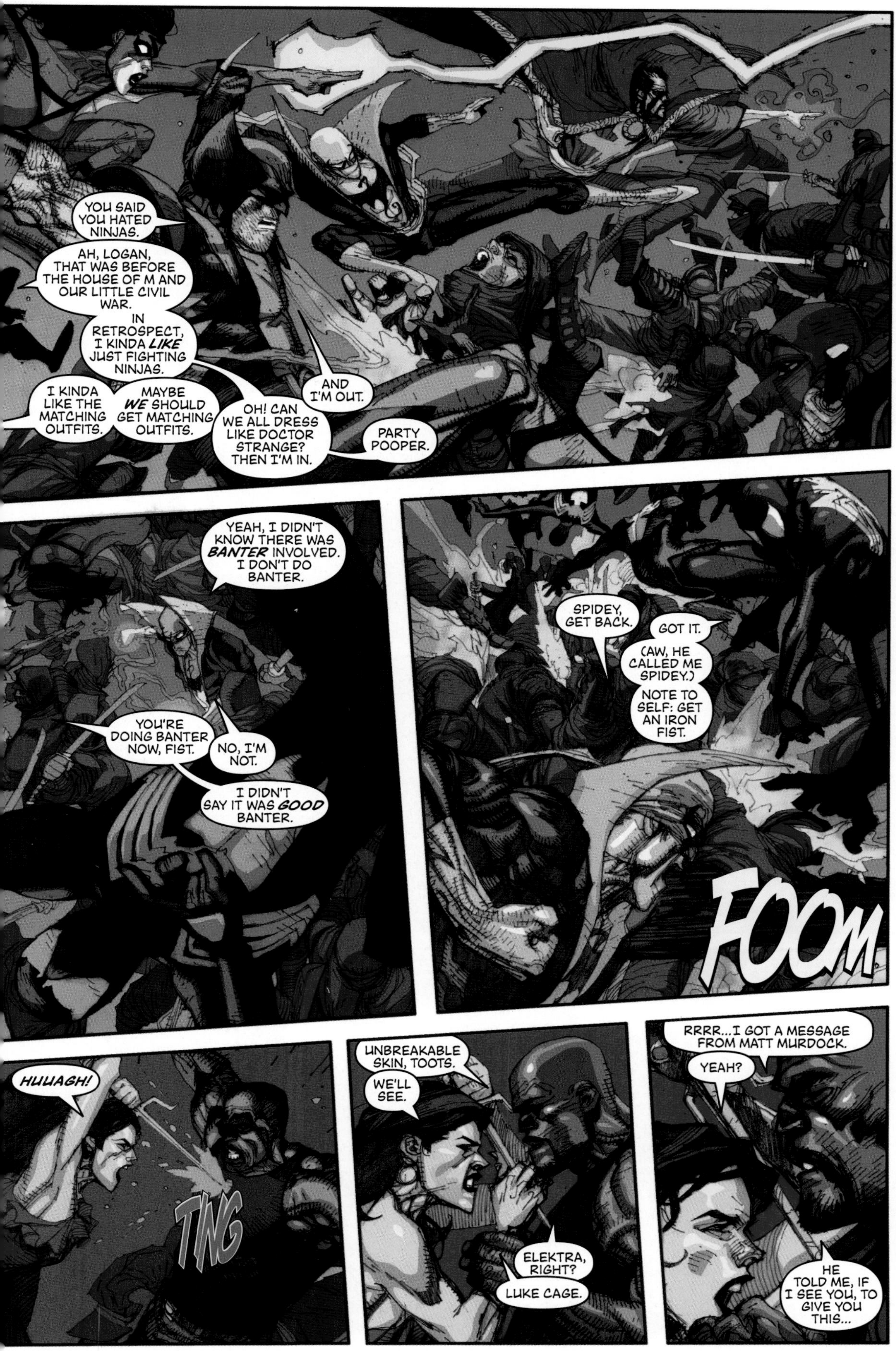
YOU SAID YOU HATED NINJAS.
AH, LOGAN, THAT WAS BEFORE THE HOUSE OF M AND OUR LITTLE CIVIL WAR.
IN RETROSPECT, I KINDA LIKE JUST FIGHTING NINJAS.
I KINDA LIKE THE MATCHING OUTFITS.
MAYBE WE SHOULD GET MATCHING OUTFITS.
OH! CAN WE ALL DRESS LIKE DOCTOR STRANGE? THEN I'M IN.
AND I'M OUT.
PARTY POOPER.
YEAH, I DIDN'T KNOW THERE WAS BANTER INVOLVED. I DON'T DO BANTER.
YOU'RE DOING BANTER NOW, FIST.
NO, I'M NOT.
I DIDN'T SAY IT WAS GOOD BANTER.
SPIDEY, GET BACK.
GOT IT.
(AW, HE CALLED ME SPIDEY.)
NOTE TO SELF: GET AN IRON FIST.
FOOM
HUUAGH!
TING
UNBREAKABLE SKIN, TOOTS.
WE'LL SEE.
ELEKTRA, RIGHT?
LUKE CAGE.
RRRR...I GOT A MESSAGE FROM MATT MURDOCK.
YEAH?
HE TOLD ME, IF I SEE YOU, TO GIVE YOU THIS...

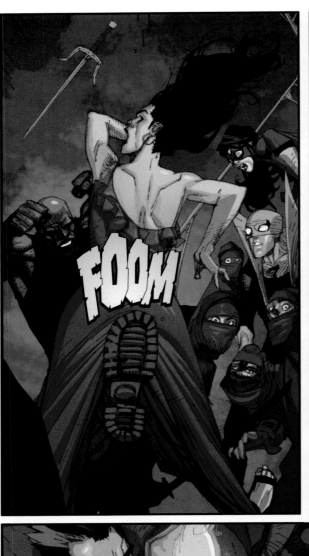

OOF!

THAT *HAD* TO HURT!

DON'T SCREW AROUND! WE GOTTA KEEP MOVING.

DO LIKE WE SAID.

OKAY, OKAY. JEEZ...

HI. MY NAME IS LUKE SKYWALKER AND I'M HERE TO RESCUE YOU.

(SORRY, I ALWAYS WANTED TO SAY THAT.)

COME ON, ALL THE COOL AVENGERS ARE HERE. CAN YOU READ MY LIPS? MATT MURDOCK SENT US TO GET YOU AND WE GOT YOU, SO LET'S...

THE AVENGERSSS BROKE UP.

I KNOW...

THISSS IS A TRICK...

WE'RE THE *NEW* NEW AVENGERS.

COME ON...

NOOO...

I PROMISE I'M HERE TO HELP YOU.

(MAN, WHAT DID THEY DO TO YOU?)

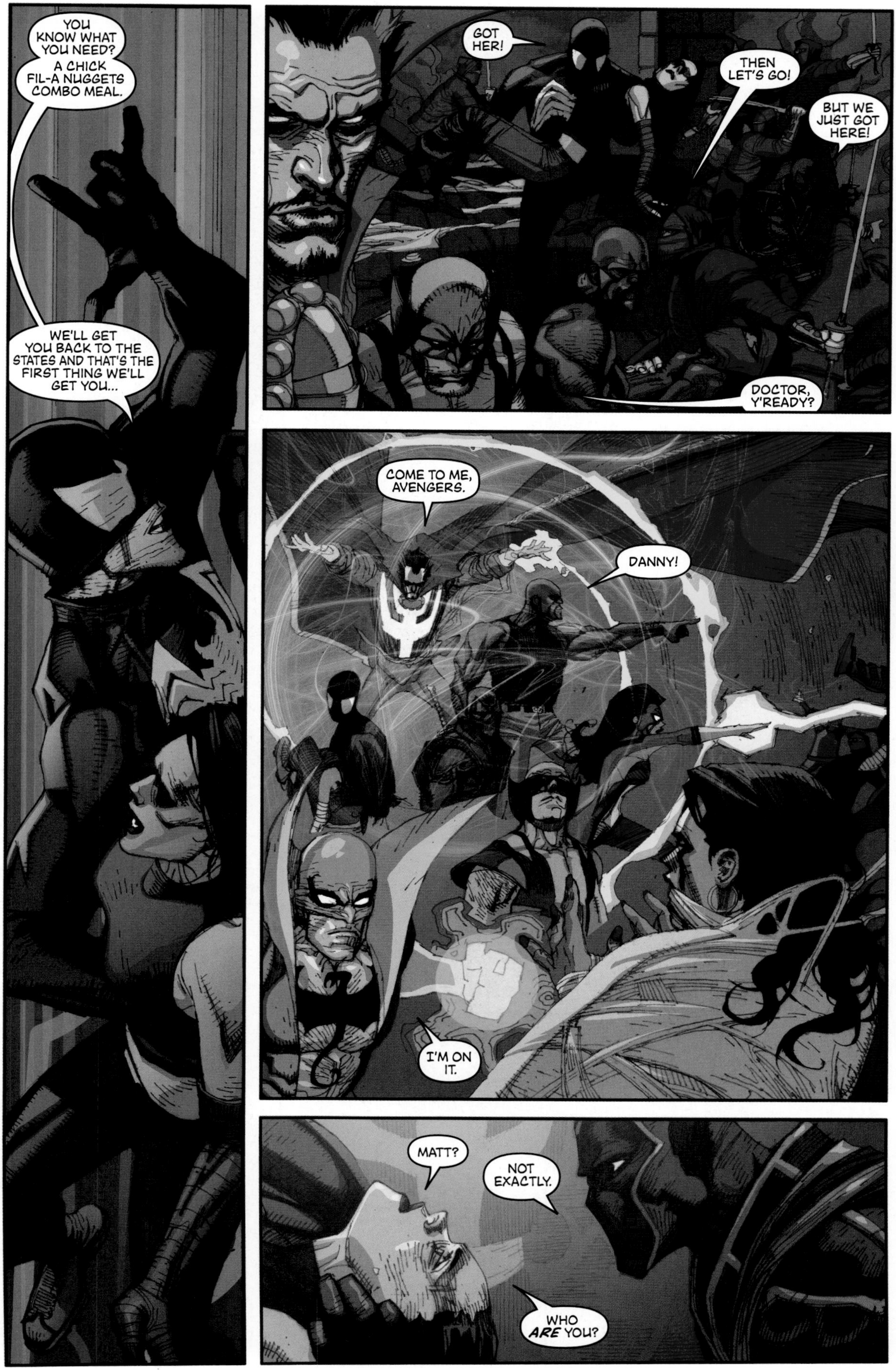
YOU KNOW WHAT YOU NEED? A CHICK FIL-A NUGGETS COMBO MEAL.
WE'LL GET YOU BACK TO THE STATES AND THAT'S THE FIRST THING WE'LL GET YOU...
GOT HER!
THEN LET'S GO!
BUT WE JUST GOT HERE!
DOCTOR, Y'READY?
COME TO ME, AVENGERS.
DANNY!
I'M ON IT.
MATT?
NOT EXACTLY.
WHO *ARE* YOU?

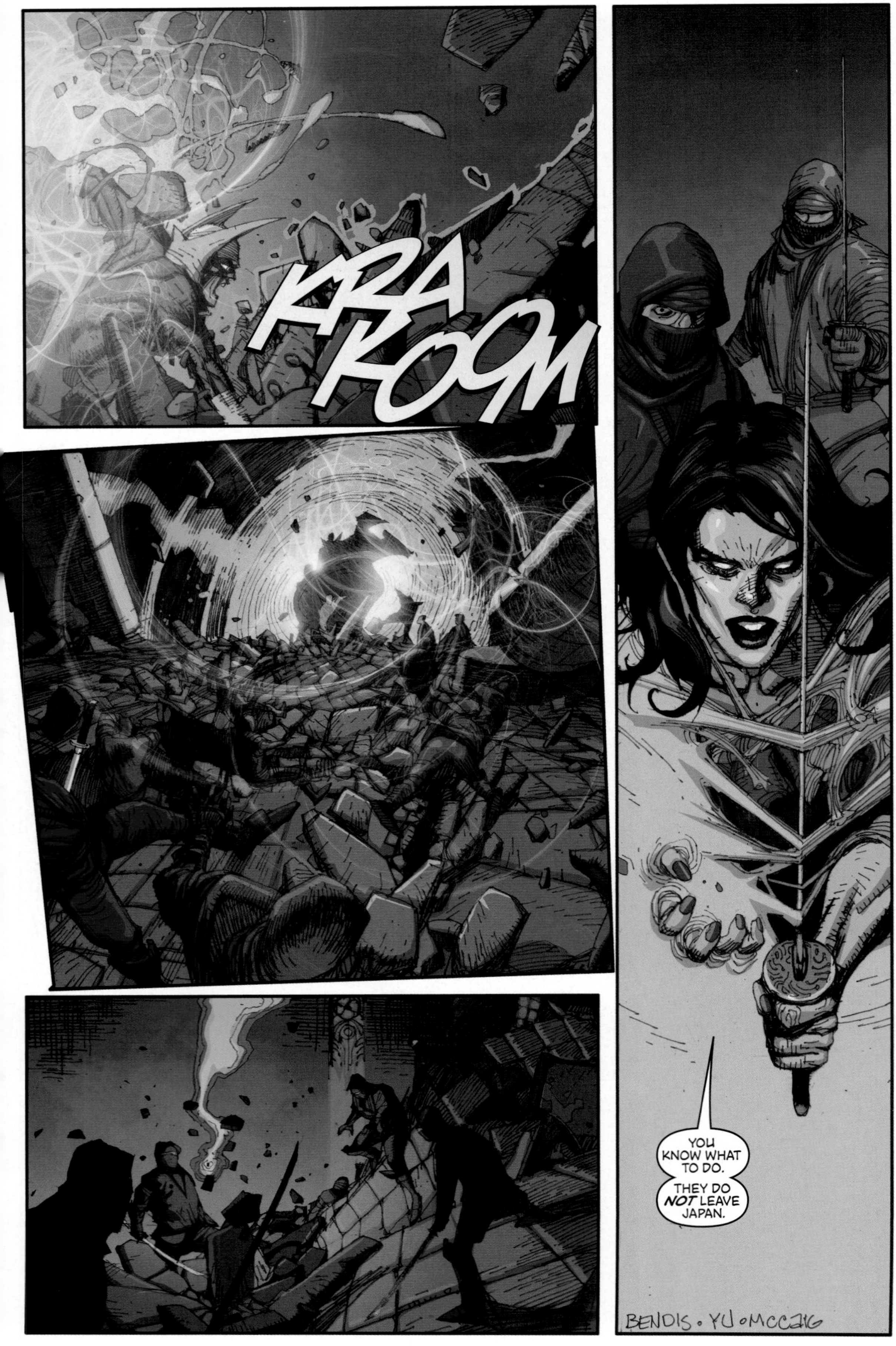
KRA KOOM
YOU KNOW WHAT TO DO.
THEY DO *NOT* LEAVE JAPAN.
BENDIS • YU • MCCAIG

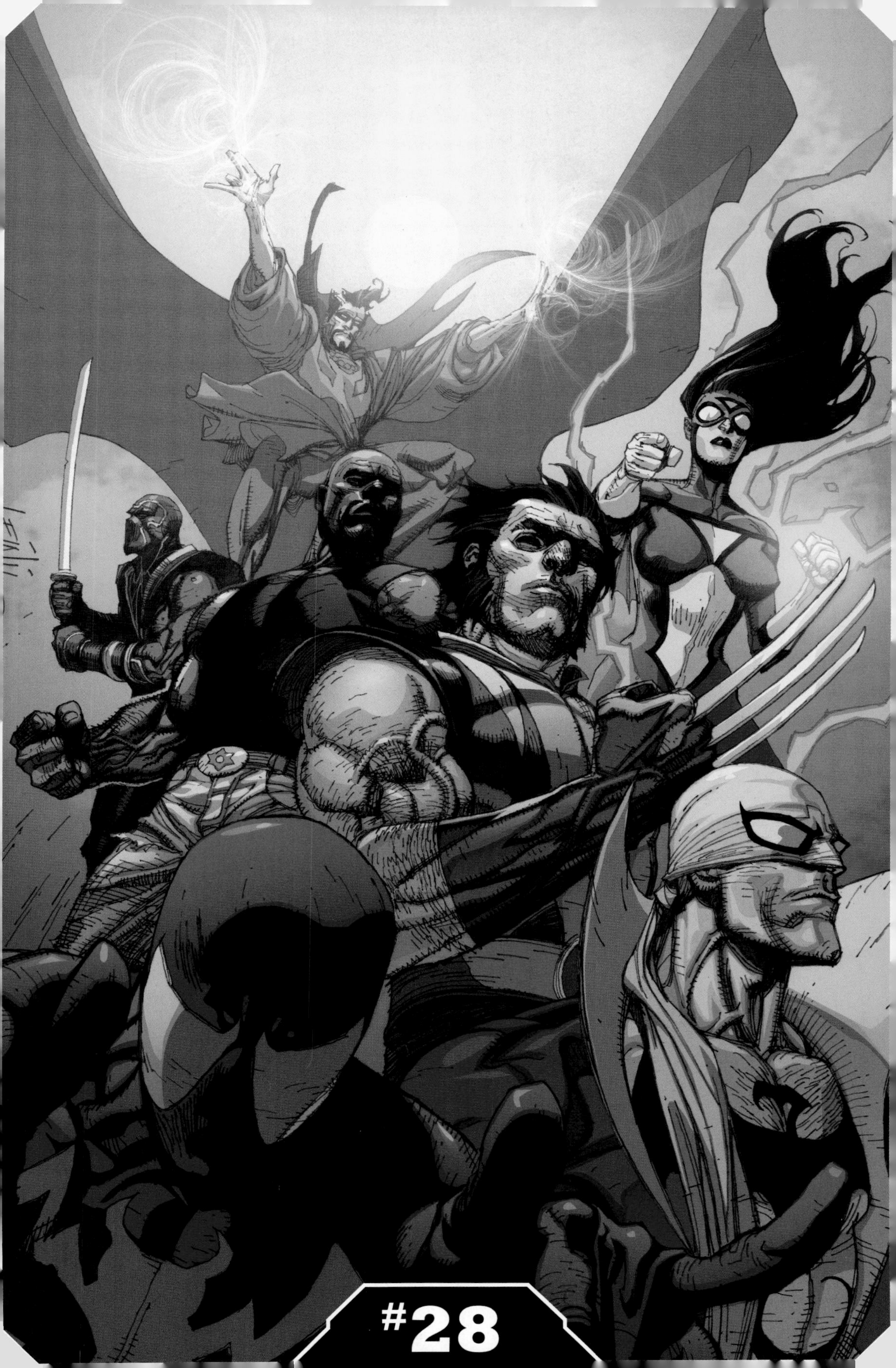
#28

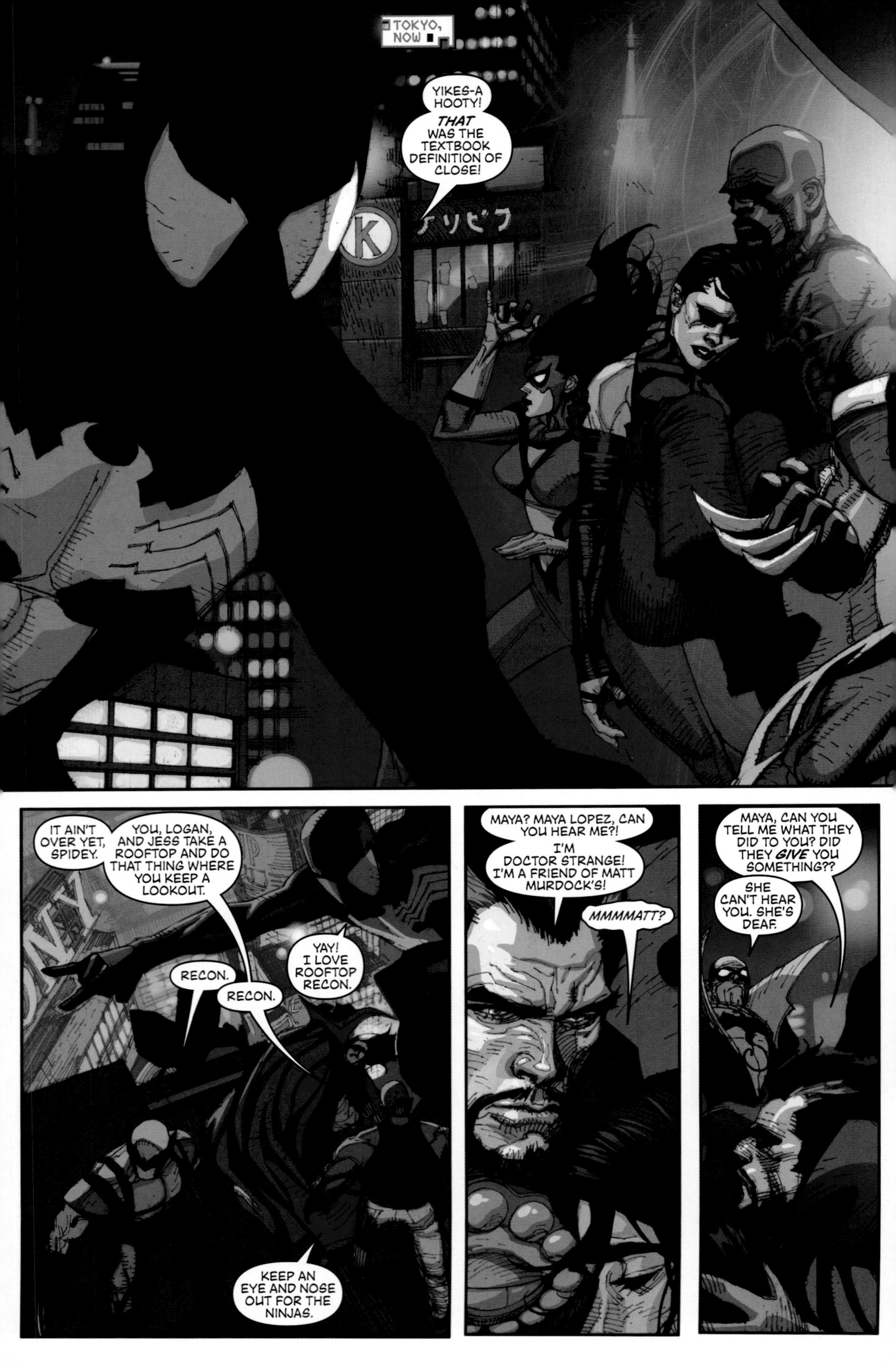
TOKYO, NOW
YIKES-A HOOTY! *THAT* WAS THE TEXTBOOK DEFINITION OF CLOSE!
IT AIN'T OVER YET, SPIDEY.
YOU, LOGAN, AND JESS TAKE A ROOFTOP AND DO THAT THING WHERE YOU KEEP A LOOKOUT.
YAY! I LOVE ROOFTOP RECON.
RECON.
RECON.
KEEP AN EYE AND NOSE OUT FOR THE NINJAS.
MAYA? MAYA LOPEZ, CAN YOU HEAR ME?!
I'M DOCTOR STRANGE! I'M A FRIEND OF MATT MURDOCK'S!
MMMMATT?
MAYA, CAN YOU TELL ME WHAT THEY DID TO YOU? DID THEY *GIVE* YOU SOMETHING??
SHE CAN'T HEAR YOU. SHE'S DEAF.

TTTHEY KILLED ME... AND THEN BROUGHT ME... TTTHEY BROUGHT ME BACK. AND THEN A BLUE DEMON.

BLUE... BLUE PILL...

BLUE PILL?

GOOD LORD, THEY WERE TRYING TO BRAINWASH HER.

REAL OLD-SCHOOL NINJA %^¢#.

IS IT TOO LATE?

NO. BUT WE HAVE TO GET HER SOMEWHERE SAFE.

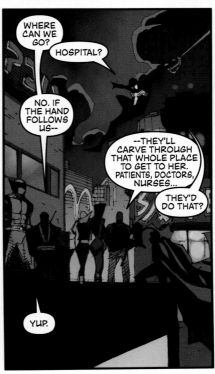

WHERE CAN WE GO?

HOSPITAL?

NO. IF THE HAND FOLLOWS US--

--THEY'LL CARVE THROUGH THAT WHOLE PLACE TO GET TO HER. PATIENTS, DOCTORS, NURSES...

THEY'D DO THAT?

YUP.

I KNOW WHERE WE CAN GO.

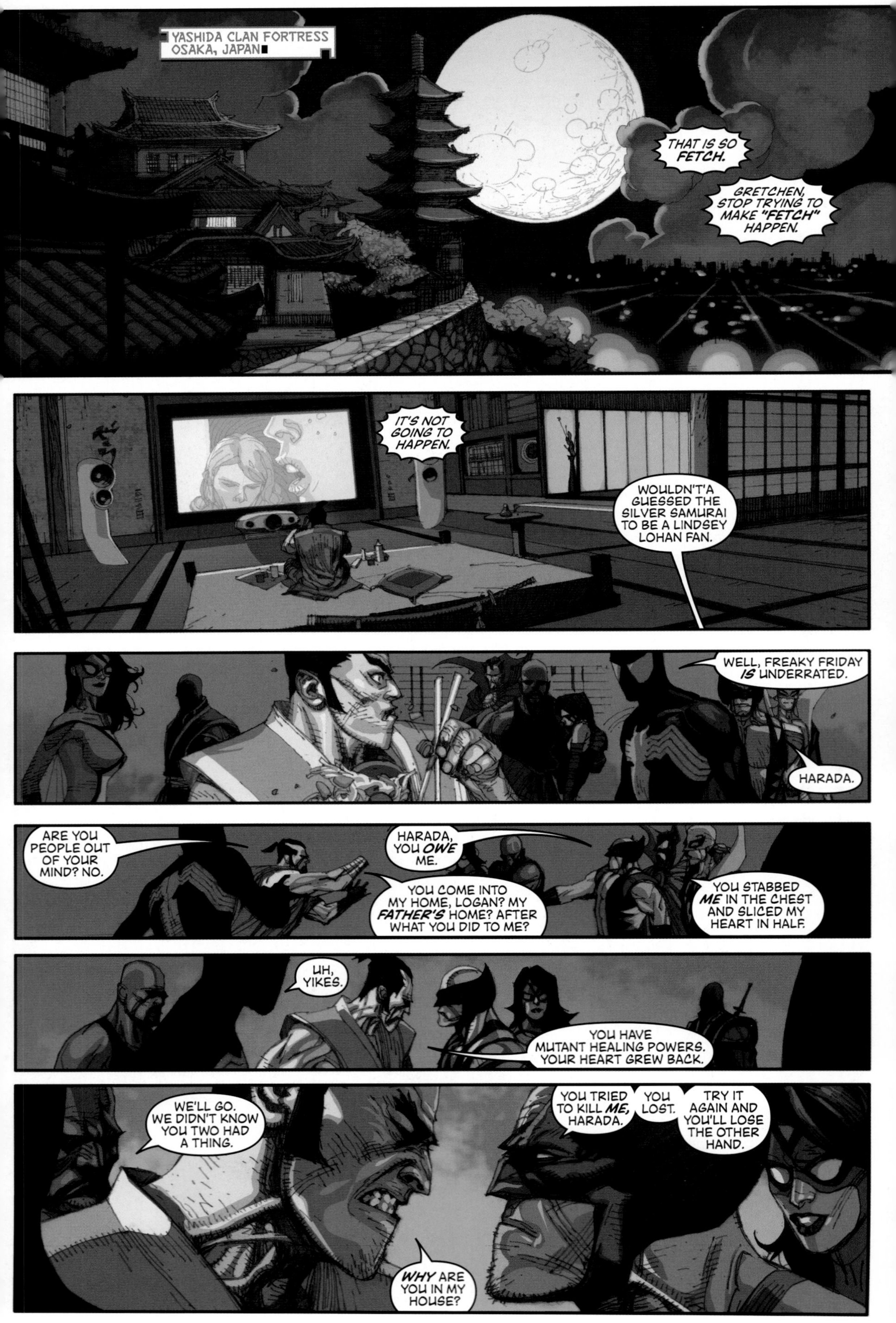

YASHIDA CLAN FORTRESS
OSAKA, JAPAN
THAT IS SO FETCH.
GRETCHEN, STOP TRYING TO MAKE "FETCH" HAPPEN.
IT'S NOT GOING TO HAPPEN.
WOULDN'T'A GUESSED THE SILVER SAMURAI TO BE A LINDSEY LOHAN FAN.
WELL, FREAKY FRIDAY IS UNDERRATED.
HARADA.
ARE YOU PEOPLE OUT OF YOUR MIND? NO.
HARADA, YOU OWE ME.
YOU COME INTO MY HOME, LOGAN? MY FATHER'S HOME? AFTER WHAT YOU DID TO ME?
YOU STABBED ME IN THE CHEST AND SLICED MY HEART IN HALF.
UH, YIKES.
YOU HAVE MUTANT HEALING POWERS. YOUR HEART GREW BACK.
WE'LL GO. WE DIDN'T KNOW YOU TWO HAD A THING.
YOU TRIED TO KILL ME, HARADA.
YOU LOST.
TRY IT AGAIN AND YOU'LL LOSE THE OTHER HAND.
WHY ARE YOU IN MY HOUSE?

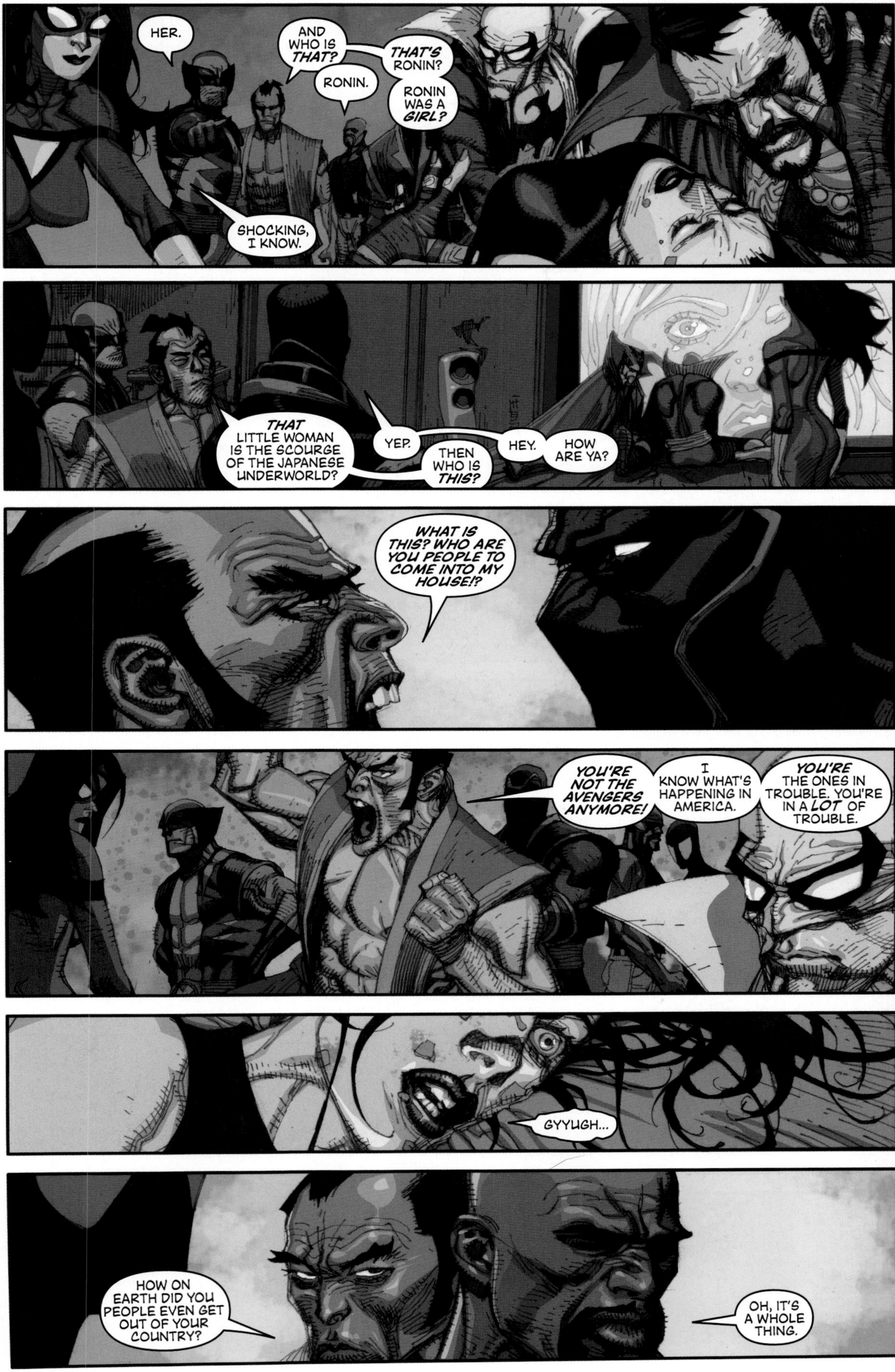
HER.
AND WHO IS THAT?
RONIN.
THAT'S RONIN?
RONIN WAS A GIRL?
SHOCKING, I KNOW.
THAT LITTLE WOMAN IS THE SCOURGE OF THE JAPANESE UNDERWORLD?
YEP.
THEN WHO IS THIS?
HEY.
HOW ARE YA?
WHAT IS THIS? WHO ARE YOU PEOPLE TO COME INTO MY HOUSE!?
YOU'RE NOT THE AVENGERS ANYMORE!
I KNOW WHAT'S HAPPENING IN AMERICA.
YOU'RE THE ONES IN TROUBLE. YOU'RE IN A LOT OF TROUBLE.
GYYUGH...
HOW ON EARTH DID YOU PEOPLE EVEN GET OUT OF YOUR COUNTRY?
OH, IT'S A WHOLE THING.

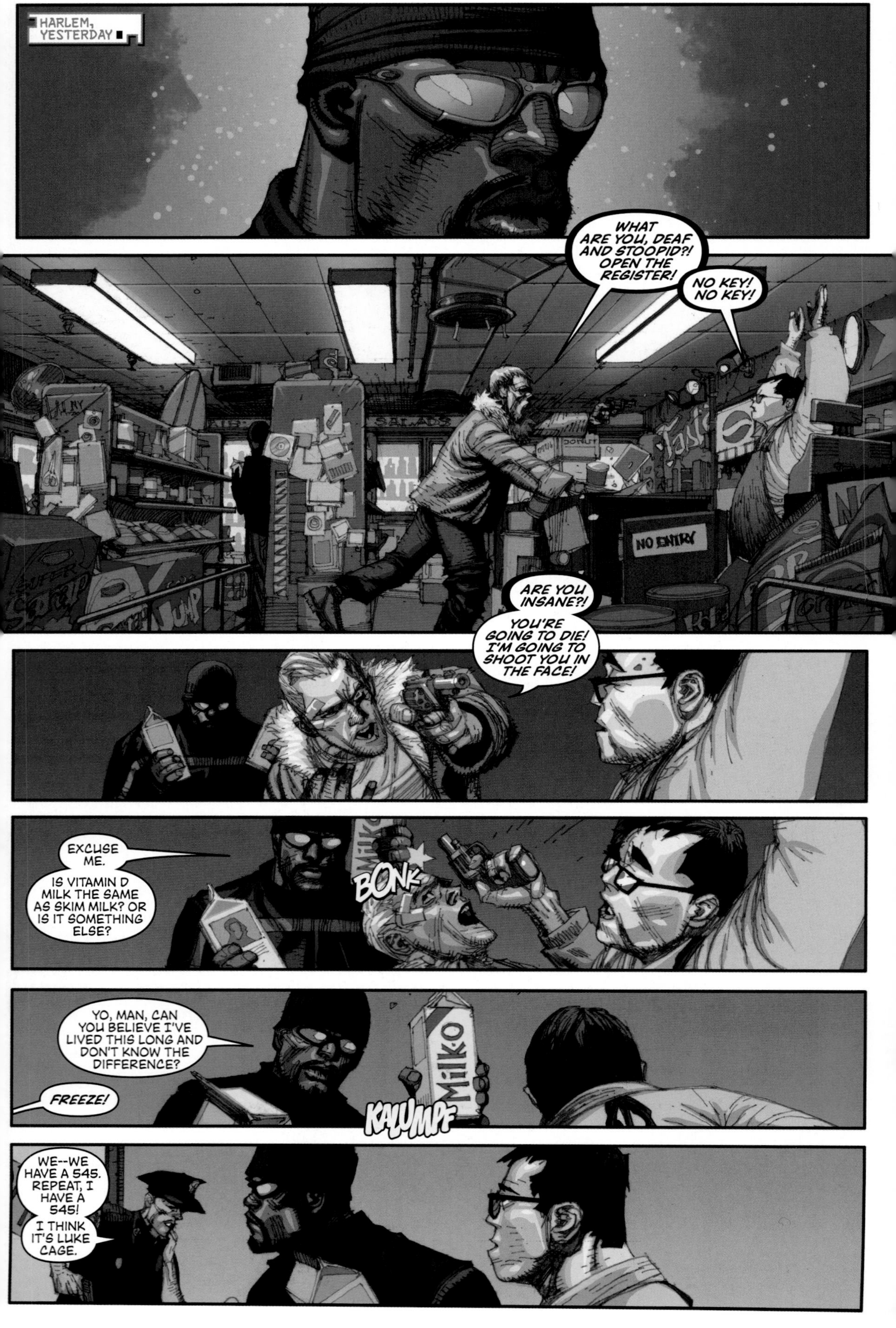
HARLEM, YESTERDAY
WHAT ARE YOU, DEAF AND STOOPID?! OPEN THE REGISTER!
NO KEY! NO KEY!
NO ENTRY
ARE YOU INSANE?!
YOU'RE GOING TO DIE! I'M GOING TO SHOOT YOU IN THE FACE!
EXCUSE ME.
IS VITAMIN D MILK THE SAME AS SKIM MILK? OR IS IT SOMETHING ELSE?
BONK
YO, MAN, CAN YOU BELIEVE I'VE LIVED THIS LONG AND DON'T KNOW THE DIFFERENCE?
FREEZE!
MilkO
KALUMPF
WE--WE HAVE A 545. REPEAT, I HAVE A 545!
I THINK IT'S LUKE CAGE.

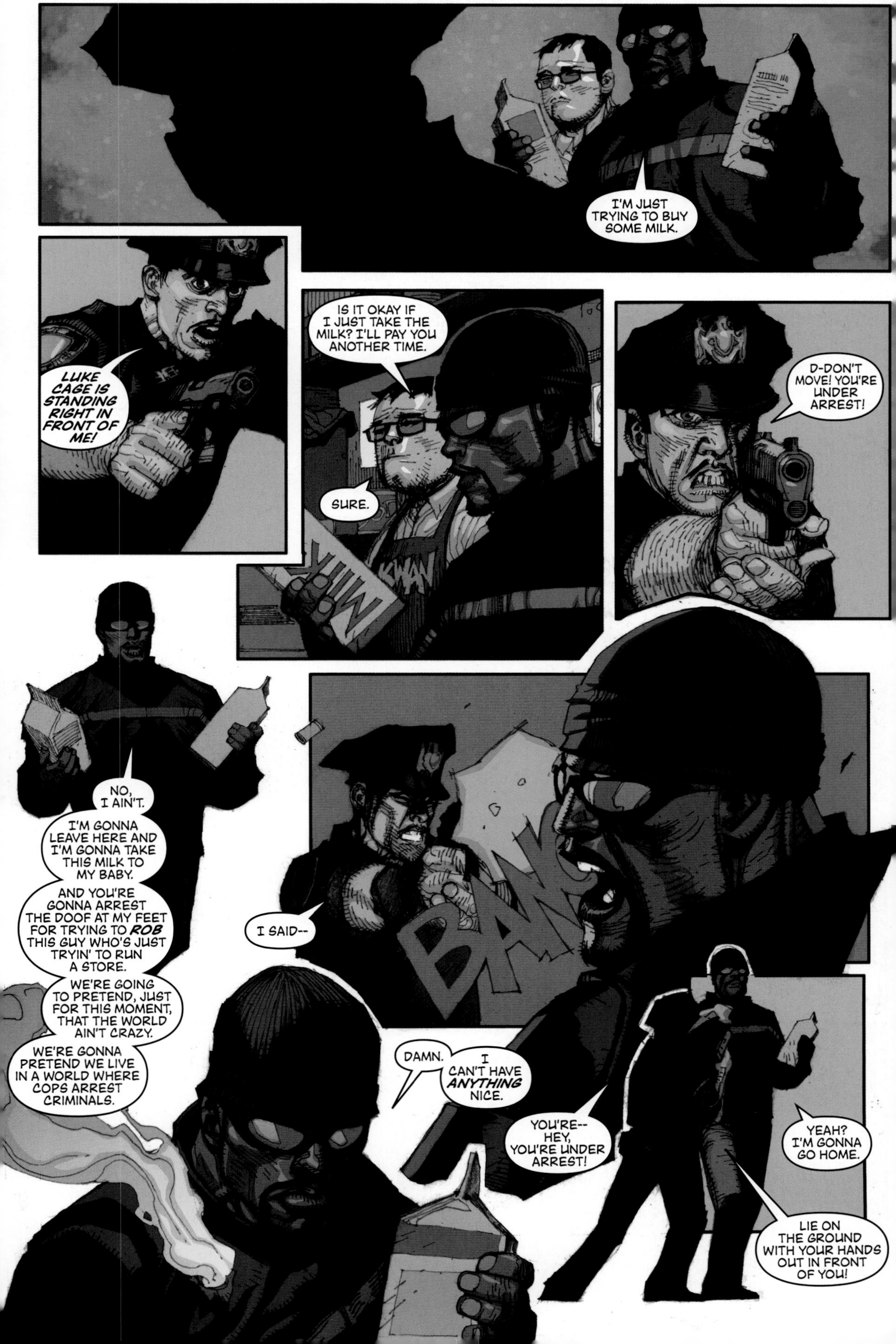
I'M JUST TRYING TO BUY SOME MILK.
LUKE CAGE IS STANDING RIGHT IN FRONT OF ME!
IS IT OKAY IF I JUST TAKE THE MILK? I'LL PAY YOU ANOTHER TIME.
SURE.
KWAN
MILK
D-DON'T MOVE! YOU'RE UNDER ARREST!
NO, I AIN'T.
I'M GONNA LEAVE HERE AND I'M GONNA TAKE THIS MILK TO MY BABY.
AND YOU'RE GONNA ARREST THE DOOF AT MY FEET FOR TRYING TO ROB THIS GUY WHO'S JUST TRYIN' TO RUN A STORE.
WE'RE GOING TO PRETEND, JUST FOR THIS MOMENT, THAT THE WORLD AIN'T CRAZY.
WE'RE GONNA PRETEND WE LIVE IN A WORLD WHERE COPS ARREST CRIMINALS.
I SAID--
BAM
DAMN.
I CAN'T HAVE ANYTHING NICE.
YOU'RE-- HEY, YOU'RE UNDER ARREST!
YEAH? I'M GONNA GO HOME.
LIE ON THE GROUND WITH YOUR HANDS OUT IN FRONT OF YOU!

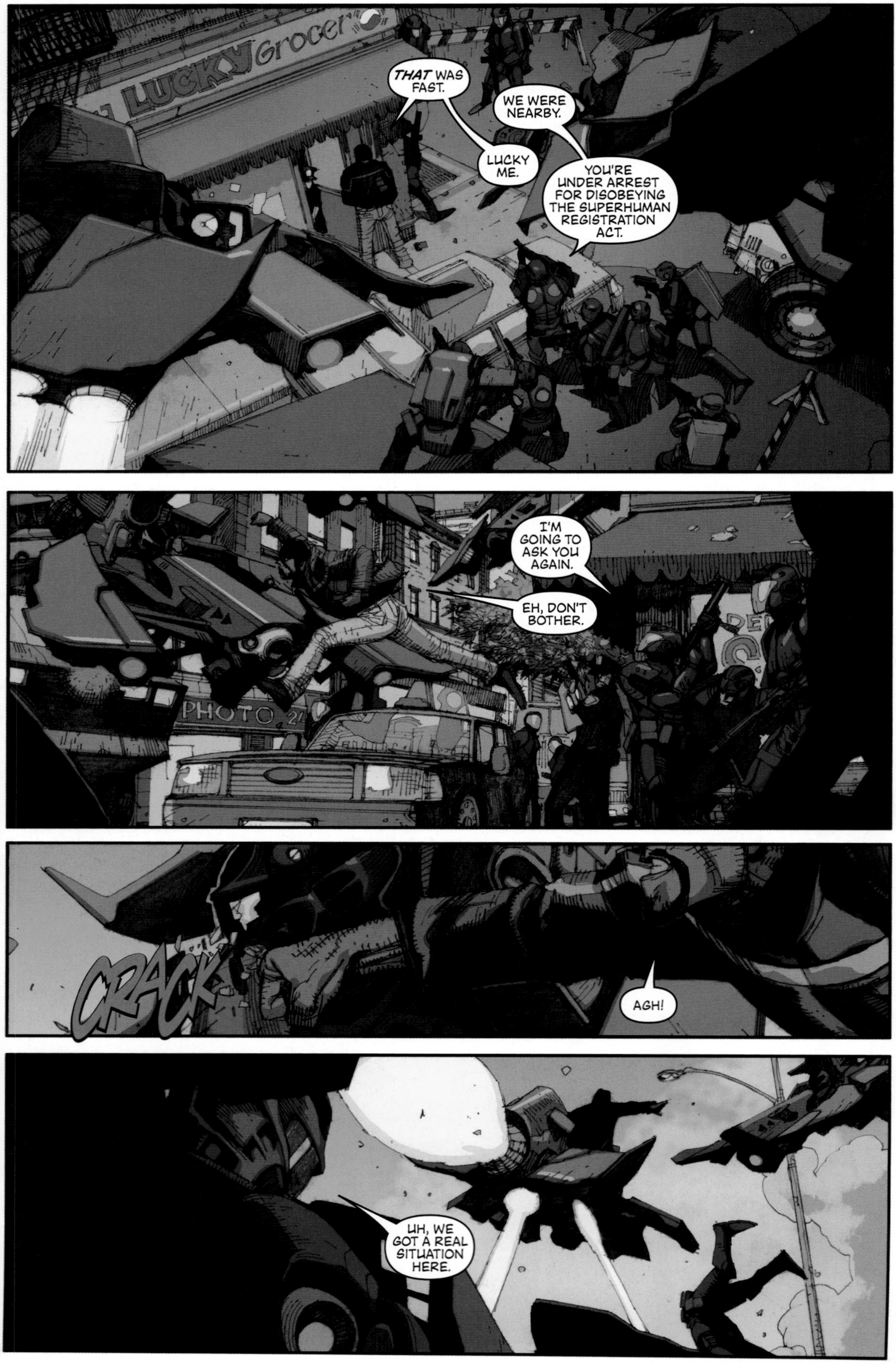
LUCKY Grocer
THAT WAS FAST.
WE WERE NEARBY.
LUCKY ME.
YOU'RE UNDER ARREST FOR DISOBEYING THE SUPERHUMAN REGISTRATION ACT.
I'M GOING TO ASK YOU AGAIN.
EH, DON'T BOTHER.
PHOTO
CRACK
AGH!
UH, WE GOT A REAL SITUATION HERE.

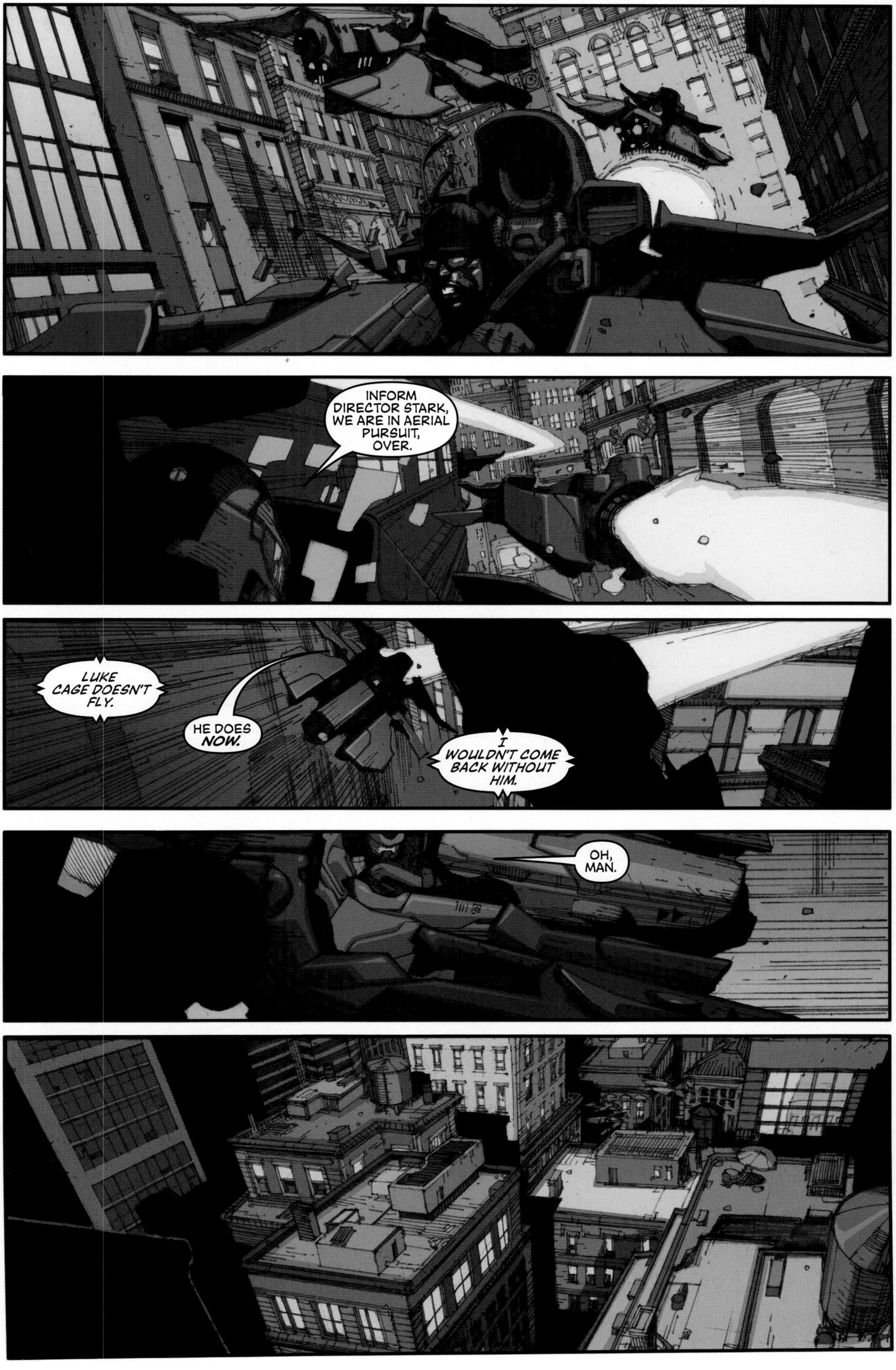
INFORM DIRECTOR STARK, WE ARE IN AERIAL PURSUIT, OVER.
LUKE CAGE DOESN'T FLY.
HE DOES NOW.
I WOULDN'T COME BACK WITHOUT HIM.
OH, MAN.

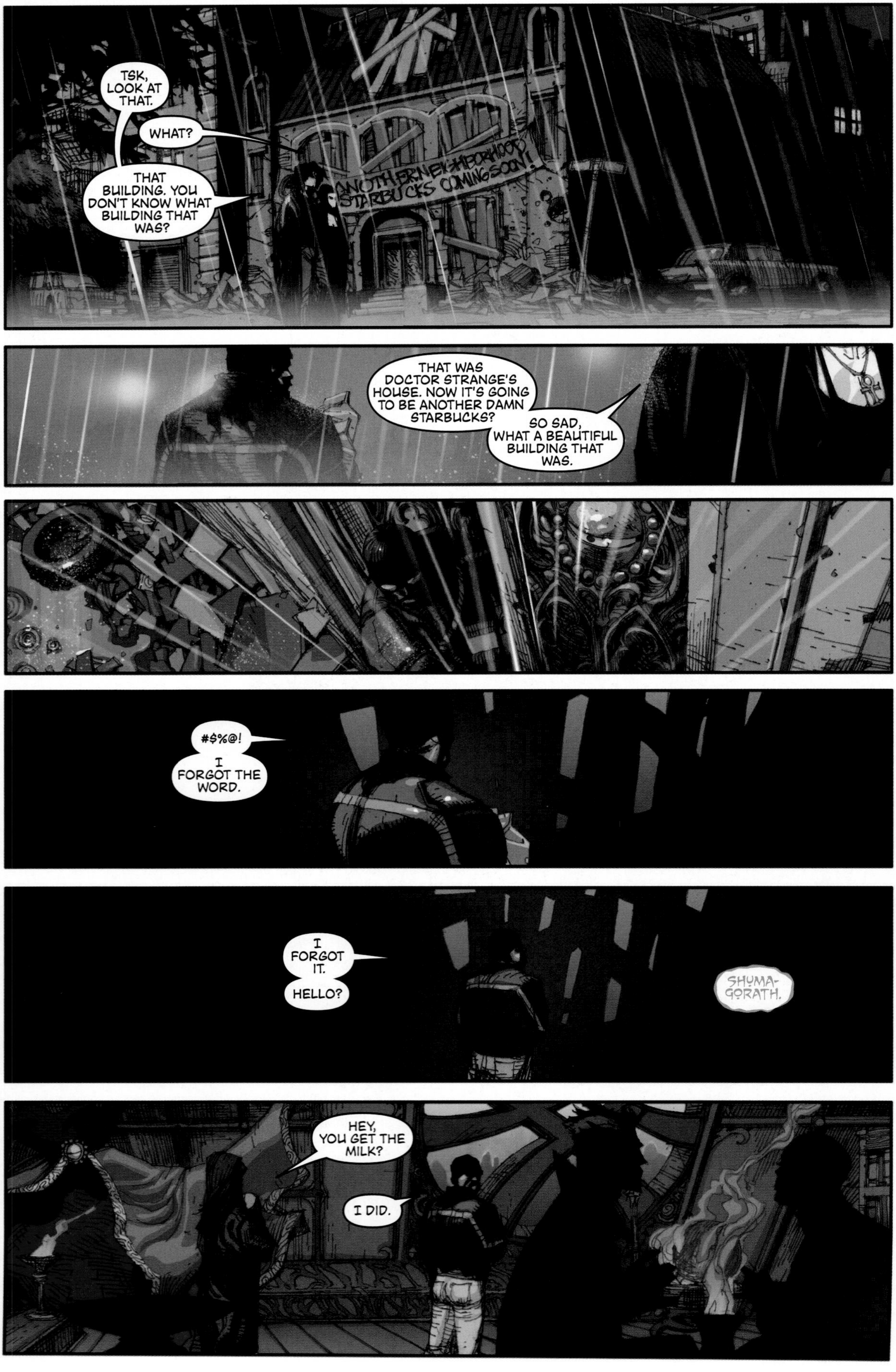
TSK, LOOK AT THAT.
WHAT?
THAT BUILDING. YOU DON'T KNOW WHAT BUILDING THAT WAS?
ANOTHER NEIGHBORHOOD STARBUCKS COMING SOON!
THAT WAS DOCTOR STRANGE'S HOUSE. NOW IT'S GOING TO BE ANOTHER DAMN STARBUCKS?
SO SAD, WHAT A BEAUTIFUL BUILDING THAT WAS.
#$%@!
I FORGOT THE WORD.
I FORGOT IT.
HELLO?
SHUMA-GORATH.
HEY, YOU GET THE MILK?
I DID.

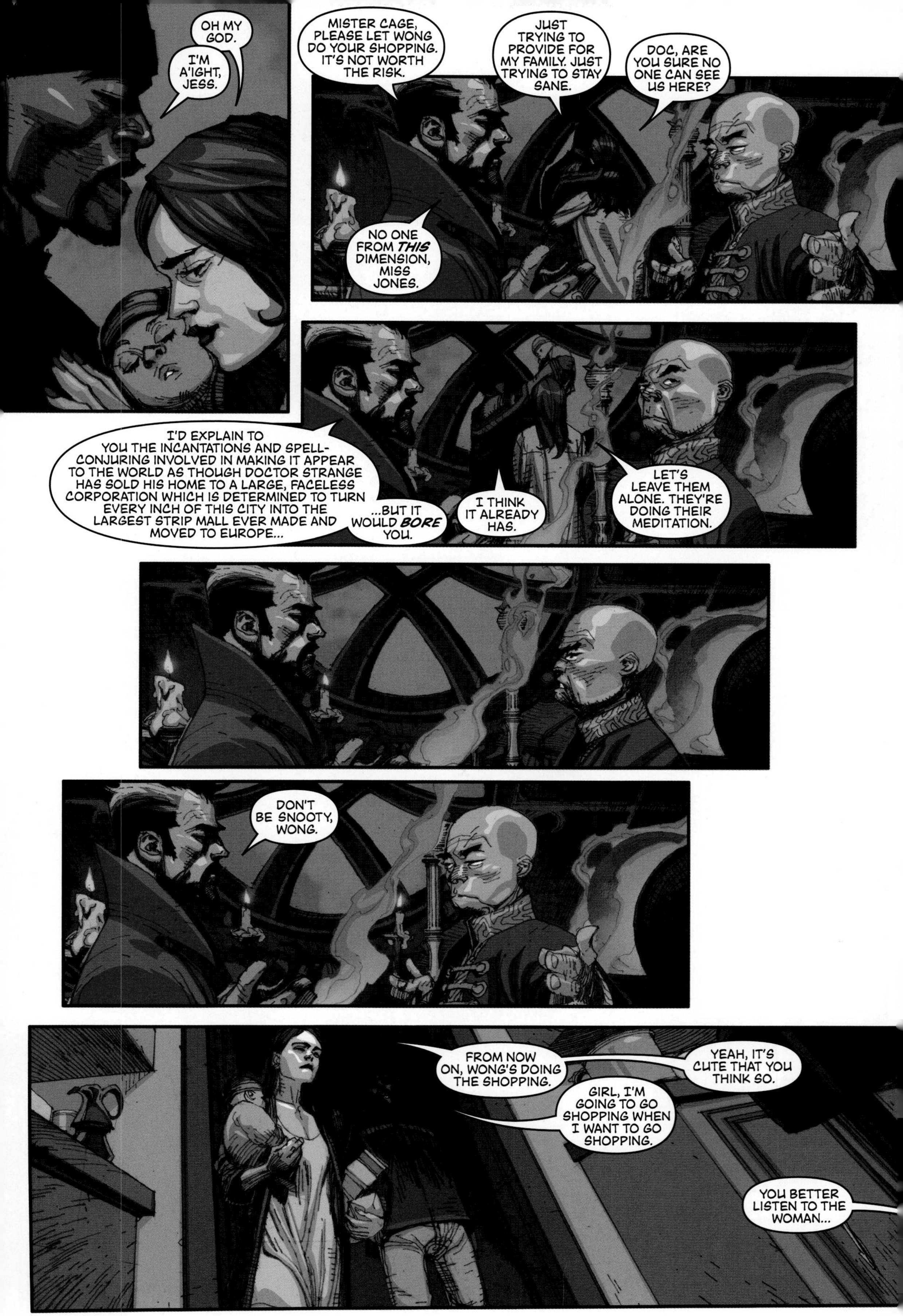
OH MY GOD.
I'M A'IGHT, JESS.
MISTER CAGE, PLEASE LET WONG DO YOUR SHOPPING. IT'S NOT WORTH THE RISK.
JUST TRYING TO PROVIDE FOR MY FAMILY. JUST TRYING TO STAY SANE.
DOC, ARE YOU SURE NO ONE CAN SEE US HERE?
NO ONE FROM *THIS* DIMENSION, MISS JONES.
I'D EXPLAIN TO YOU THE INCANTATIONS AND SPELL-CONJURING INVOLVED IN MAKING IT APPEAR TO THE WORLD AS THOUGH DOCTOR STRANGE HAS SOLD HIS HOME TO A LARGE, FACELESS CORPORATION WHICH IS DETERMINED TO TURN EVERY INCH OF THIS CITY INTO THE LARGEST STRIP MALL EVER MADE AND MOVED TO EUROPE...
...BUT IT WOULD *BORE* YOU.
I THINK IT ALREADY HAS.
LET'S LEAVE THEM ALONE. THEY'RE DOING THEIR MEDITATION.
DON'T BE SNOOTY, WONG.
FROM NOW ON, WONG'S DOING THE SHOPPING.
YEAH, IT'S CUTE THAT YOU THINK SO.
GIRL, I'M GOING TO GO SHOPPING WHEN I WANT TO GO SHOPPING.
YOU BETTER LISTEN TO THE WOMAN...

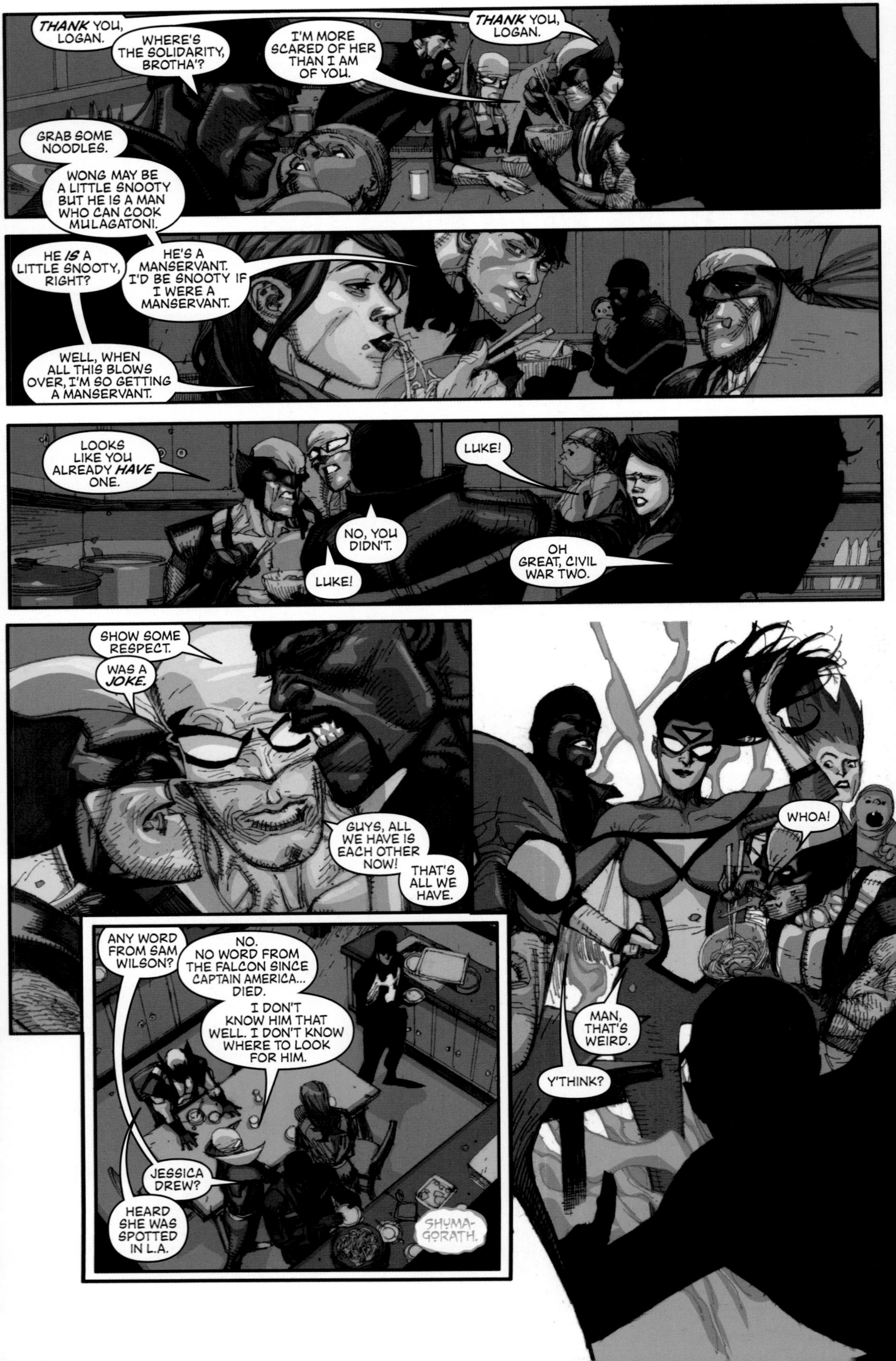
THANK YOU, LOGAN.
WHERE'S THE SOLIDARITY, BROTHA'?
I'M MORE SCARED OF HER THAN I AM OF YOU.
THANK YOU, LOGAN.
GRAB SOME NOODLES.
WONG MAY BE A LITTLE SNOOTY BUT HE IS A MAN WHO CAN COOK MULAGATONI.
HE IS A LITTLE SNOOTY, RIGHT?
HE'S A MANSERVANT. I'D BE SNOOTY IF I WERE A MANSERVANT.
WELL, WHEN ALL THIS BLOWS OVER, I'M SO GETTING A MANSERVANT.
LOOKS LIKE YOU ALREADY HAVE ONE.
LUKE!
NO, YOU DIDN'T.
LUKE!
OH GREAT, CIVIL WAR TWO.
SHOW SOME RESPECT.
WAS A JOKE.
GUYS, ALL WE HAVE IS EACH OTHER NOW!
THAT'S ALL WE HAVE.
ANY WORD FROM SAM WILSON?
NO. NO WORD FROM THE FALCON SINCE CAPTAIN AMERICA... DIED.
I DON'T KNOW HIM THAT WELL. I DON'T KNOW WHERE TO LOOK FOR HIM.
JESSICA DREW?
HEARD SHE WAS SPOTTED IN L.A.
SHUMA-GORATH.
WHOA!
MAN, THAT'S WEIRD.
Y'THINK?

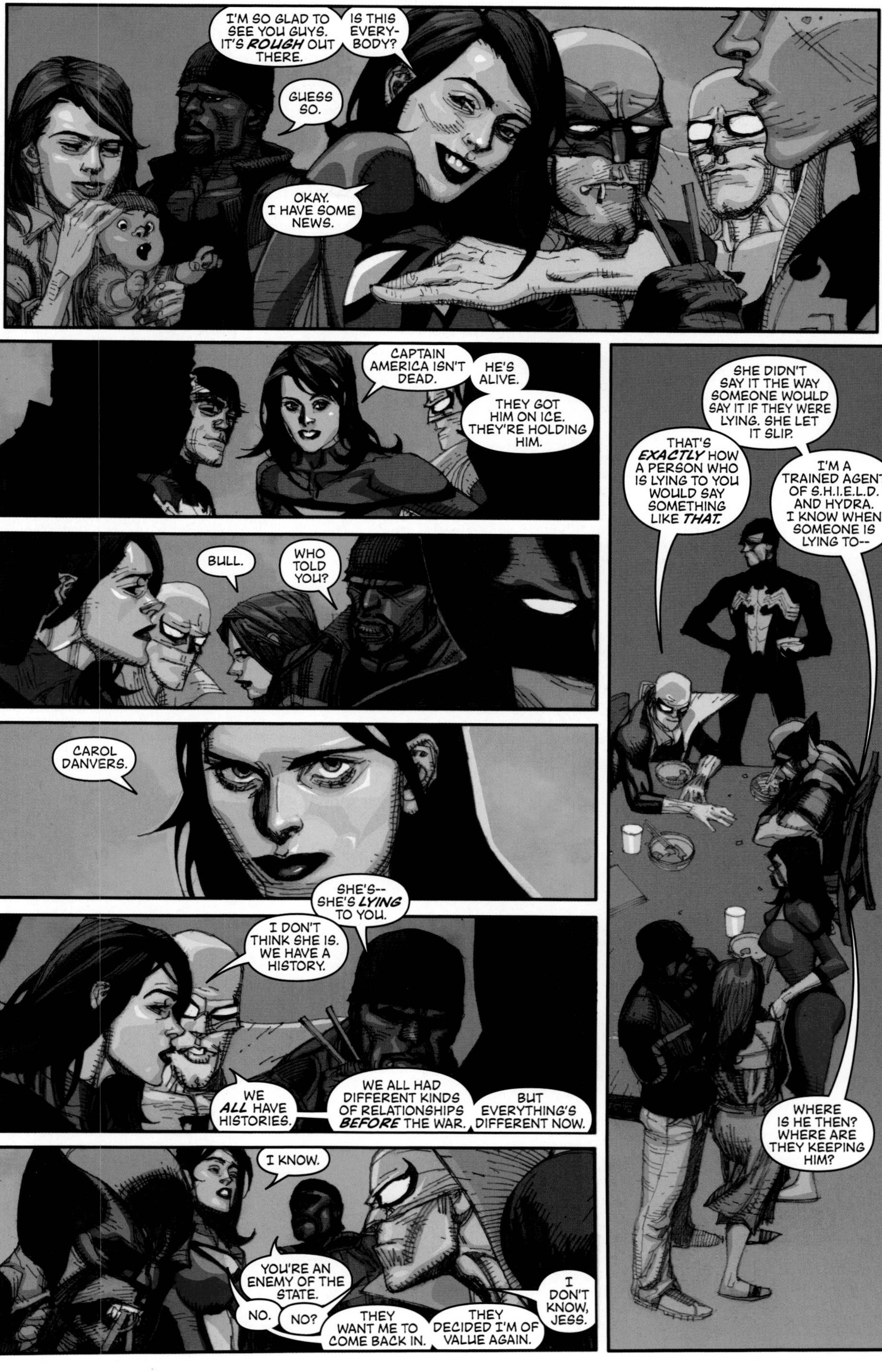
I'M SO GLAD TO SEE YOU GUYS. IT'S ROUGH OUT THERE.
IS THIS EVERY-BODY?
GUESS SO.
OKAY. I HAVE SOME NEWS.
CAPTAIN AMERICA ISN'T DEAD.
HE'S ALIVE.
THEY GOT HIM ON ICE. THEY'RE HOLDING HIM.
BULL.
WHO TOLD YOU?
CAROL DANVERS.
SHE'S-- SHE'S LYING TO YOU.
I DON'T THINK SHE IS. WE HAVE A HISTORY.
WE ALL HAVE HISTORIES.
WE ALL HAD DIFFERENT KINDS OF RELATIONSHIPS BEFORE THE WAR.
BUT EVERYTHING'S DIFFERENT NOW.
I KNOW.
YOU'RE AN ENEMY OF THE STATE.
NO.
NO?
THEY WANT ME TO COME BACK IN.
THEY DECIDED I'M OF VALUE AGAIN.
SHE DIDN'T SAY IT THE WAY SOMEONE WOULD SAY IT IF THEY WERE LYING. SHE LET IT SLIP.
THAT'S EXACTLY HOW A PERSON WHO IS LYING TO YOU WOULD SAY SOMETHING LIKE THAT.
I'M A TRAINED AGENT OF S.H.I.E.L.D. AND HYDRA. I KNOW WHEN SOMEONE IS LYING TO--
WHERE IS HE THEN? WHERE ARE THEY KEEPING HIM?
I DON'T KNOW, JESS.

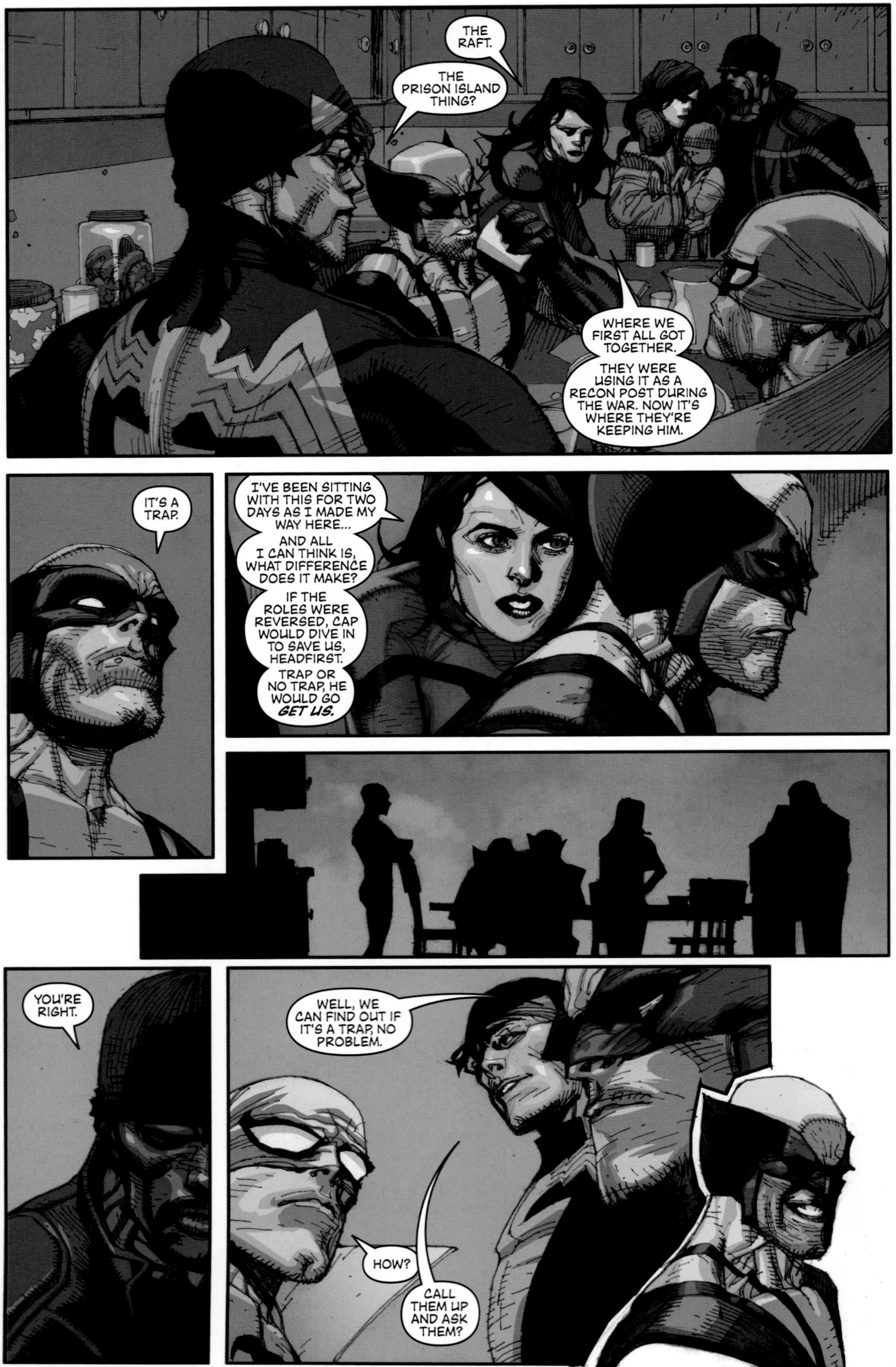
THE RAFT.
THE PRISON ISLAND THING?
WHERE WE FIRST ALL GOT TOGETHER.
THEY WERE USING IT AS A RECON POST DURING THE WAR. NOW IT'S WHERE THEY'RE KEEPING HIM.
IT'S A TRAP.
I'VE BEEN SITTING WITH THIS FOR TWO DAYS AS I MADE MY WAY HERE...
AND ALL I CAN THINK IS, WHAT DIFFERENCE DOES IT MAKE?
IF THE ROLES WERE REVERSED, CAP WOULD DIVE IN TO SAVE US, HEADFIRST.
TRAP OR NO TRAP, HE WOULD GO ***GET US.***
YOU'RE RIGHT.
WELL, WE CAN FIND OUT IF IT'S A TRAP, NO PROBLEM.
HOW?
CALL THEM UP AND ASK THEM?

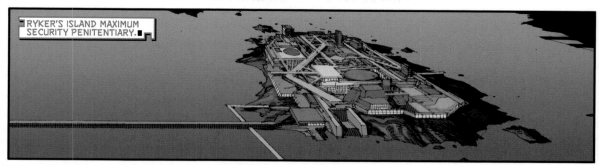

RYKER'S ISLAND MAXIMUM SECURITY PENITENTIARY. ■

THE RAFT, RYKER'S MAXIMUM-MAXIMUM SECURITY INSTALLATION. ■

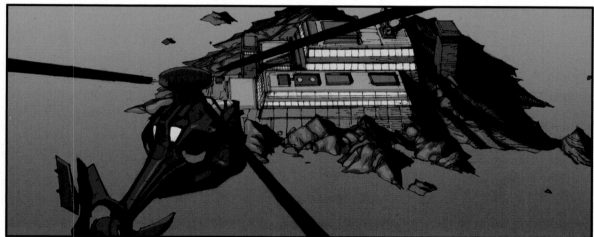

LET ME SEE HIM.

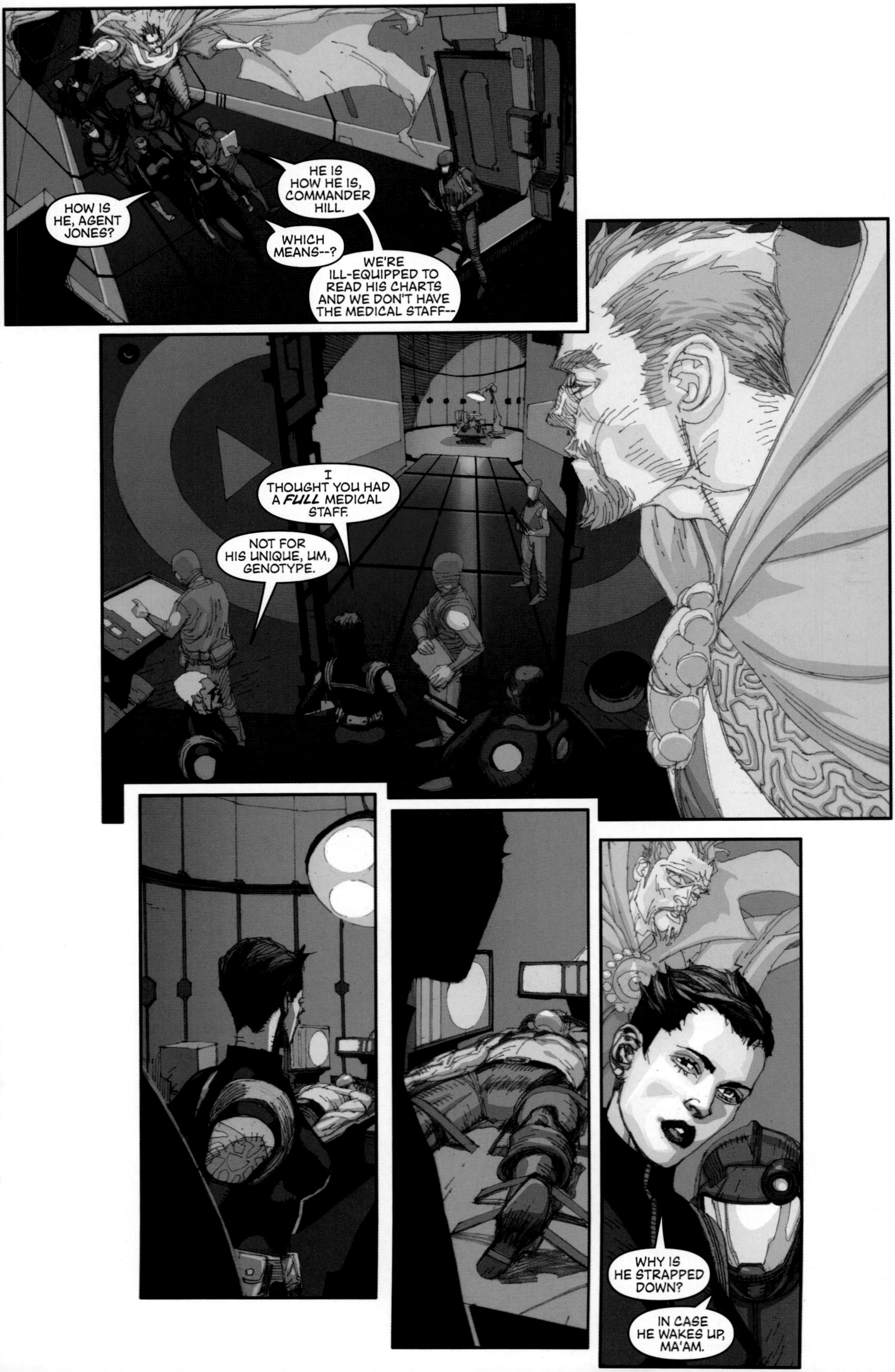
HOW IS HE, AGENT JONES?
HE IS HOW HE IS, COMMANDER HILL.
WHICH MEANS--?
WE'RE ILL-EQUIPPED TO READ HIS CHARTS AND WE DON'T HAVE THE MEDICAL STAFF--
I THOUGHT YOU HAD A FULL MEDICAL STAFF.
NOT FOR HIS UNIQUE, UM, GENOTYPE.
WHY IS HE STRAPPED DOWN?
IN CASE HE WAKES UP, MA'AM.

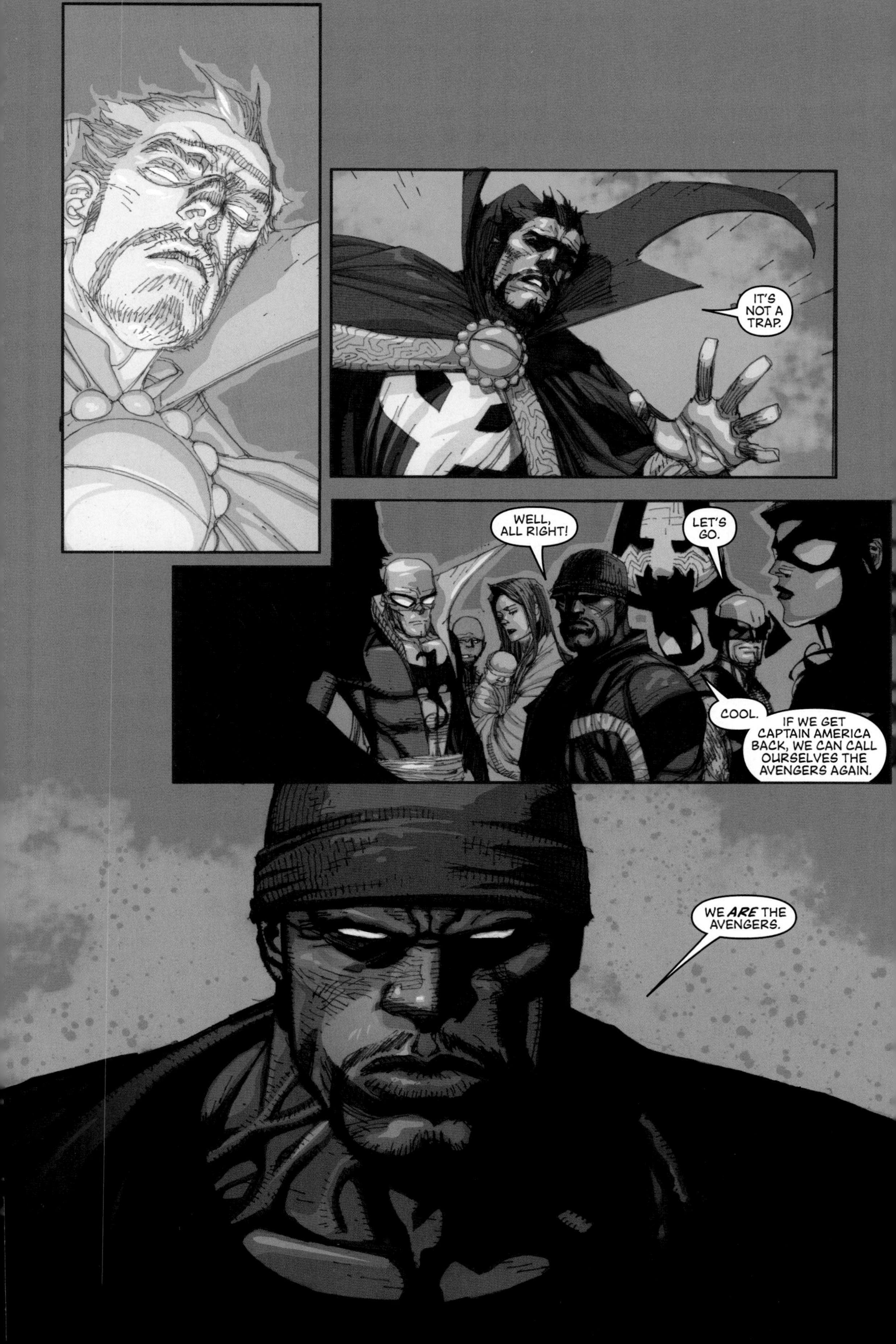
IT'S NOT A TRAP.
WELL, ALL RIGHT!
LET'S GO.
COOL.
IF WE GET CAPTAIN AMERICA BACK, WE CAN CALL OURSELVES THE AVENGERS AGAIN.
WE *ARE* THE AVENGERS.

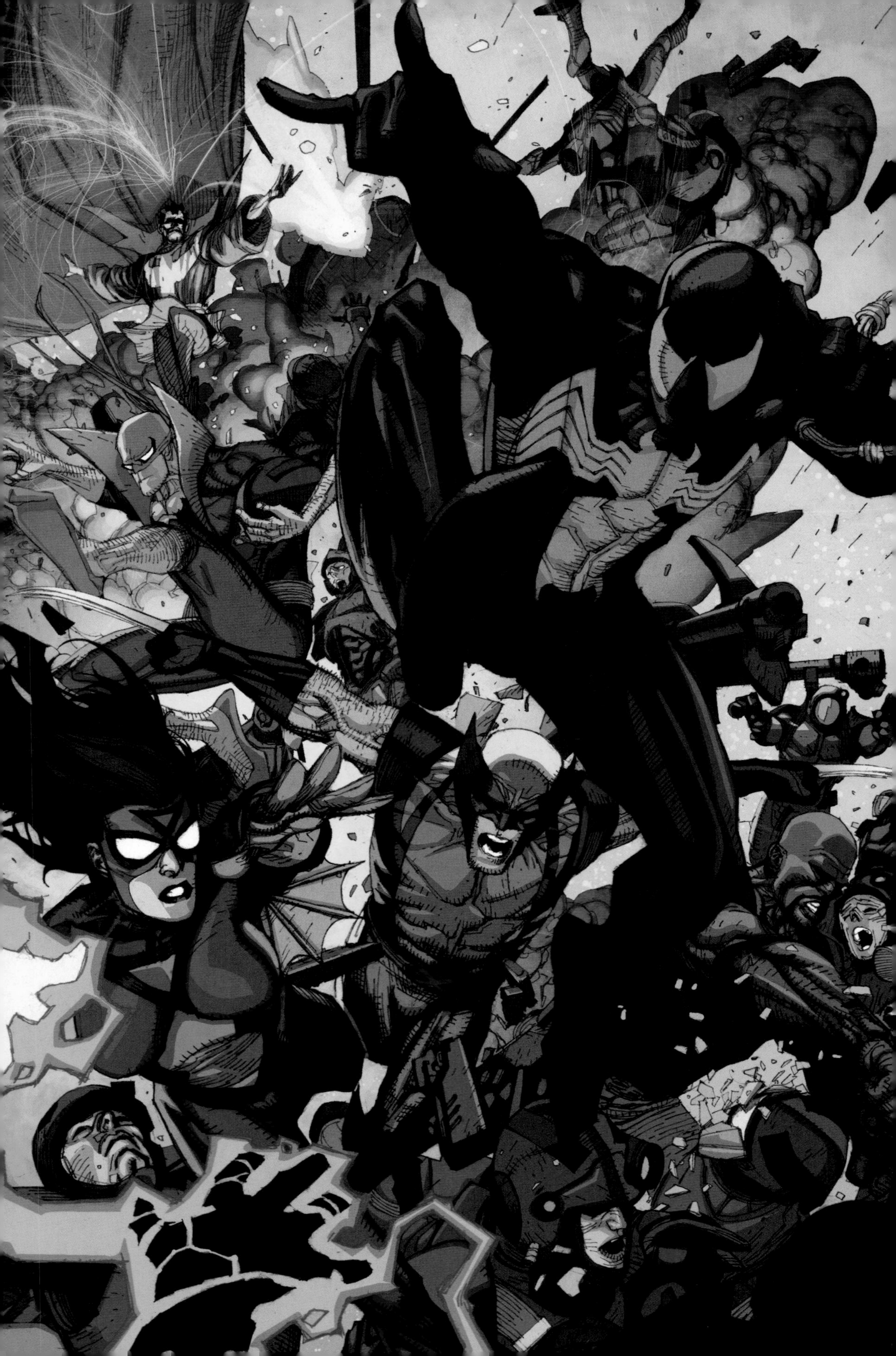

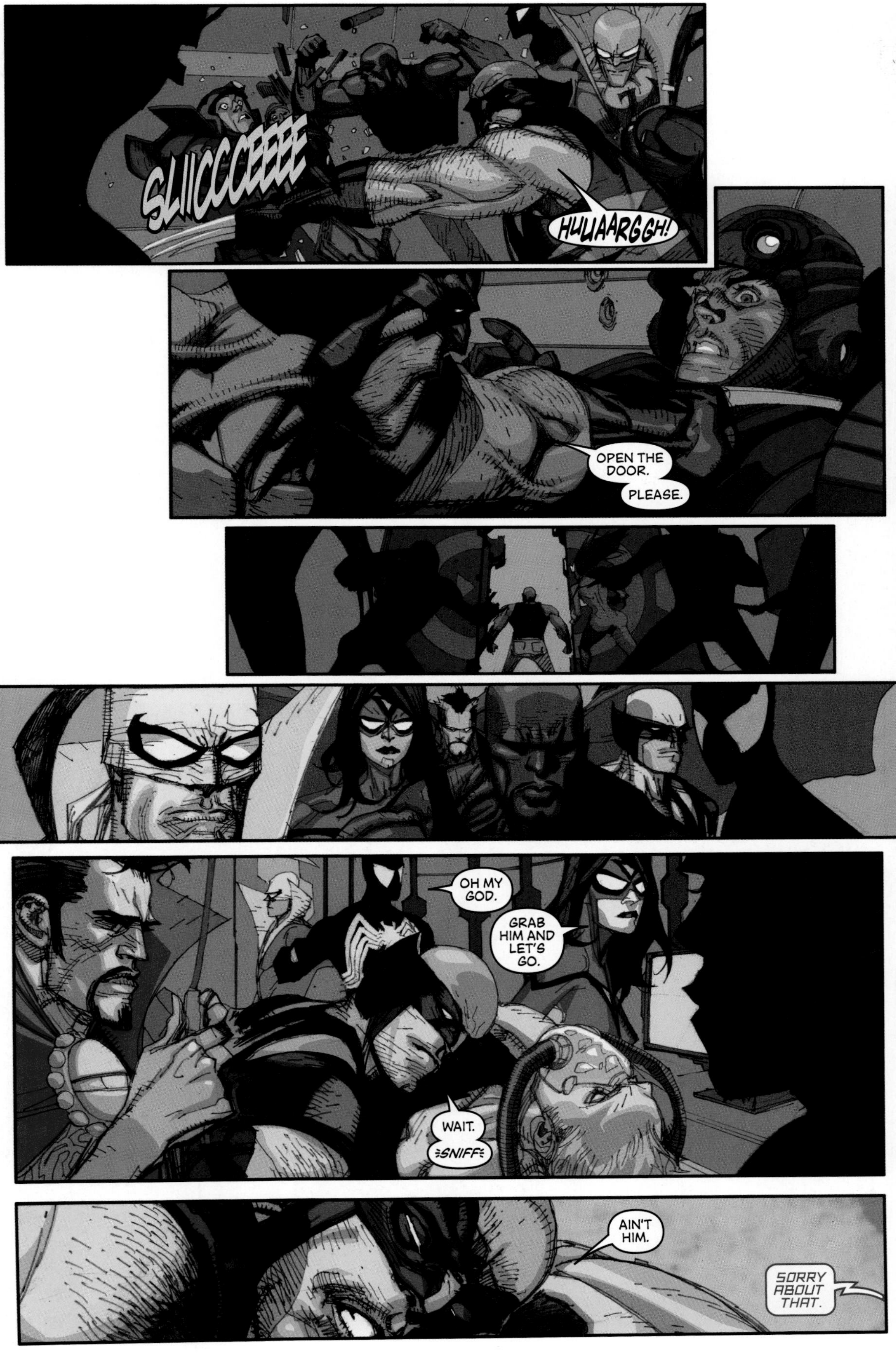
SLIICCCEEEE
HUUAARGGH!
OPEN THE DOOR.
PLEASE.
OH MY GOD.
GRAB HIM AND LET'S GO.
WAIT.
SNIFF
AIN'T HIM.
SORRY ABOUT THAT.

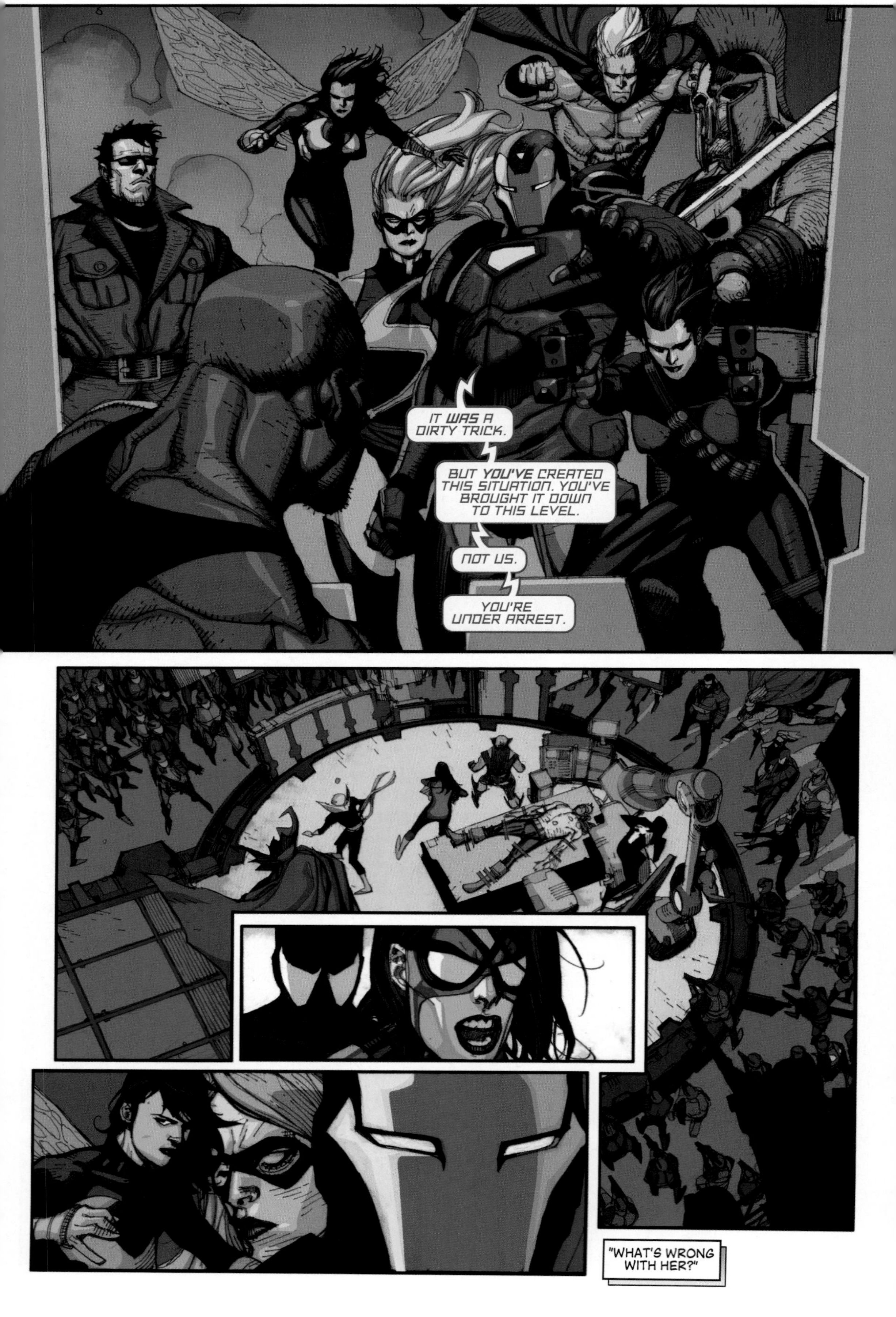
IT WAS A DIRTY TRICK.
BUT YOU'VE CREATED THIS SITUATION. YOU'VE BROUGHT IT DOWN TO THIS LEVEL.
NOT US.
YOU'RE UNDER ARREST.
"WHAT'S WRONG WITH HER?"

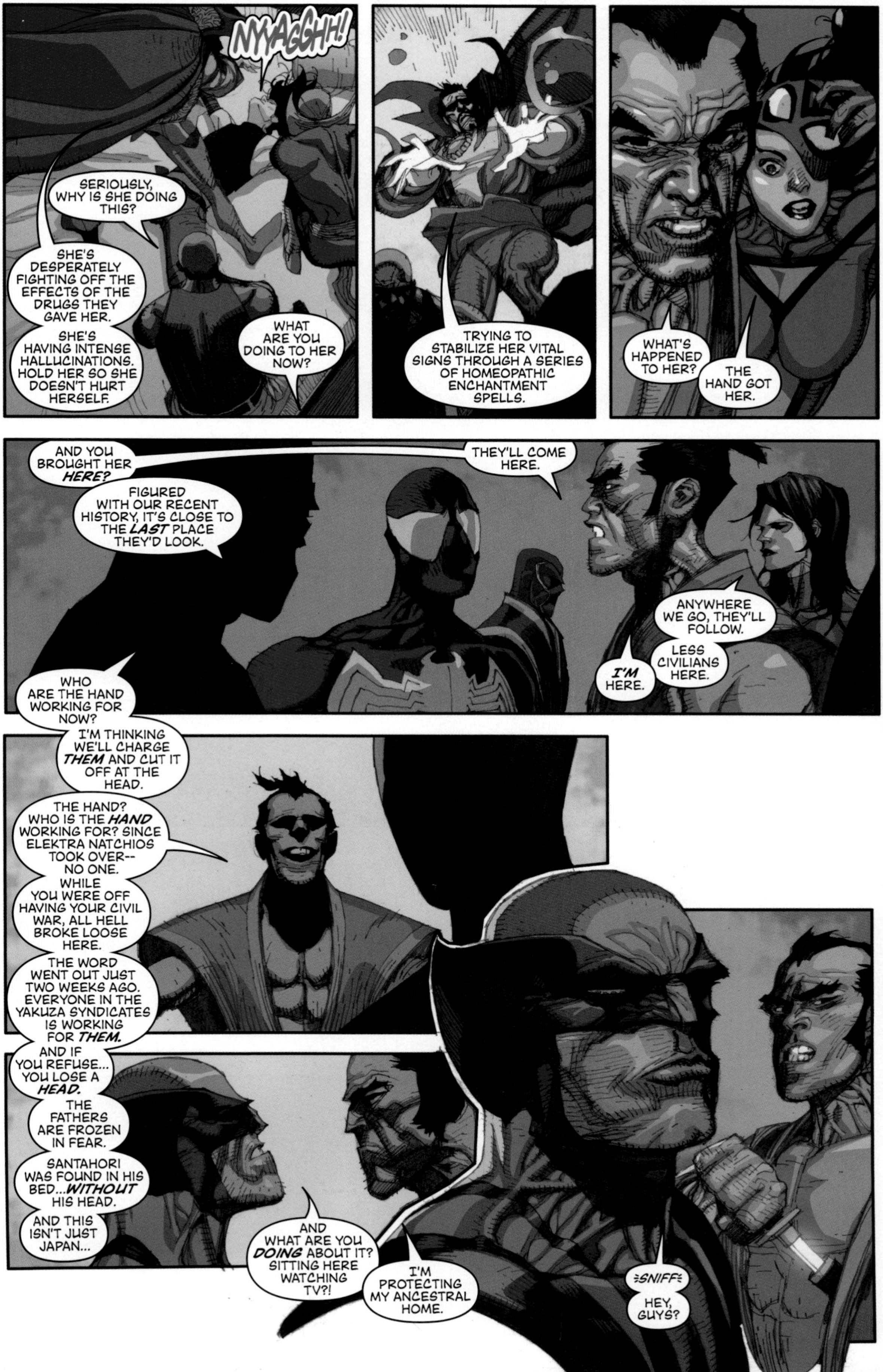
NYYAGGHH!
SERIOUSLY, WHY IS SHE DOING THIS?
SHE'S DESPERATELY FIGHTING OFF THE EFFECTS OF THE DRUGS THEY GAVE HER.
SHE'S HAVING INTENSE HALLUCINATIONS. HOLD HER SO SHE DOESN'T HURT HERSELF.
WHAT ARE YOU DOING TO HER NOW?
TRYING TO STABILIZE HER VITAL SIGNS THROUGH A SERIES OF HOMEOPATHIC ENCHANTMENT SPELLS.
WHAT'S HAPPENED TO HER?
THE HAND GOT HER.
AND YOU BROUGHT HER HERE?
THEY'LL COME HERE.
FIGURED WITH OUR RECENT HISTORY, IT'S CLOSE TO THE LAST PLACE THEY'D LOOK.
ANYWHERE WE GO, THEY'LL FOLLOW.
LESS CIVILIANS HERE.
I'M HERE.
WHO ARE THE HAND WORKING FOR NOW?
I'M THINKING WE'LL CHARGE THEM AND CUT IT OFF AT THE HEAD.
THE HAND? WHO IS THE HAND WORKING FOR? SINCE ELEKTRA NATCHIOS TOOK OVER-- NO ONE.
WHILE YOU WERE OFF HAVING YOUR CIVIL WAR, ALL HELL BROKE LOOSE HERE.
THE WORD WENT OUT JUST TWO WEEKS AGO. EVERYONE IN THE YAKUZA SYNDICATES IS WORKING FOR THEM.
AND IF YOU REFUSE... YOU LOSE A HEAD.
THE FATHERS ARE FROZEN IN FEAR.
SANTAHORI WAS FOUND IN HIS BED...WITHOUT HIS HEAD.
AND THIS ISN'T JUST JAPAN...
AND WHAT ARE YOU DOING ABOUT IT? SITTING HERE WATCHING TV?!
I'M PROTECTING MY ANCESTRAL HOME.
SNIFF
HEY, GUYS?

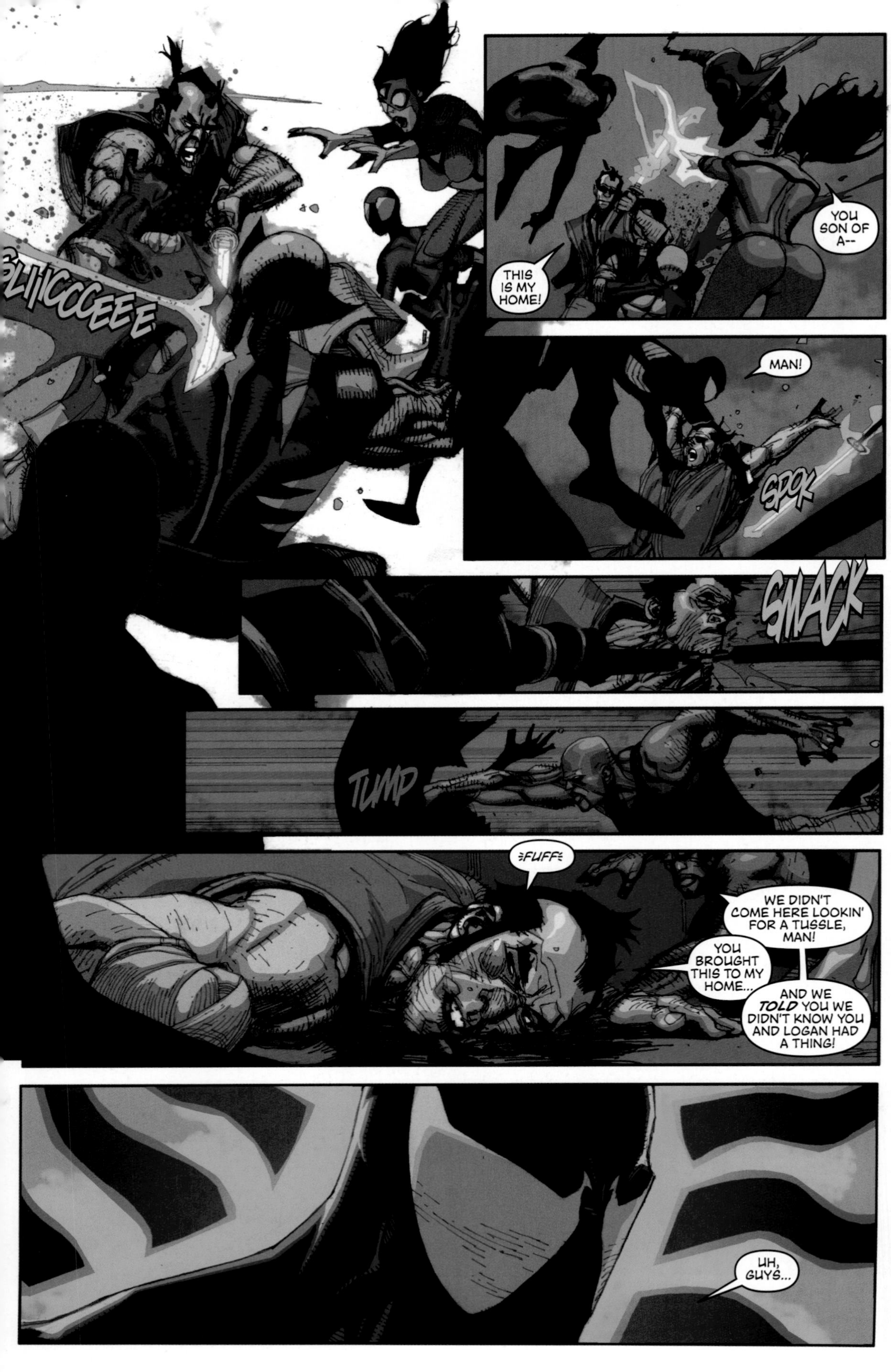

SLIIICCCEEEE
THIS IS MY HOME!
YOU SON OF A--
MAN!
SPOK
SMACK
TUMP
FUFF
WE DIDN'T COME HERE LOOKIN' FOR A TUSSLE, MAN!
YOU BROUGHT THIS TO MY HOME...
AND WE *TOLD* YOU WE DIDN'T KNOW YOU AND LOGAN HAD A THING!
UH, GUYS...

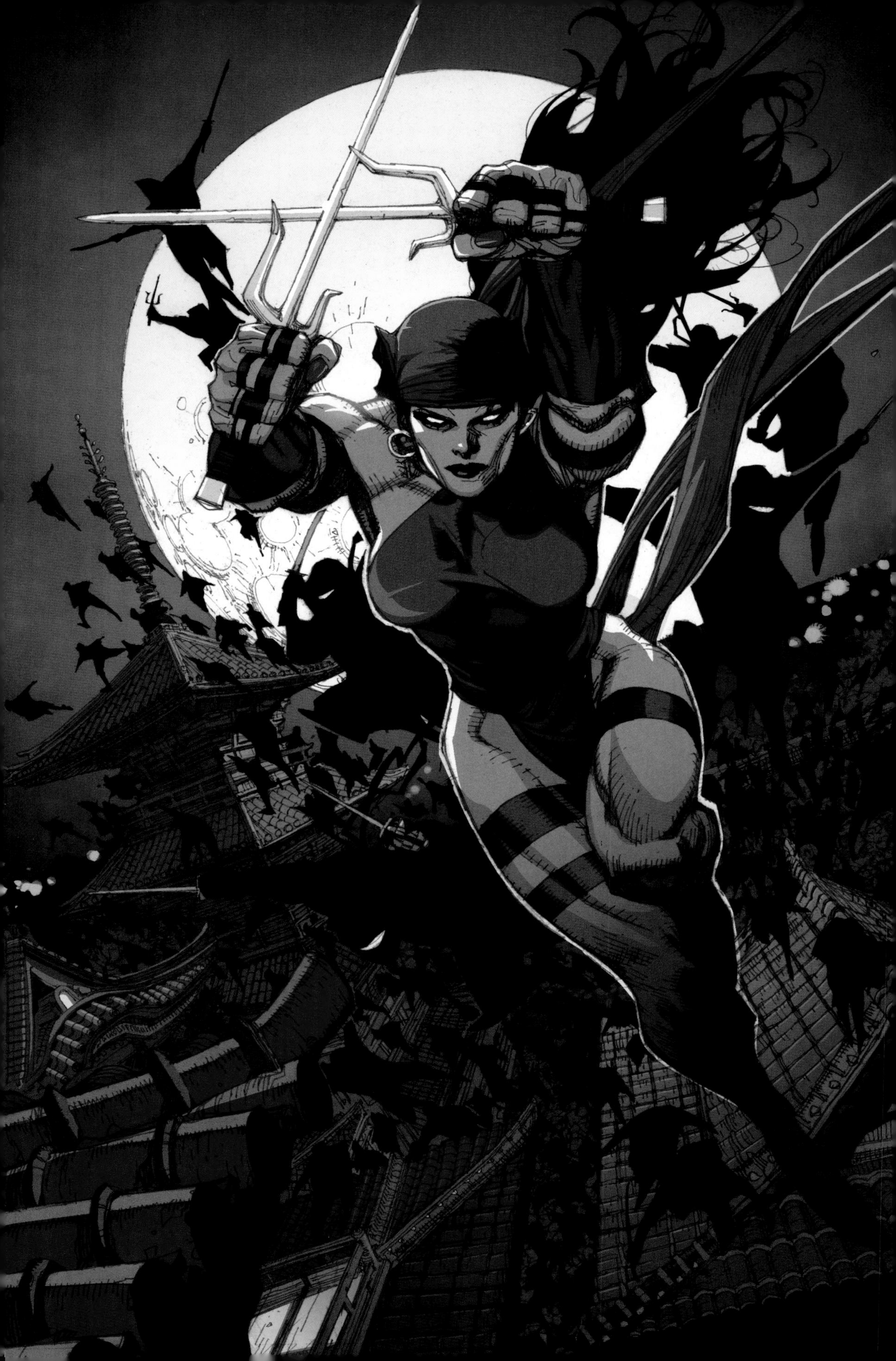

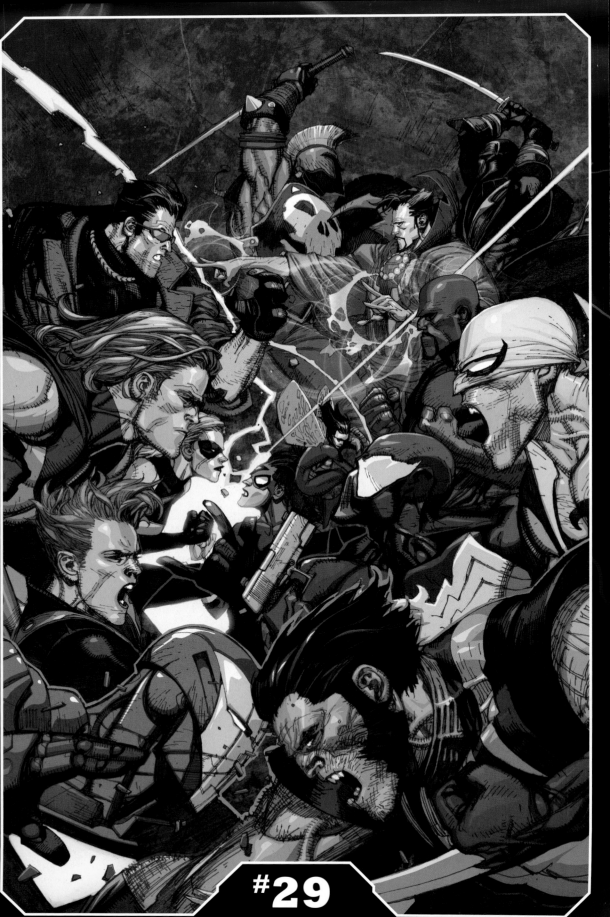

#29

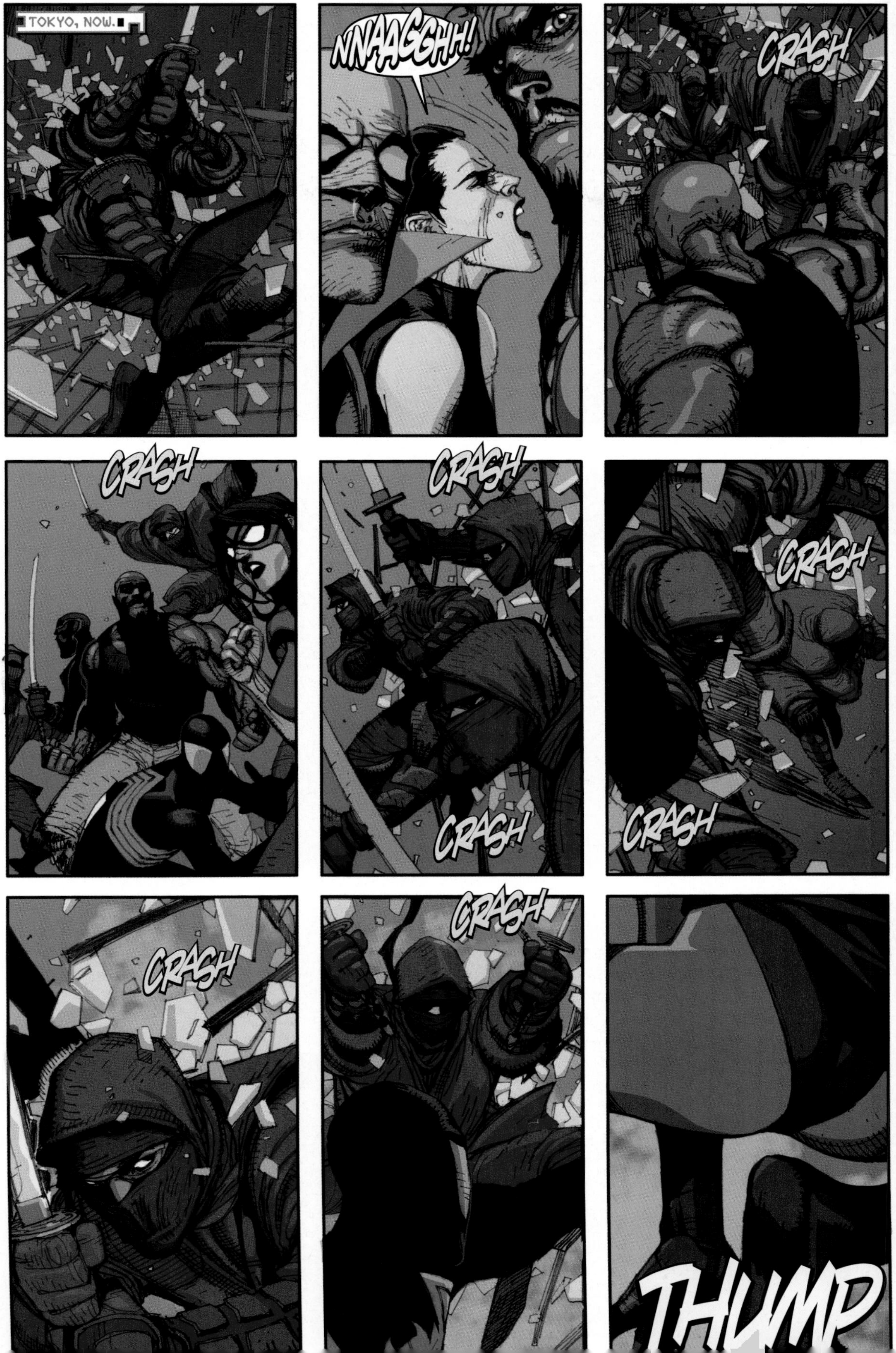
TOKYO, NOW.
NNAAGGHH!
CRASH
CRASH
CRASH
CRASH
CRASH
CRASH
CRASH
CRASH
THUMP

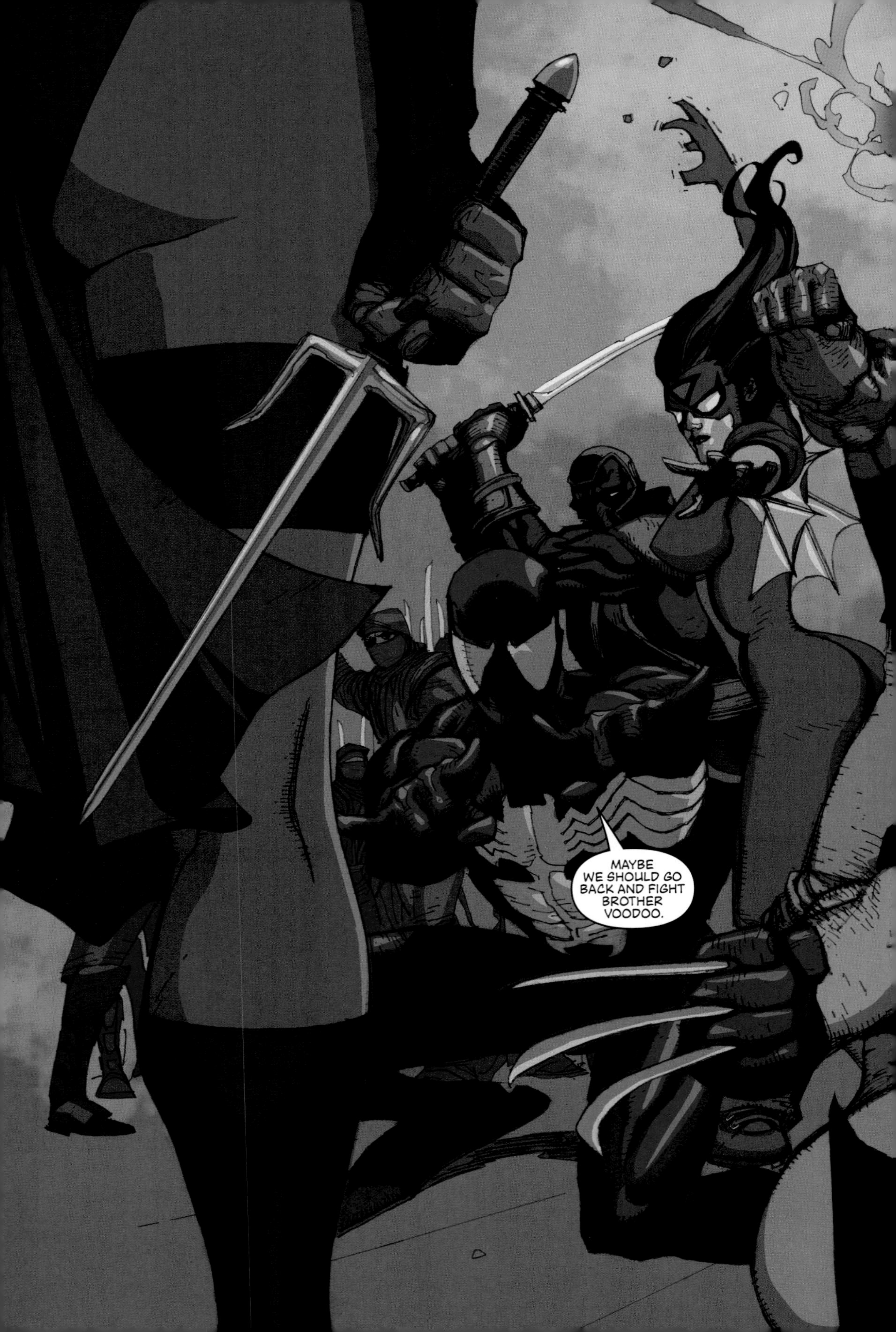
MAYBE WE SHOULD GO BACK AND FIGHT BROTHER VOODOO.

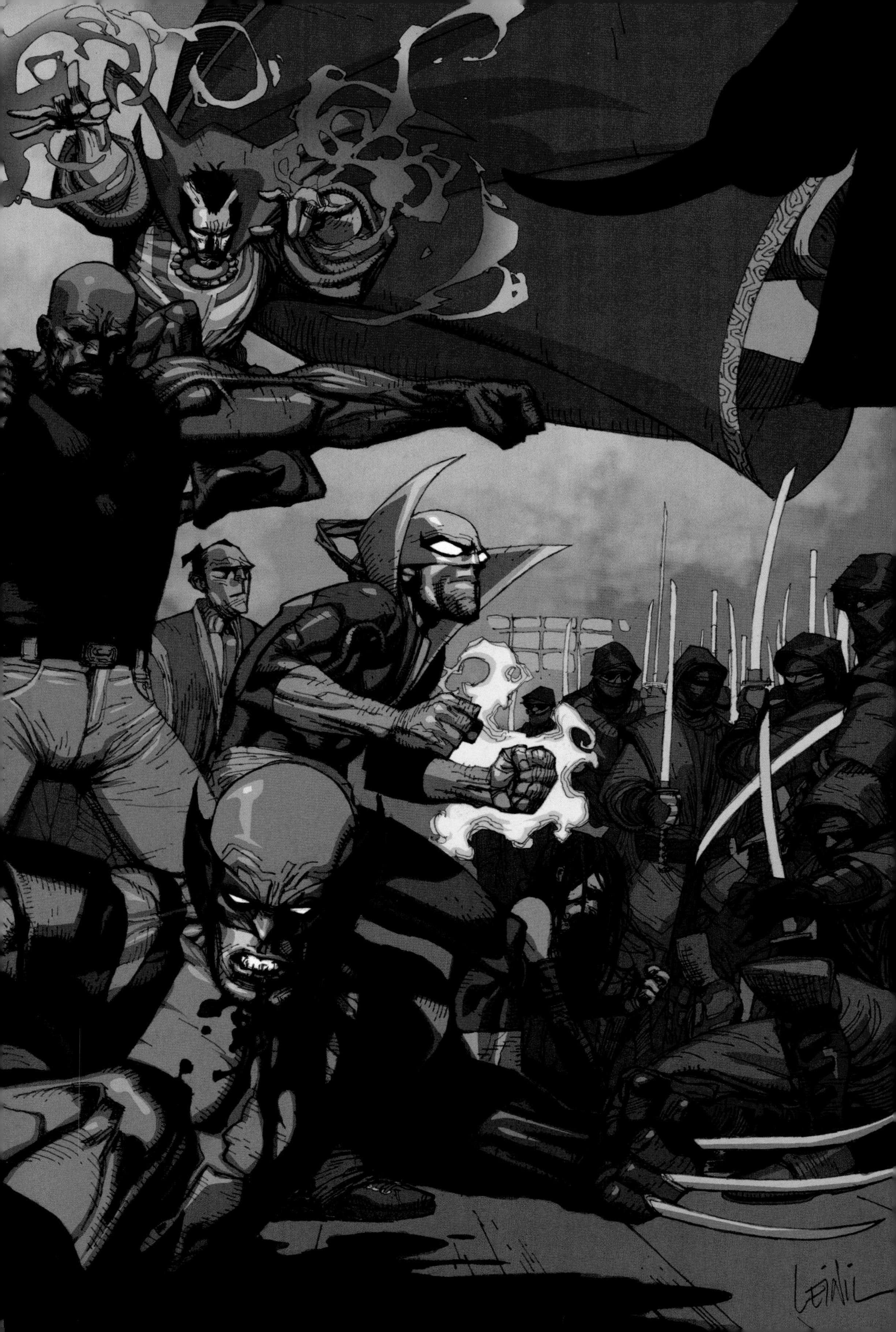

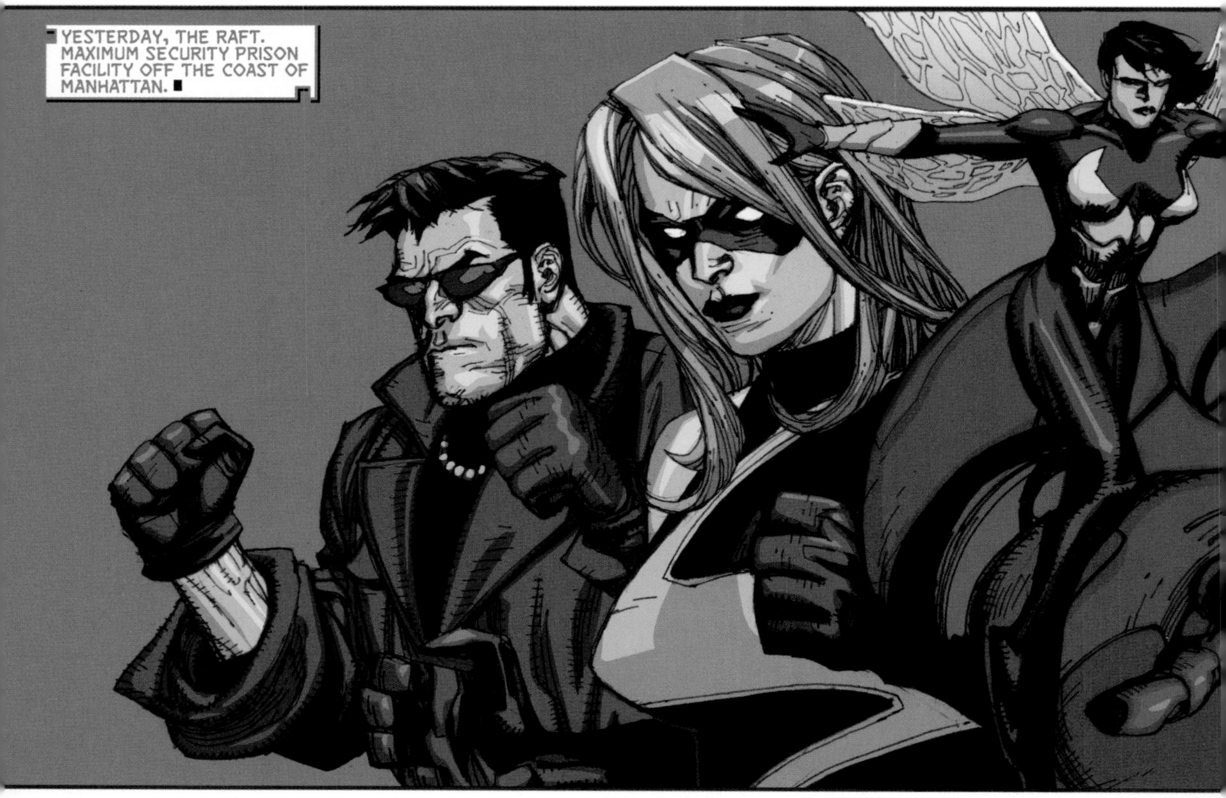
YESTERDAY, THE RAFT. MAXIMUM SECURITY PRISON FACILITY OFF THE COAST OF MANHATTAN.

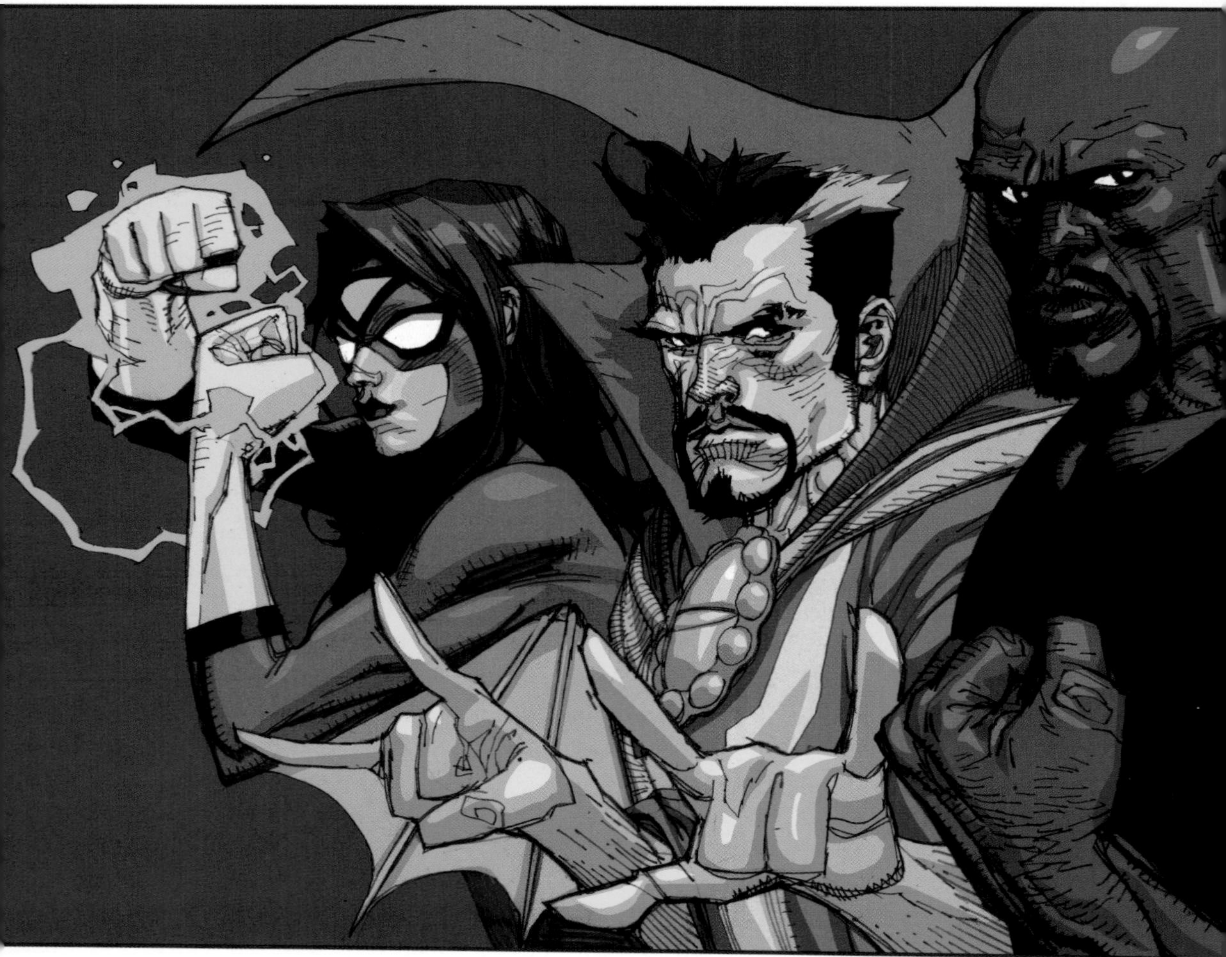

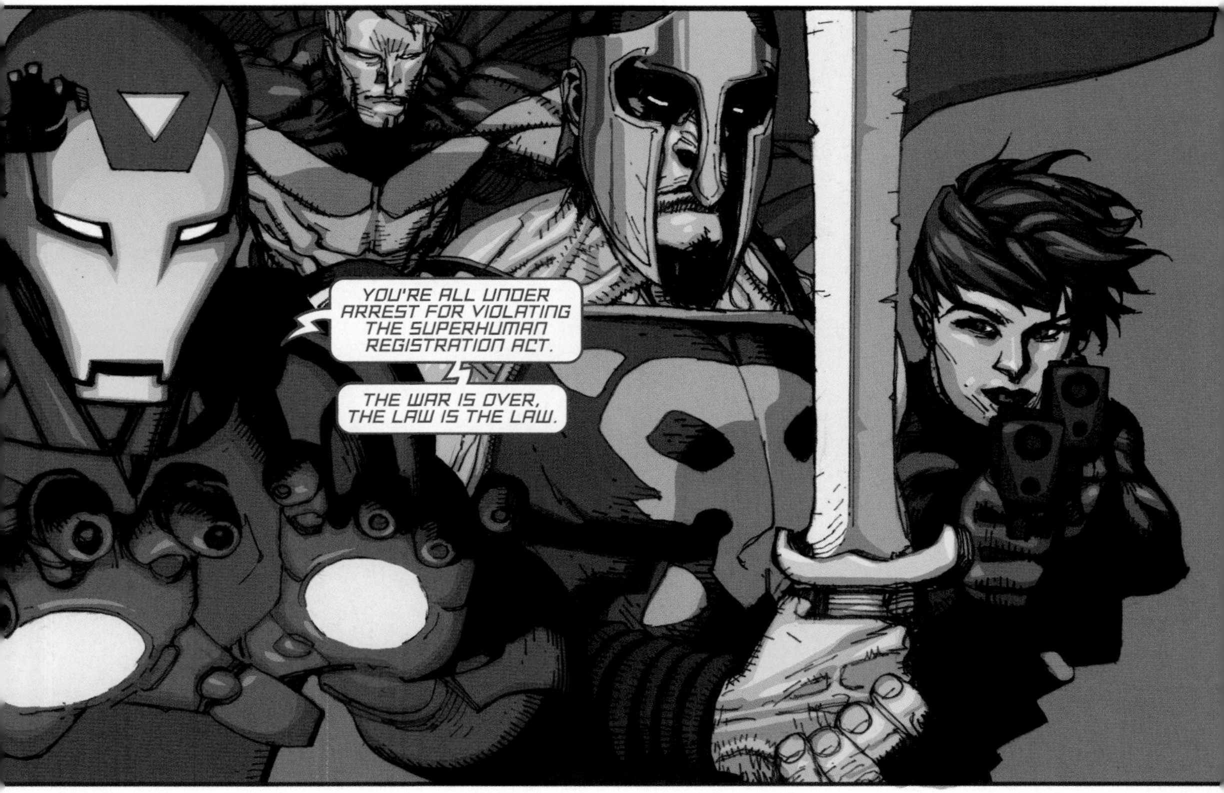
YOU'RE ALL UNDER ARREST FOR VIOLATING THE SUPERHUMAN REGISTRATION ACT.
THE WAR IS OVER, THE LAW IS THE LAW.

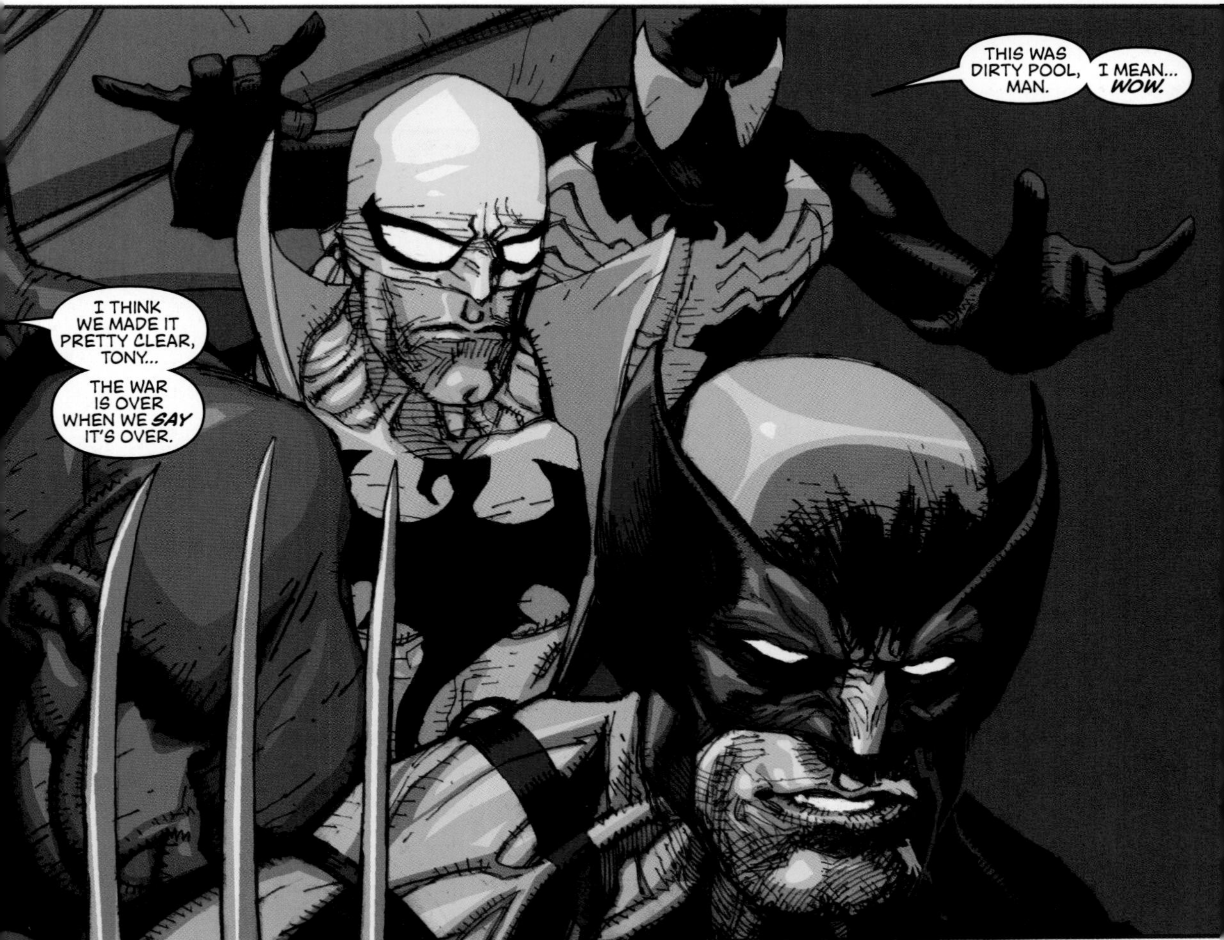
THIS WAS DIRTY POOL, MAN.
I MEAN... **WOW.**
I THINK WE MADE IT PRETTY CLEAR, TONY...
THE WAR IS OVER WHEN WE ***SAY*** IT'S OVER.

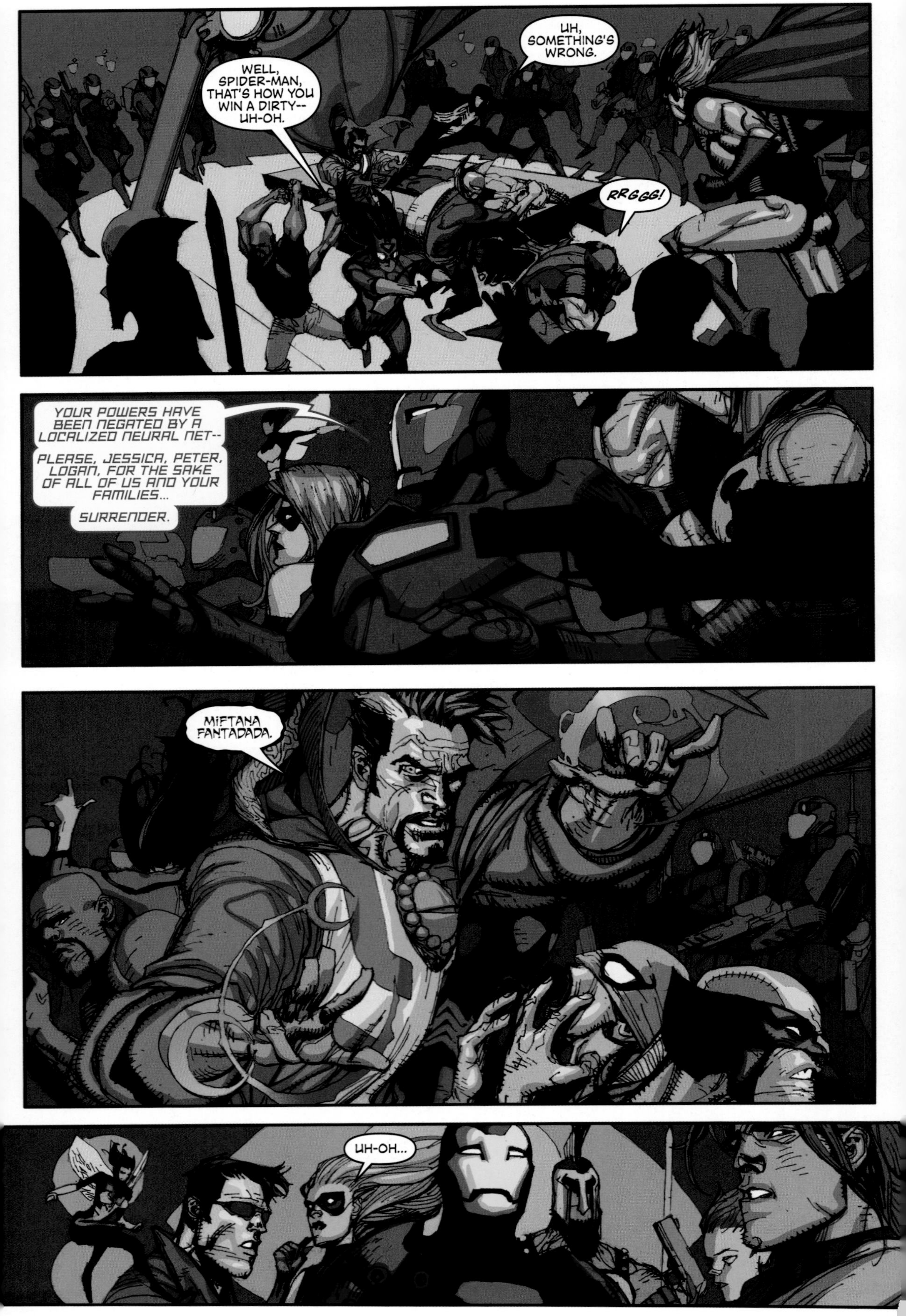
WELL, SPIDER-MAN, THAT'S HOW YOU WIN A DIRTY-- UH-OH.
UH, SOMETHING'S WRONG.
RRGGG!
YOUR POWERS HAVE BEEN NEGATED BY A LOCALIZED NEURAL NET--
PLEASE, JESSICA, PETER, LOGAN, FOR THE SAKE OF ALL OF US AND YOUR FAMILIES...
SURRENDER.
MIFTANA FANTADADA.
UH-OH...

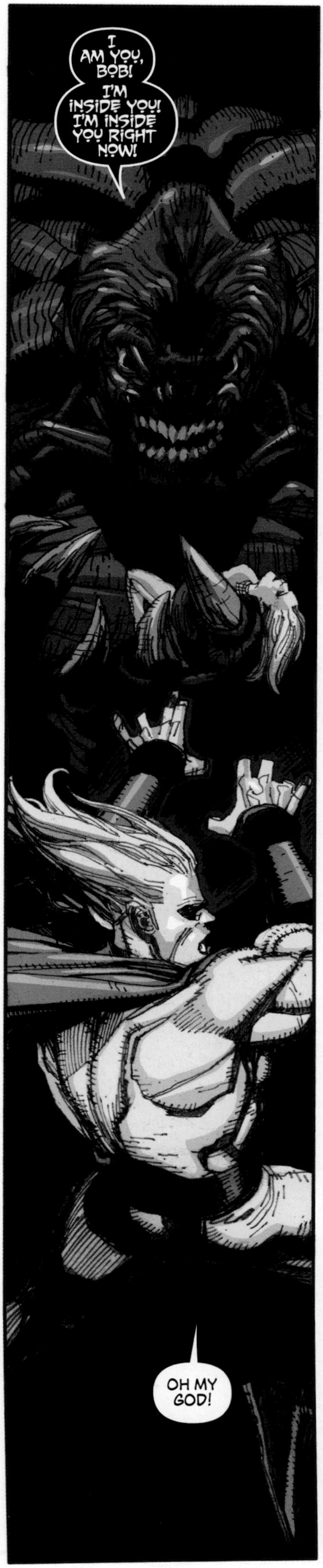
I AM YOU, BOB! I'M INSIDE YOU! I'M INSIDE YOU RIGHT NOW!
OH MY GOD!
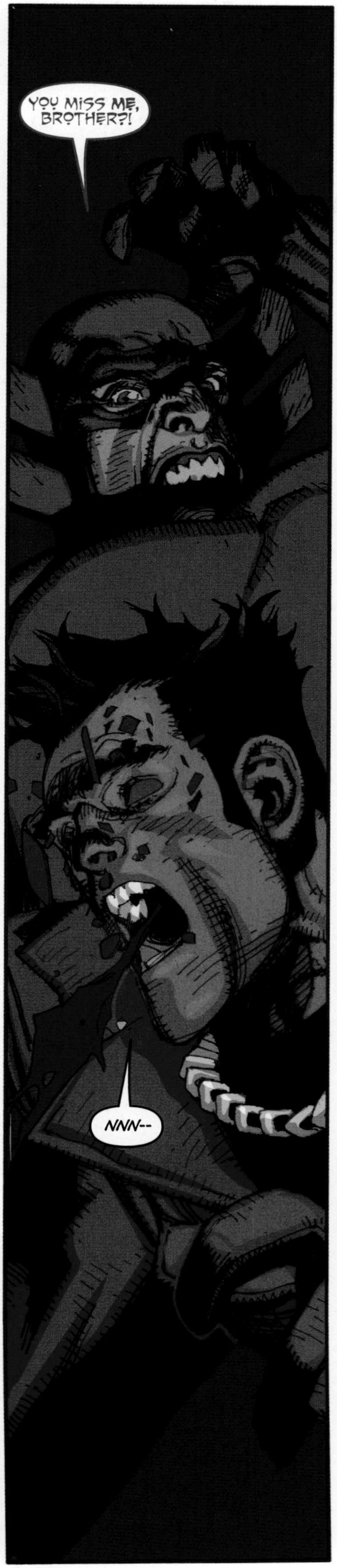
YOU MISS ME, BROTHER?!
NNN--
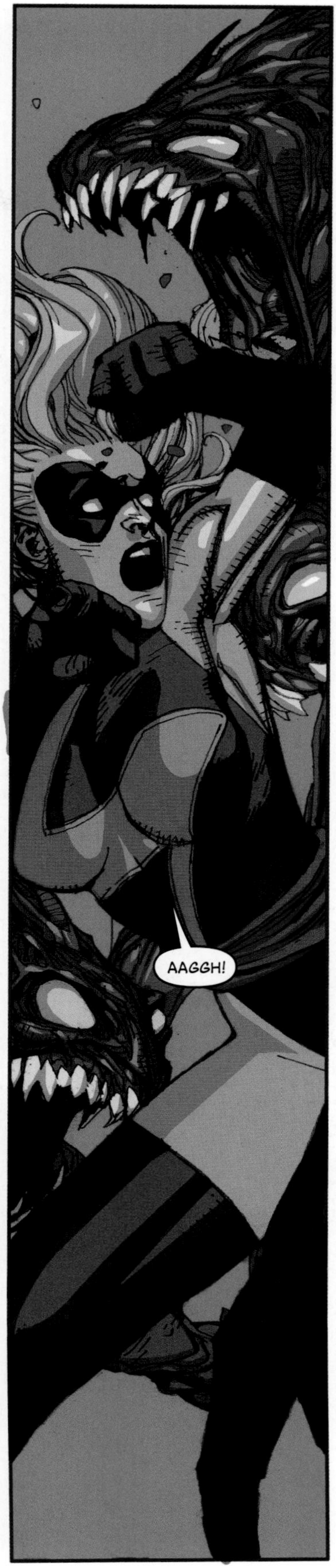
AAGGH!

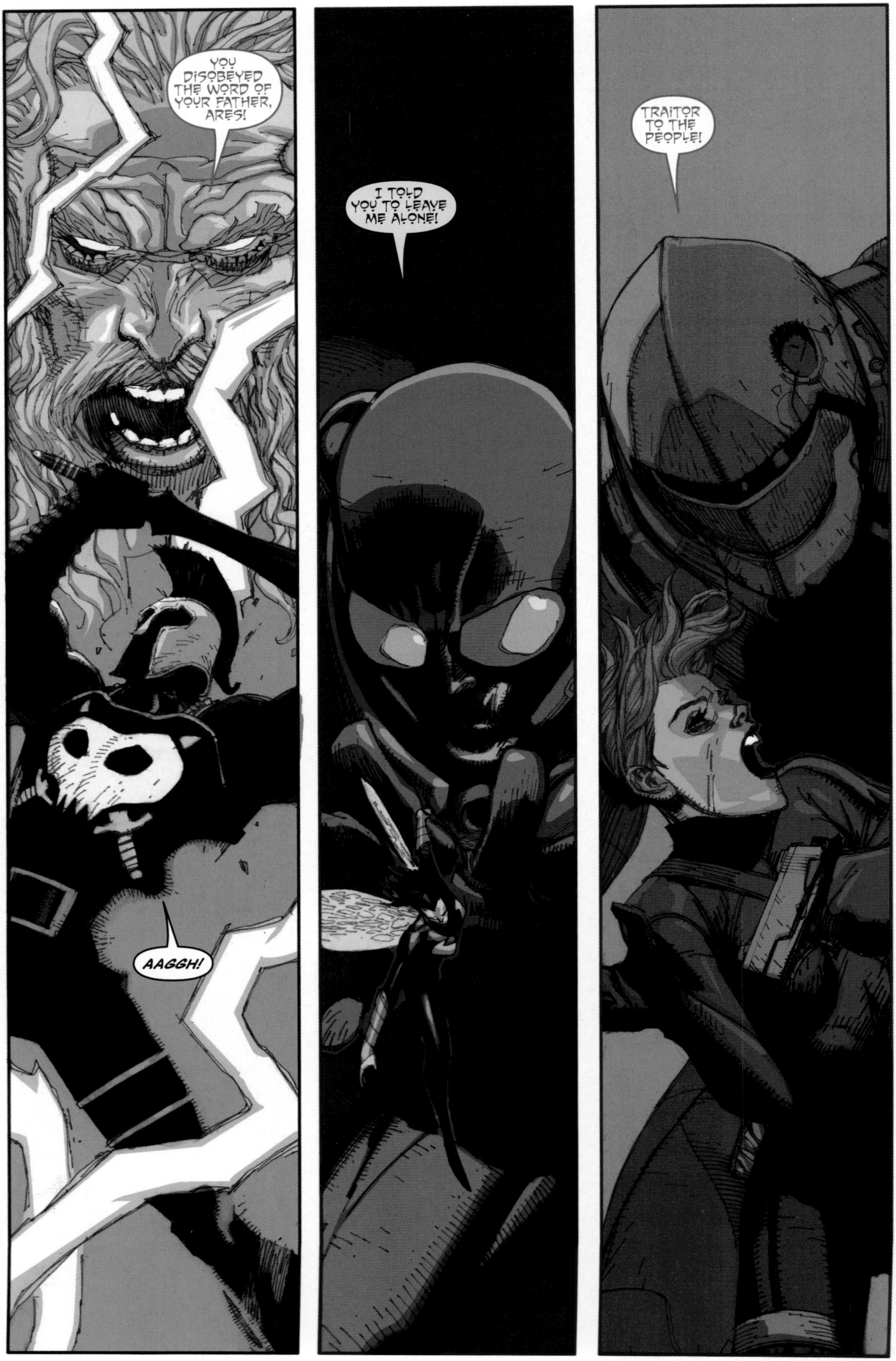
YOU DISOBEYED THE WORD OF YOUR FATHER, ARES!
AAGGH!
I TOLD YOU TO LEAVE ME ALONE!
TRAITOR TO THE PEOPLE!

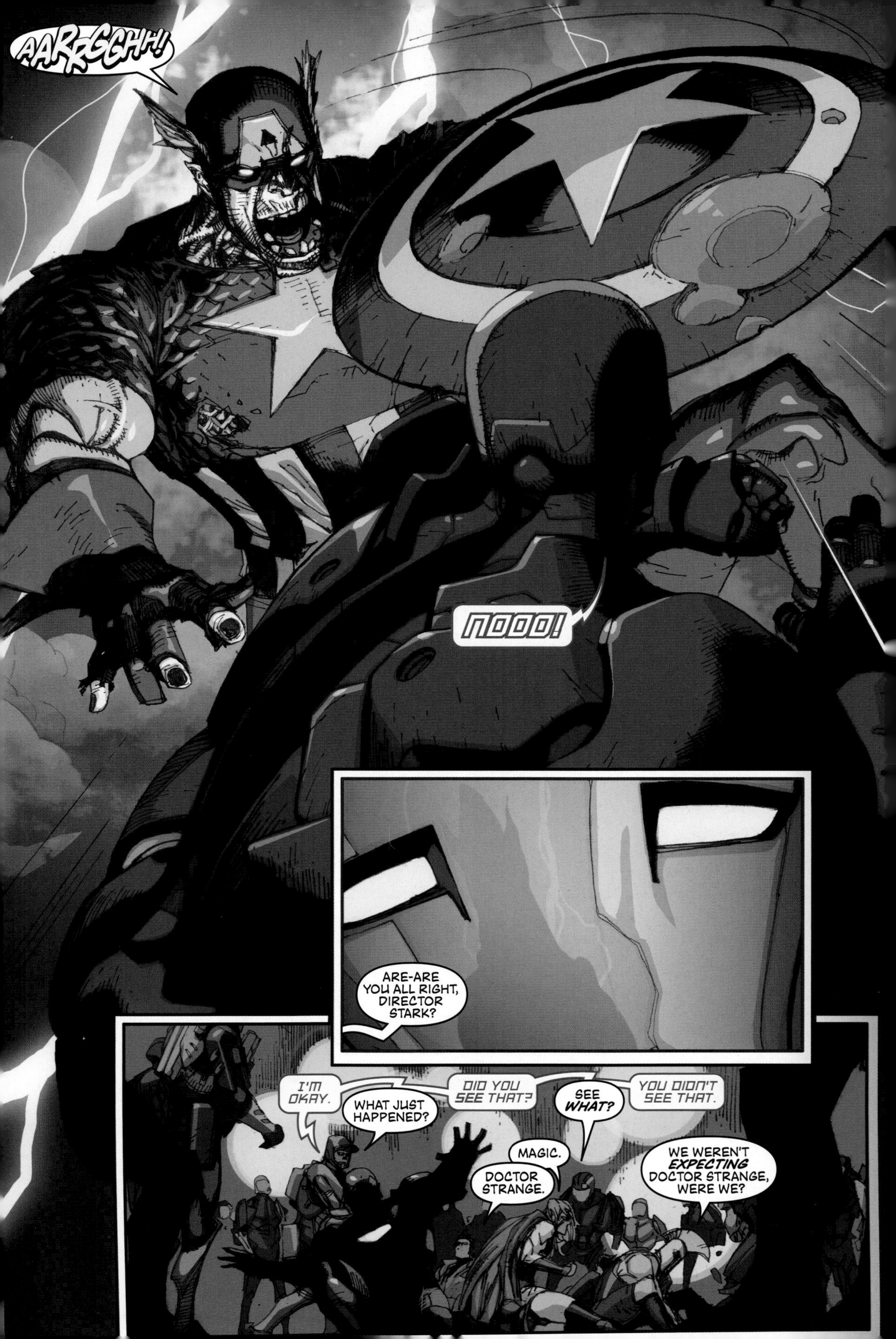
AARRGGHH!
NOOO!
ARE-ARE YOU ALL RIGHT, DIRECTOR STARK?
I'M OKAY.
WHAT JUST HAPPENED?
DID YOU SEE THAT?
SEE WHAT?
YOU DIDN'T SEE THAT.
MAGIC.
DOCTOR STRANGE.
WE WEREN'T EXPECTING DOCTOR STRANGE, WERE WE?

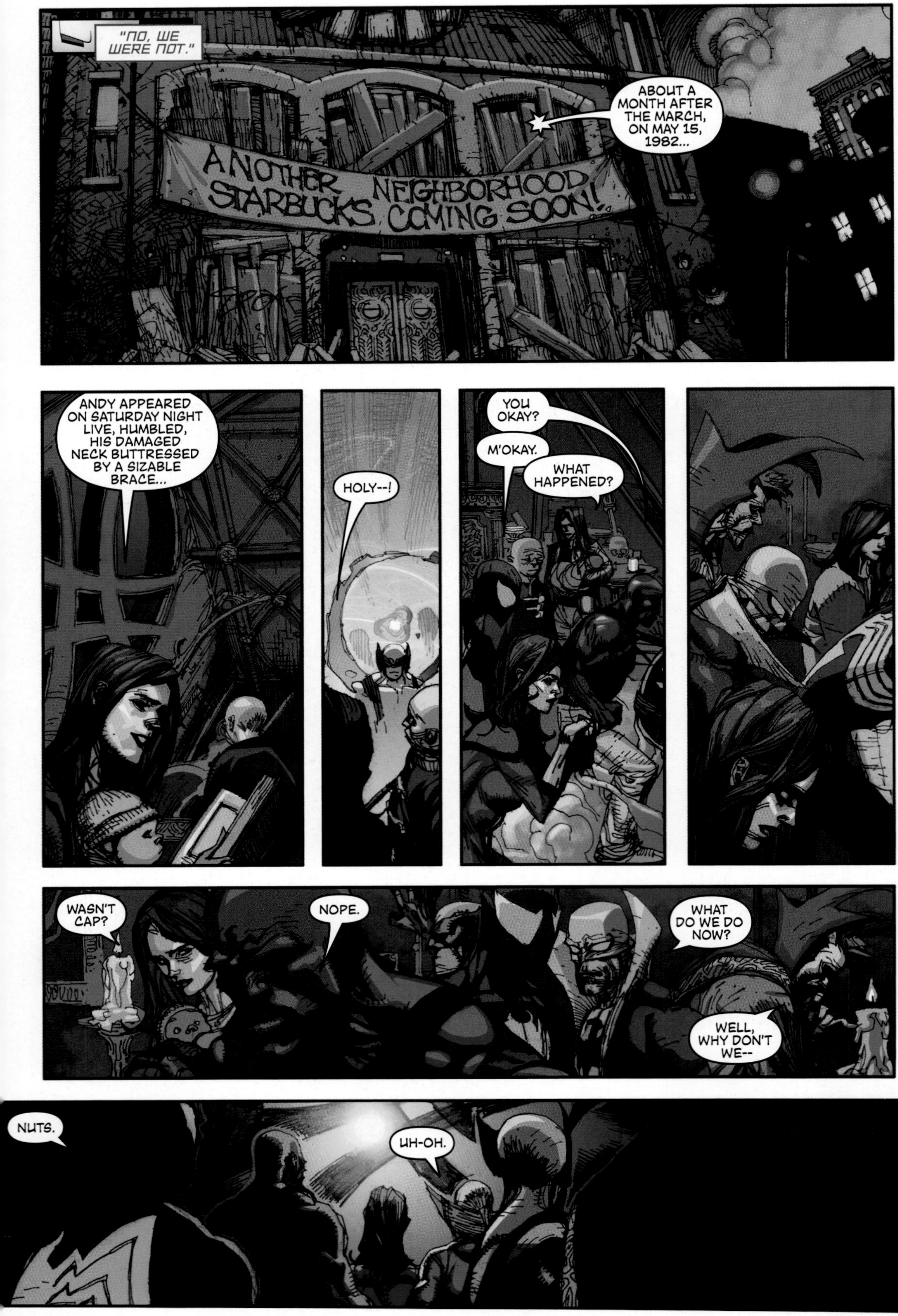
"NO, WE WERE NOT."
ABOUT A MONTH AFTER THE MARCH, ON MAY 15, 1982...
ANOTHER NEIGHBORHOOD STARBUCKS COMING SOON!
ANDY APPEARED ON SATURDAY NIGHT LIVE, HUMBLED, HIS DAMAGED NECK BUTTRESSED BY A SIZABLE BRACE...
HOLY--!
YOU OKAY?
M'OKAY.
WHAT HAPPENED?
WASN'T CAP?
NOPE.
WHAT DO WE DO NOW?
WELL, WHY DON'T WE--
NUTS.
UH-OH.

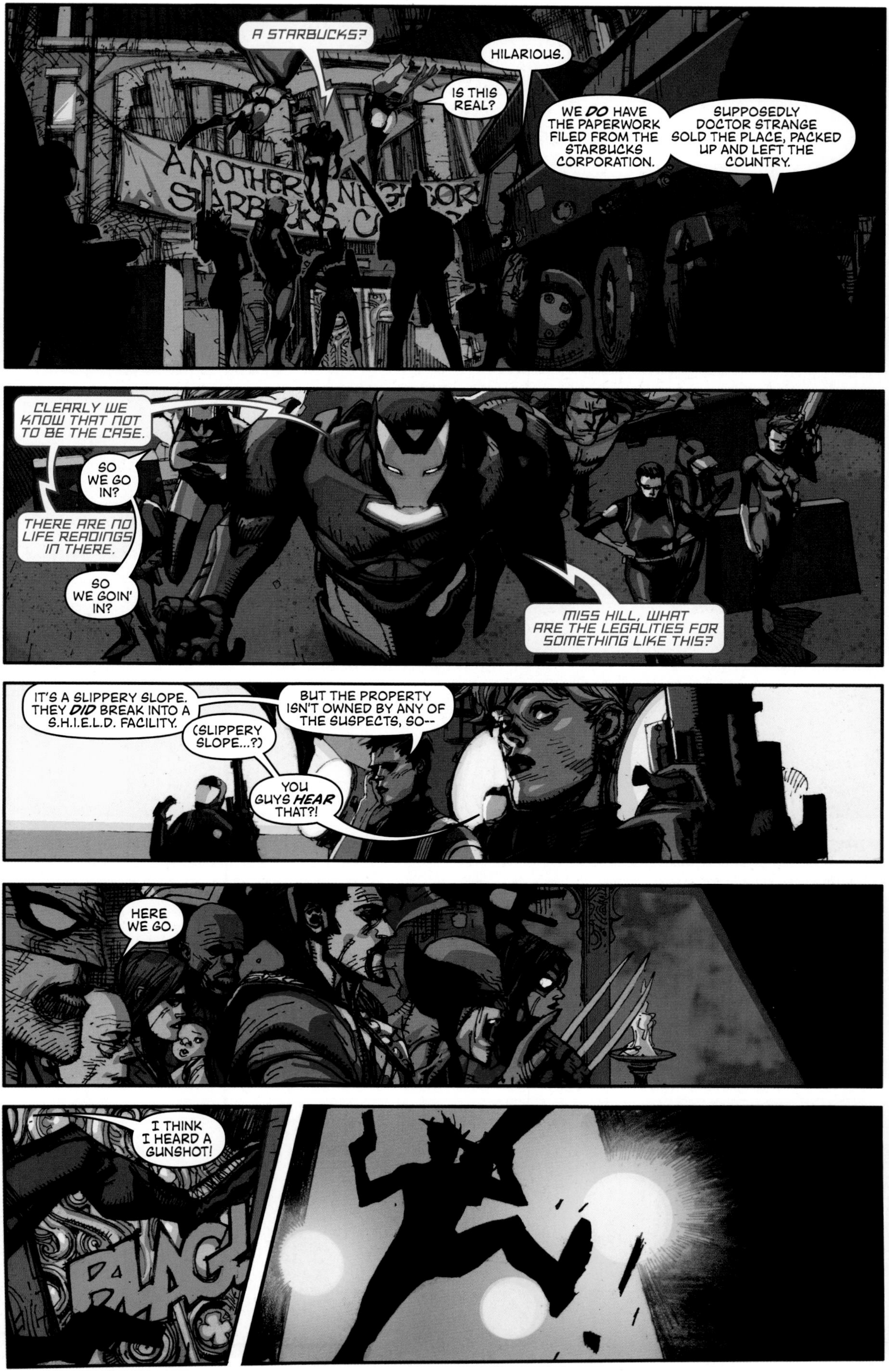
A STARBUCKS?
IS THIS REAL?
HILARIOUS.
WE DO HAVE THE PAPERWORK FILED FROM THE STARBUCKS CORPORATION.
SUPPOSEDLY DOCTOR STRANGE SOLD THE PLACE, PACKED UP AND LEFT THE COUNTRY.
CLEARLY WE KNOW THAT NOT TO BE THE CASE.
SO WE GO IN?
THERE ARE NO LIFE READINGS IN THERE.
SO WE GOIN' IN?
MISS HILL, WHAT ARE THE LEGALITIES FOR SOMETHING LIKE THIS?
IT'S A SLIPPERY SLOPE. THEY DID BREAK INTO A S.H.I.E.L.D. FACILITY.
BUT THE PROPERTY ISN'T OWNED BY ANY OF THE SUSPECTS, SO--
(SLIPPERY SLOPE...?)
YOU GUYS HEAR THAT?!
HERE WE GO.
I THINK I HEARD A GUNSHOT!

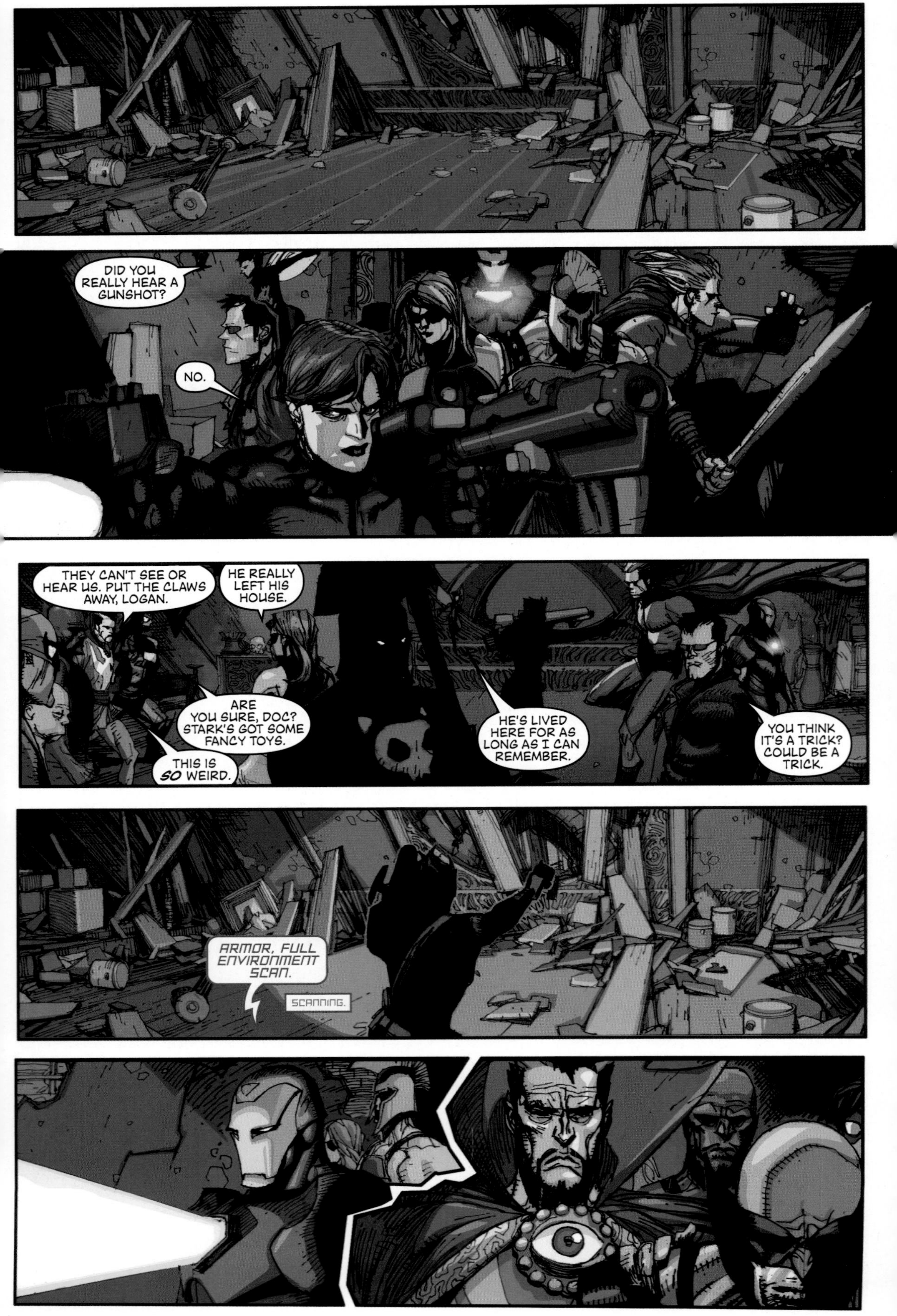
DID YOU REALLY HEAR A GUNSHOT?
NO.
THEY CAN'T SEE OR HEAR US. PUT THE CLAWS AWAY, LOGAN.
HE REALLY LEFT HIS HOUSE.
ARE YOU SURE, DOC? STARK'S GOT SOME FANCY TOYS.
THIS IS *SO* WEIRD.
HE'S LIVED HERE FOR AS LONG AS I CAN REMEMBER.
YOU THINK IT'S A TRICK? COULD BE A TRICK.
ARMOR, FULL ENVIRONMENT SCAN.
SCANNING.

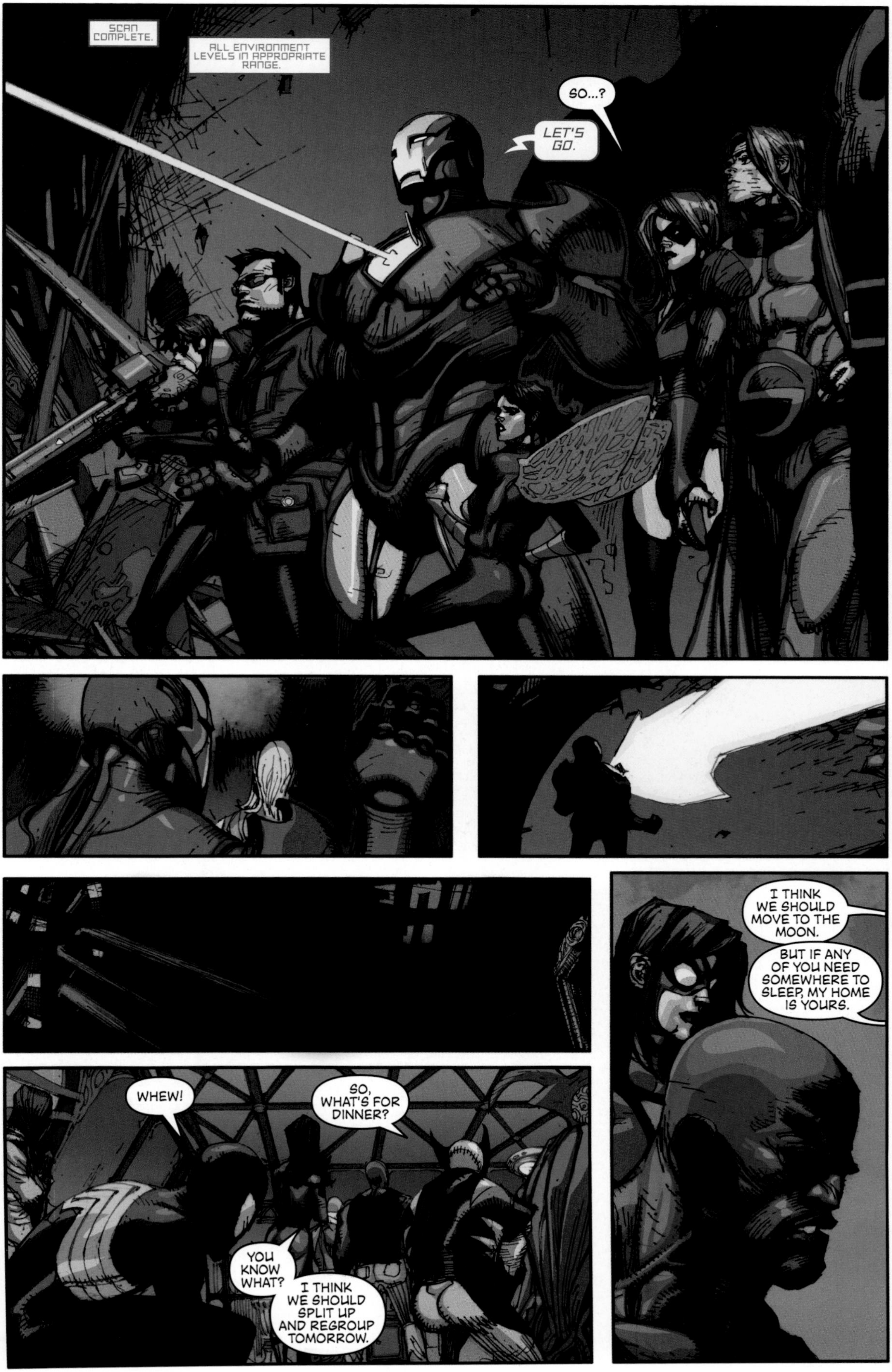
SCAN COMPLETE.
ALL ENVIRONMENT LEVELS IN APPROPRIATE RANGE.
SO...?
LET'S GO.
WHEW!
SO, WHAT'S FOR DINNER?
YOU KNOW WHAT?
I THINK WE SHOULD SPLIT UP AND REGROUP TOMORROW.
I THINK WE SHOULD MOVE TO THE MOON.
BUT IF ANY OF YOU NEED SOMEWHERE TO SLEEP, MY HOME IS YOURS.

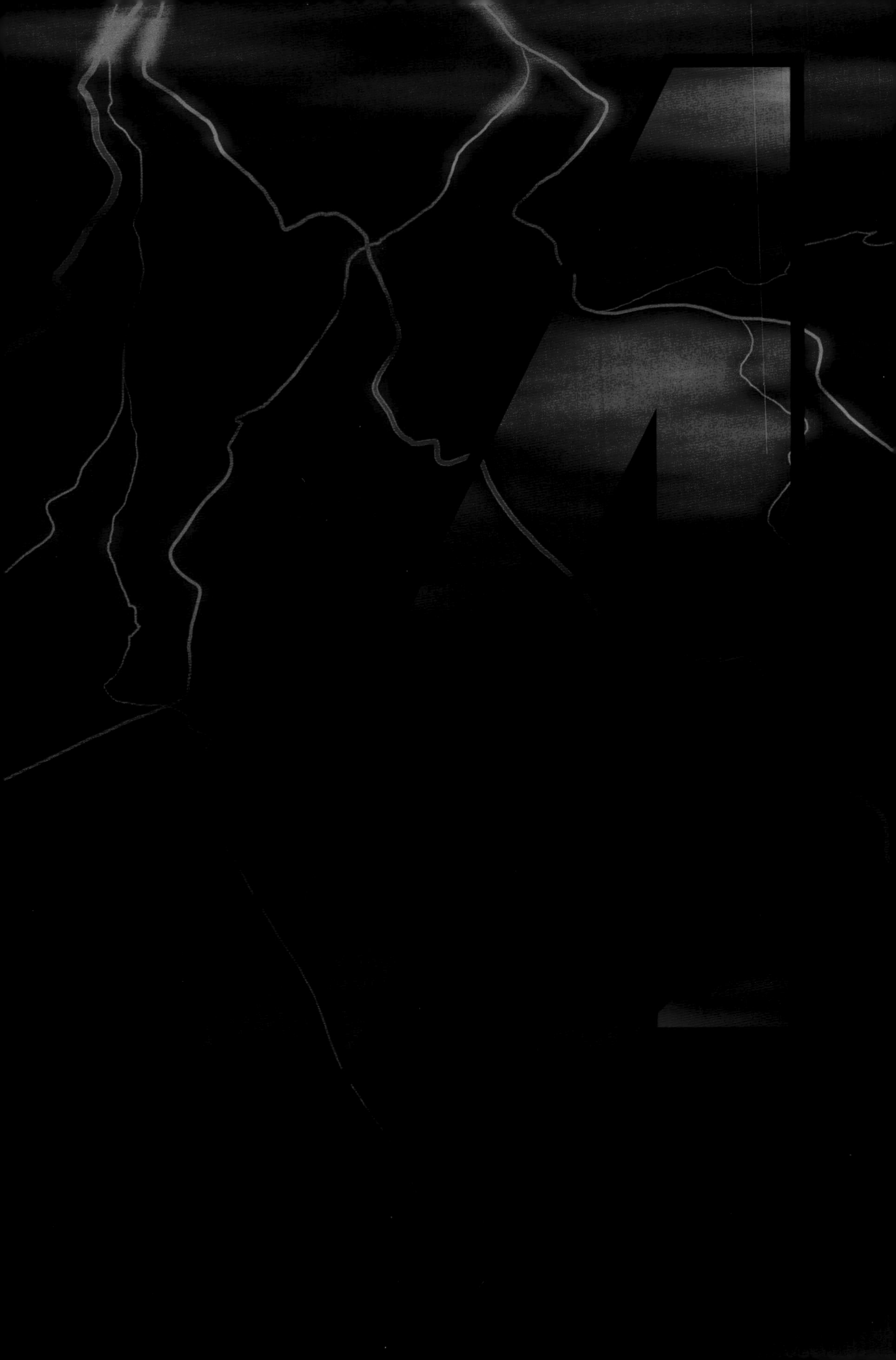

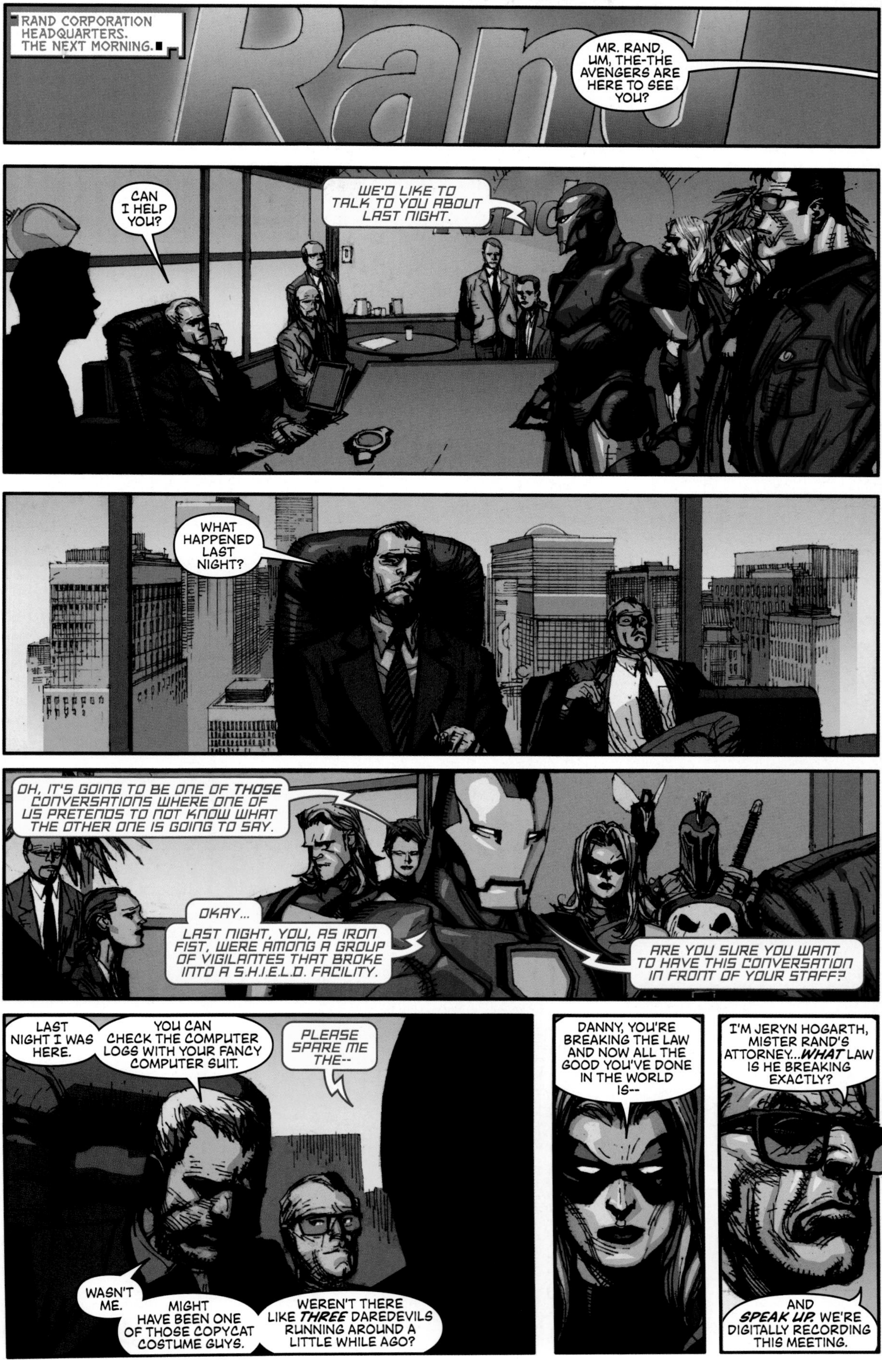
RAND CORPORATION HEADQUARTERS. THE NEXT MORNING.
MR. RAND, UM, THE-THE AVENGERS ARE HERE TO SEE YOU?
CAN I HELP YOU?
WE'D LIKE TO TALK TO YOU ABOUT LAST NIGHT.
WHAT HAPPENED LAST NIGHT?
OH, IT'S GOING TO BE ONE OF THOSE CONVERSATIONS WHERE ONE OF US PRETENDS TO NOT KNOW WHAT THE OTHER ONE IS GOING TO SAY.
OKAY... LAST NIGHT, YOU, AS IRON FIST, WERE AMONG A GROUP OF VIGILANTES THAT BROKE INTO A S.H.I.E.L.D. FACILITY.
ARE YOU SURE YOU WANT TO HAVE THIS CONVERSATION IN FRONT OF YOUR STAFF?
LAST NIGHT I WAS HERE.
YOU CAN CHECK THE COMPUTER LOGS WITH YOUR FANCY COMPUTER SUIT.
PLEASE SPARE ME THE--
WASN'T ME.
MIGHT HAVE BEEN ONE OF THOSE COPYCAT COSTUME GUYS.
WEREN'T THERE LIKE THREE DAREDEVILS RUNNING AROUND A LITTLE WHILE AGO?
DANNY, YOU'RE BREAKING THE LAW AND NOW ALL THE GOOD YOU'VE DONE IN THE WORLD IS--
I'M JERYN HOGARTH, MISTER RAND'S ATTORNEY...WHAT LAW IS HE BREAKING EXACTLY?
AND SPEAK UP. WE'RE DIGITALLY RECORDING THIS MEETING.

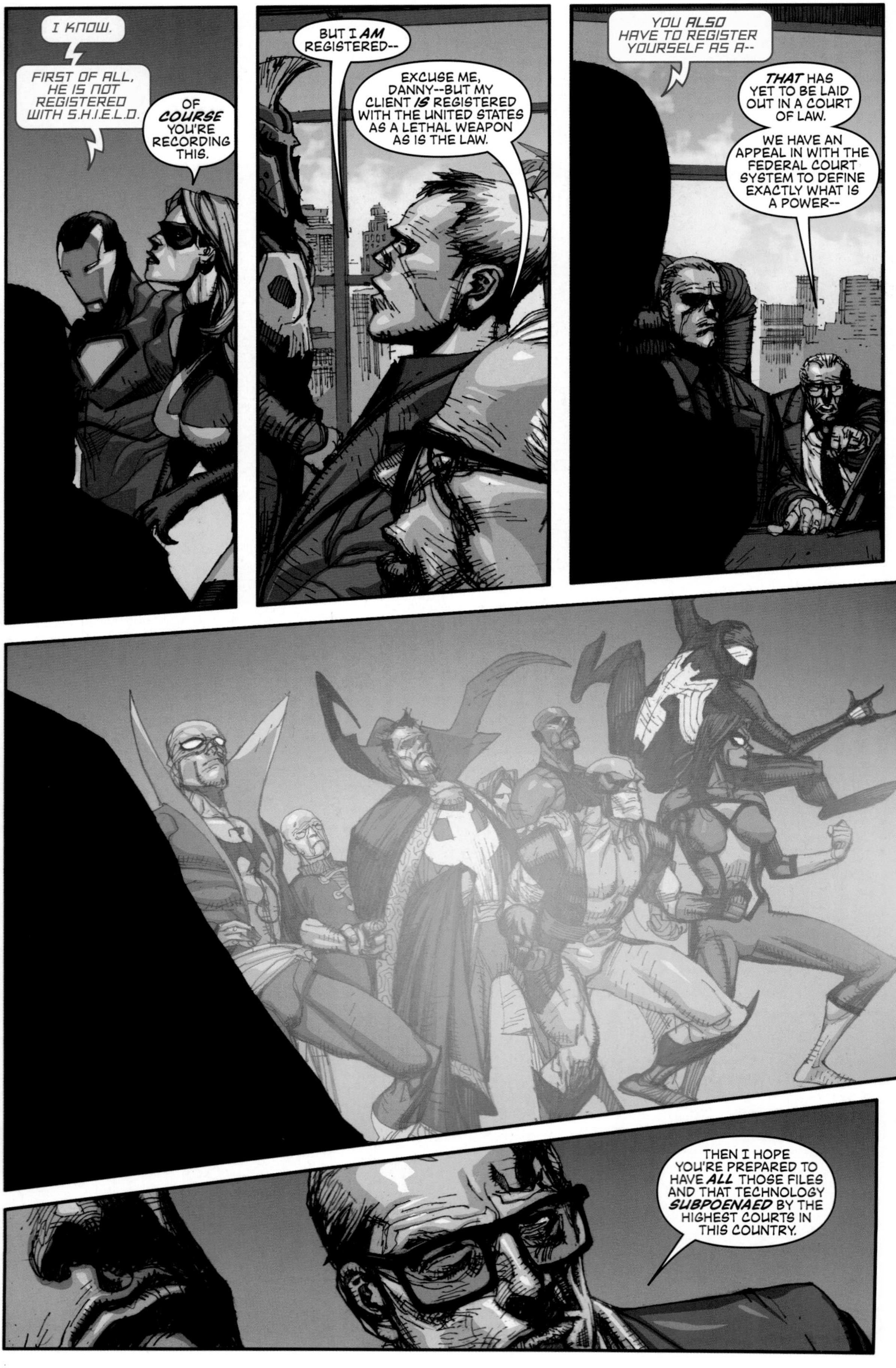
I KNOW.
FIRST OF ALL, HE IS NOT REGISTERED WITH S.H.I.E.L.D.
OF COURSE YOU'RE RECORDING THIS.
BUT I AM REGISTERED--
EXCUSE ME, DANNY--BUT MY CLIENT IS REGISTERED WITH THE UNITED STATES AS A LETHAL WEAPON AS IS THE LAW.
YOU ALSO HAVE TO REGISTER YOURSELF AS A--
THAT HAS YET TO BE LAID OUT IN A COURT OF LAW.
WE HAVE AN APPEAL IN WITH THE FEDERAL COURT SYSTEM TO DEFINE EXACTLY WHAT IS A POWER--
THEN I HOPE YOU'RE PREPARED TO HAVE ALL THOSE FILES AND THAT TECHNOLOGY SUBPOENAED BY THE HIGHEST COURTS IN THIS COUNTRY.

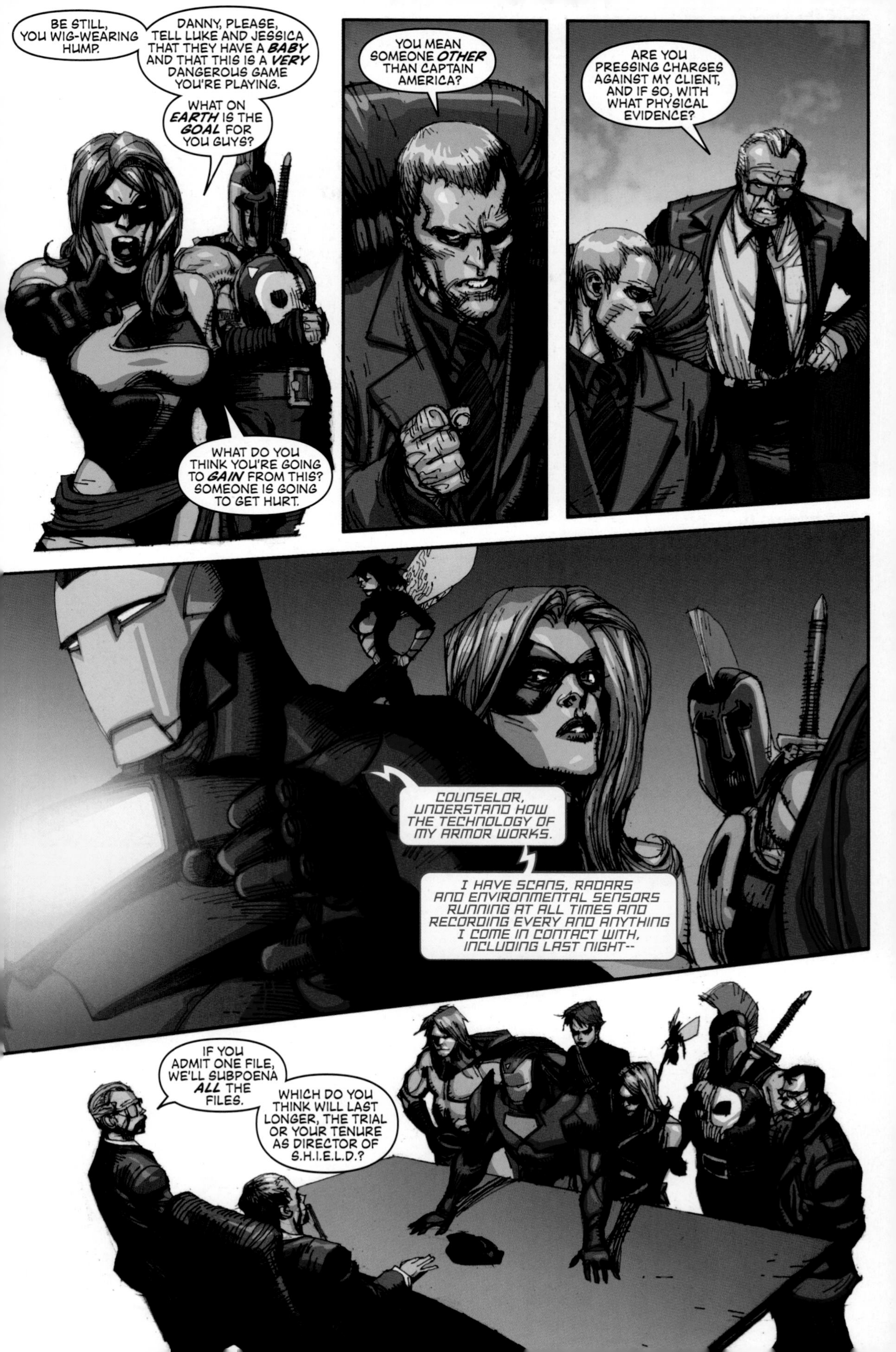

BE STILL, YOU WIG-WEARING HUMP.
DANNY, PLEASE, TELL LUKE AND JESSICA THAT THEY HAVE A BABY AND THAT THIS IS A VERY DANGEROUS GAME YOU'RE PLAYING.
WHAT ON EARTH IS THE GOAL FOR YOU GUYS?
WHAT DO YOU THINK YOU'RE GOING TO GAIN FROM THIS? SOMEONE IS GOING TO GET HURT.
YOU MEAN SOMEONE OTHER THAN CAPTAIN AMERICA?
ARE YOU PRESSING CHARGES AGAINST MY CLIENT, AND IF SO, WITH WHAT PHYSICAL EVIDENCE?
COUNSELOR, UNDERSTAND HOW THE TECHNOLOGY OF MY ARMOR WORKS.
I HAVE SCANS, RADARS AND ENVIRONMENTAL SENSORS RUNNING AT ALL TIMES AND RECORDING EVERY AND ANYTHING I COME IN CONTACT WITH, INCLUDING LAST NIGHT--
IF YOU ADMIT ONE FILE, WE'LL SUBPOENA ALL THE FILES.
WHICH DO YOU THINK WILL LAST LONGER, THE TRIAL OR YOUR TENURE AS DIRECTOR OF S.H.I.E.L.D.?

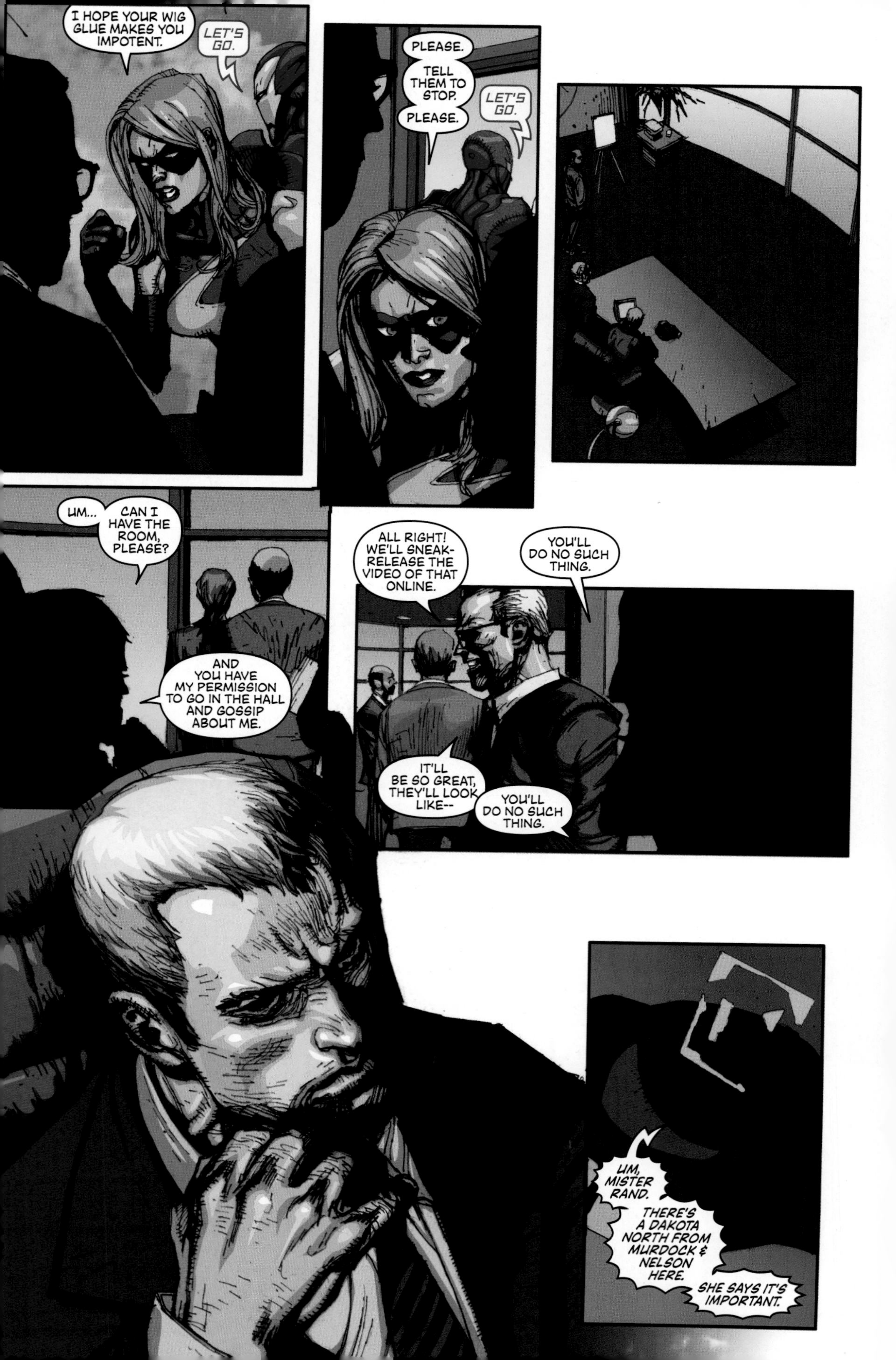

I HOPE YOUR WIG GLUE MAKES YOU IMPOTENT.
LET'S GO.
PLEASE.
TELL THEM TO STOP.
PLEASE.
LET'S GO.
UM...
CAN I HAVE THE ROOM, PLEASE?
AND YOU HAVE MY PERMISSION TO GO IN THE HALL AND GOSSIP ABOUT ME.
ALL RIGHT! WE'LL SNEAK-RELEASE THE VIDEO OF THAT ONLINE.
YOU'LL DO NO SUCH THING.
IT'LL BE SO GREAT, THEY'LL LOOK LIKE--
YOU'LL DO NO SUCH THING.
UM, MISTER RAND.
THERE'S A DAKOTA NORTH FROM MURDOCK & NELSON HERE.
SHE SAYS IT'S IMPORTANT.

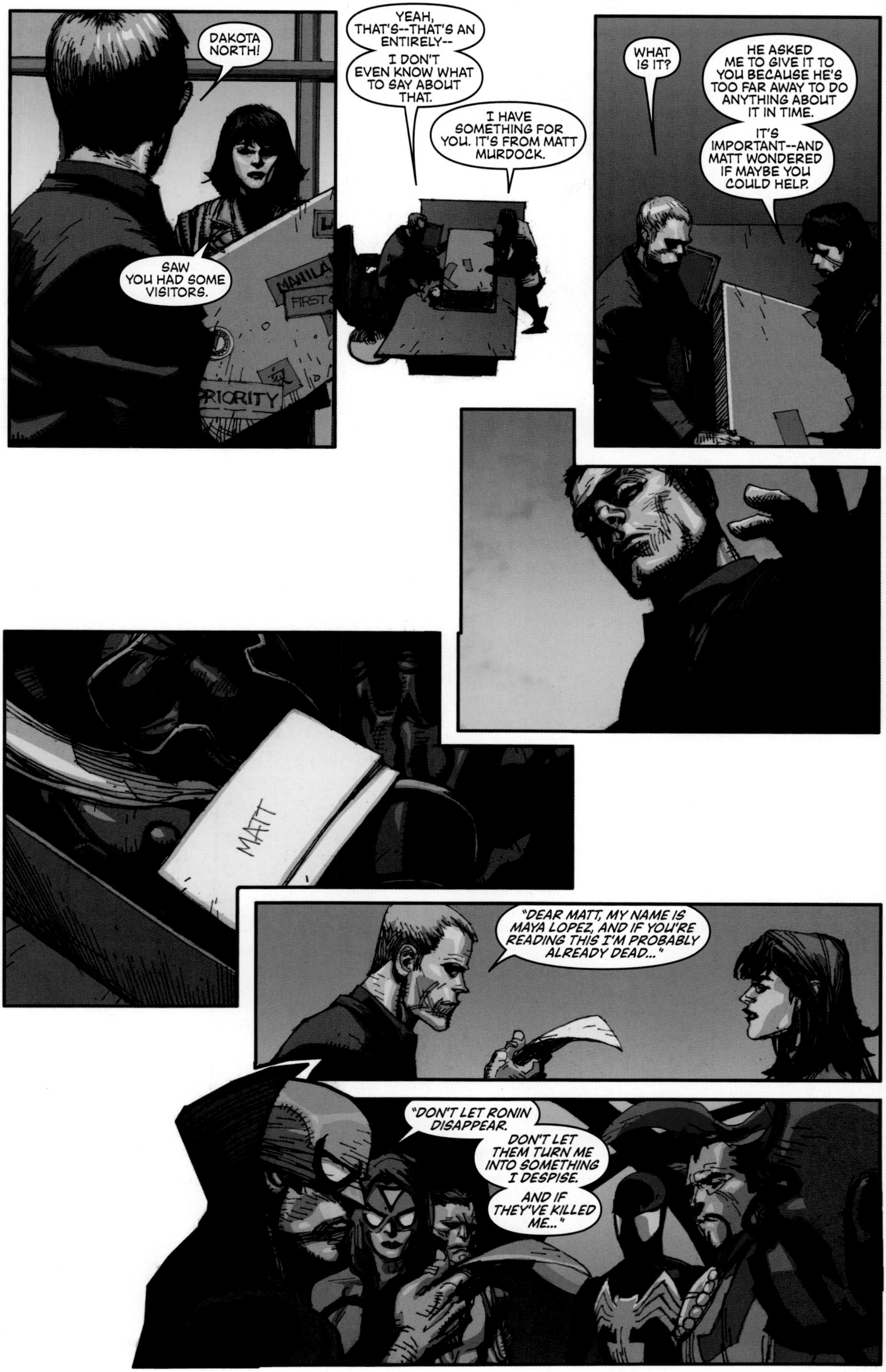
DAKOTA NORTH!
SAW YOU HAD SOME VISITORS.
MANILA
FIRST
PRIORITY
YEAH, THAT'S--THAT'S AN ENTIRELY-- I DON'T EVEN KNOW WHAT TO SAY ABOUT THAT.
I HAVE SOMETHING FOR YOU. IT'S FROM MATT MURDOCK.
WHAT IS IT?
HE ASKED ME TO GIVE IT TO YOU BECAUSE HE'S TOO FAR AWAY TO DO ANYTHING ABOUT IT IN TIME.
IT'S IMPORTANT--AND MATT WONDERED IF MAYBE YOU COULD HELP.
MATT
"DEAR MATT, MY NAME IS MAYA LOPEZ, AND IF YOU'RE READING THIS I'M PROBABLY ALREADY DEAD..."
"DON'T LET RONIN DISAPPEAR.
DON'T LET THEM TURN ME INTO SOMETHING I DESPISE.
AND IF THEY'VE KILLED ME..."

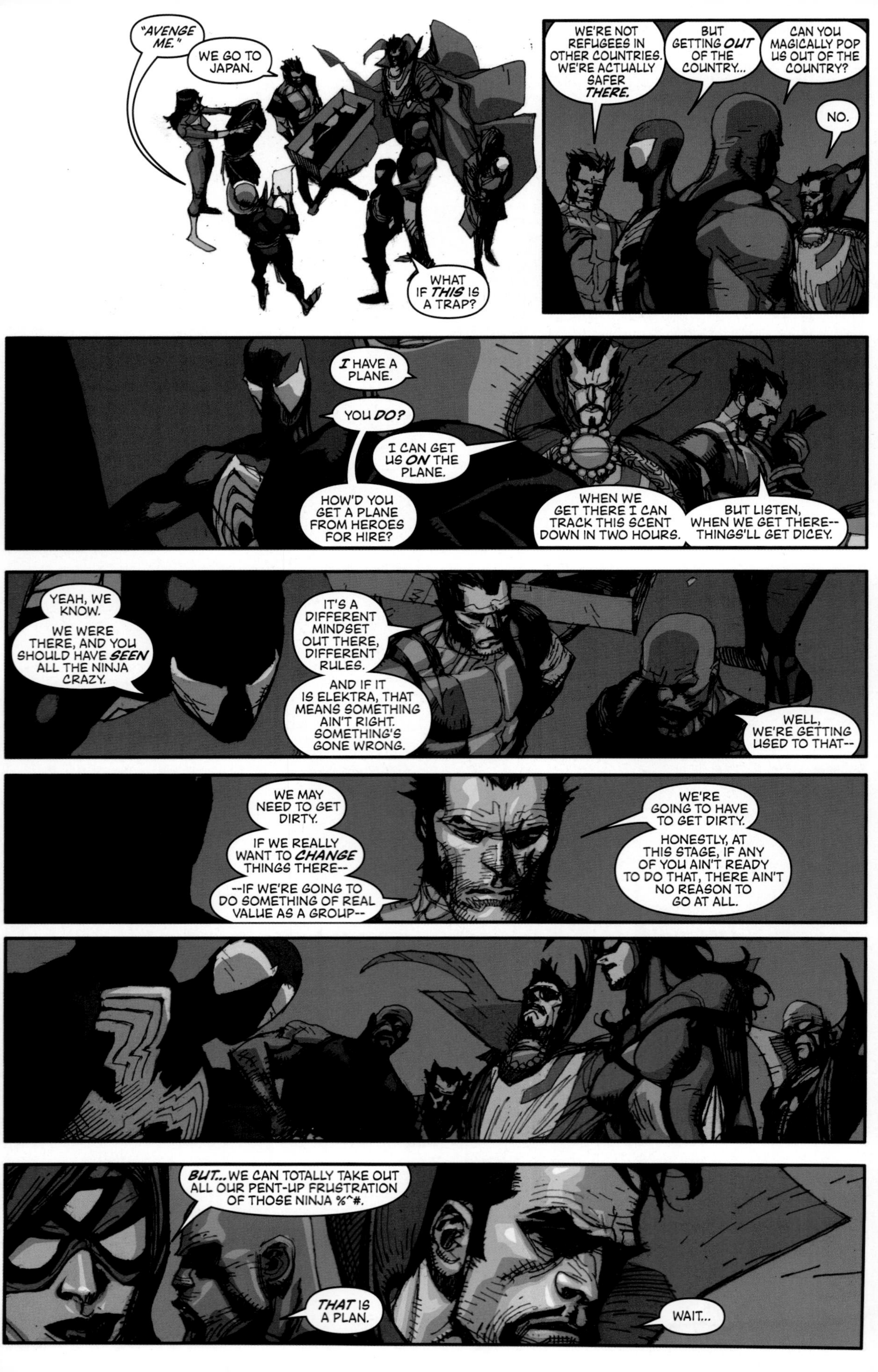
"AVENGE ME."
WE GO TO JAPAN.
WHAT IF THIS IS A TRAP?
WE'RE NOT REFUGEES IN OTHER COUNTRIES. WE'RE ACTUALLY SAFER THERE.
BUT GETTING OUT OF THE COUNTRY...
CAN YOU MAGICALLY POP US OUT OF THE COUNTRY?
NO.
I HAVE A PLANE.
YOU DO?
I CAN GET US ON THE PLANE.
HOW'D YOU GET A PLANE FROM HEROES FOR HIRE?
WHEN WE GET THERE I CAN TRACK THIS SCENT DOWN IN TWO HOURS.
BUT LISTEN, WHEN WE GET THERE-- THINGS'LL GET DICEY.
YEAH, WE KNOW.
WE WERE THERE, AND YOU SHOULD HAVE SEEN ALL THE NINJA CRAZY.
IT'S A DIFFERENT MINDSET OUT THERE, DIFFERENT RULES.
AND IF IT IS ELEKTRA, THAT MEANS SOMETHING AIN'T RIGHT. SOMETHING'S GONE WRONG.
WELL, WE'RE GETTING USED TO THAT--
WE MAY NEED TO GET DIRTY.
IF WE REALLY WANT TO CHANGE THINGS THERE--
--IF WE'RE GOING TO DO SOMETHING OF REAL VALUE AS A GROUP--
WE'RE GOING TO HAVE TO GET DIRTY.
HONESTLY, AT THIS STAGE, IF ANY OF YOU AIN'T READY TO DO THAT, THERE AIN'T NO REASON TO GO AT ALL.
BUT... WE CAN TOTALLY TAKE OUT ALL OUR PENT-UP FRUSTRATION OF THOSE NINJA %^#.
THAT IS A PLAN.
WAIT...

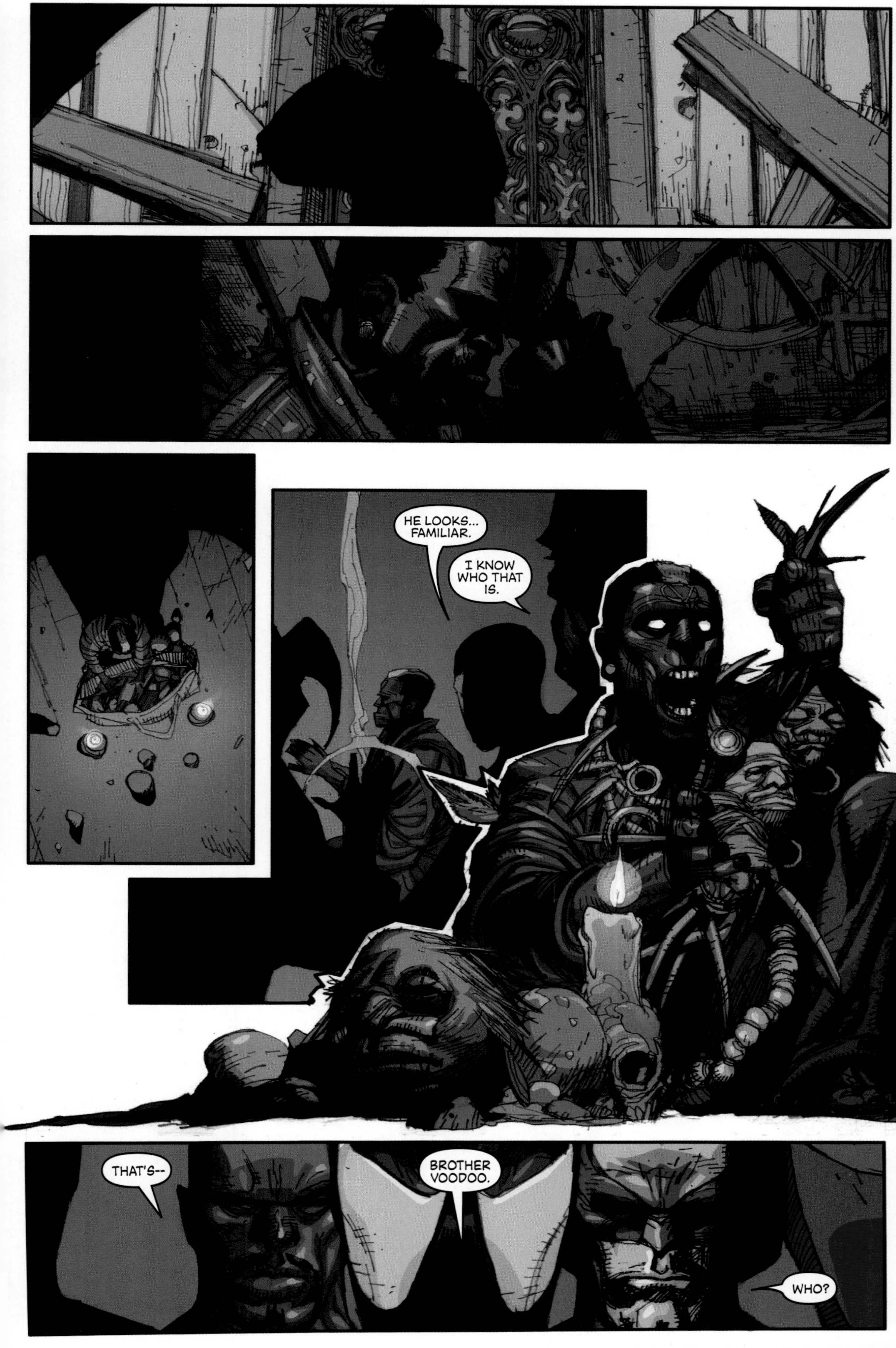
HE LOOKS... FAMILIAR.
I KNOW WHO THAT IS.
THAT'S--
BROTHER VOODOO.
WHO?

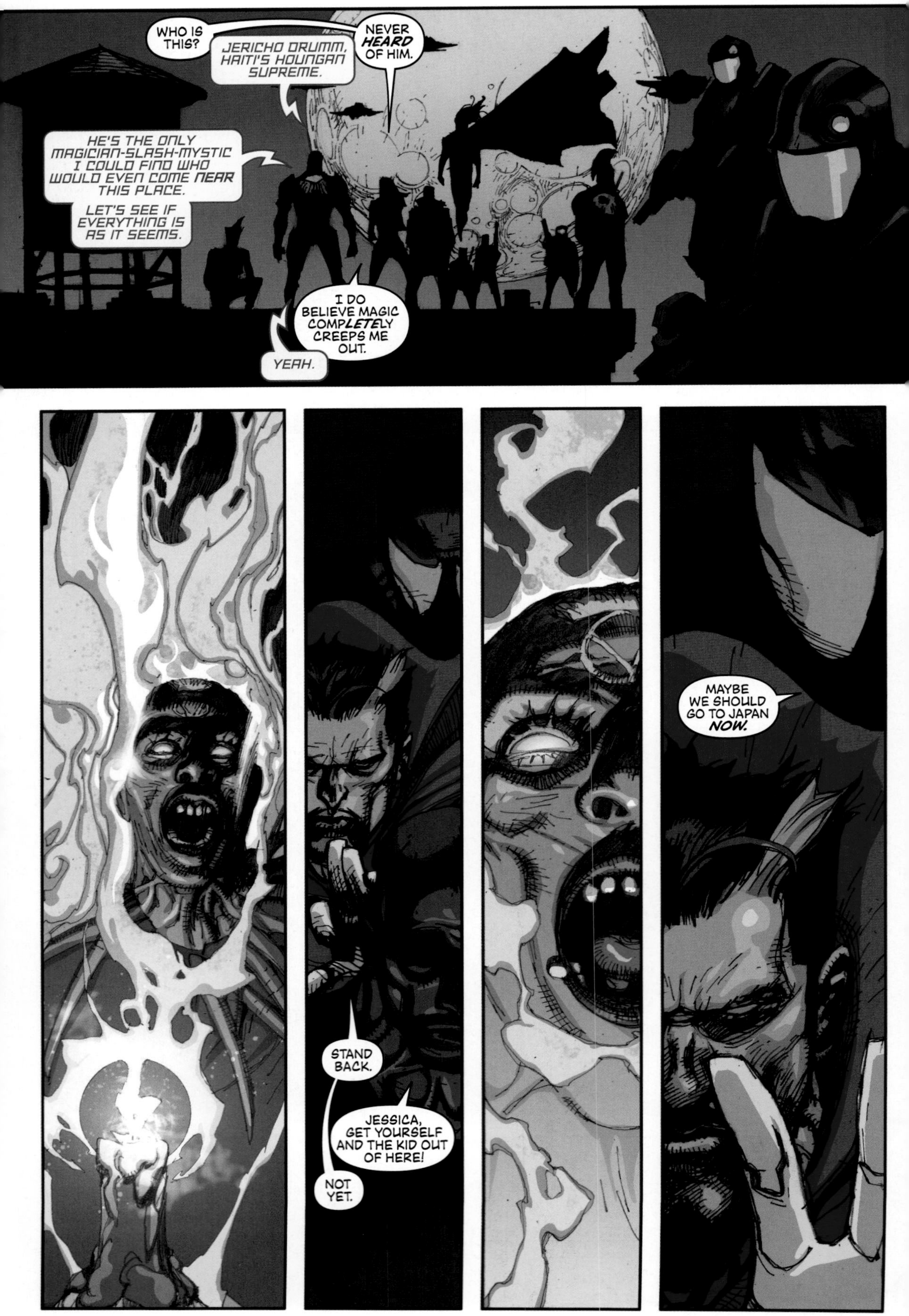
WHO IS THIS?
JERICHO DRUMM, HAITI'S HOUNGAN SUPREME.
NEVER HEARD OF HIM.
HE'S THE ONLY MAGICIAN-SLASH-MYSTIC I COULD FIND WHO WOULD EVEN COME NEAR THIS PLACE.
LET'S SEE IF EVERYTHING IS AS IT SEEMS.
I DO BELIEVE MAGIC COMPLETELY CREEPS ME OUT.
YEAH.
STAND BACK.
JESSICA, GET YOURSELF AND THE KID OUT OF HERE!
NOT YET.
MAYBE WE SHOULD GO TO JAPAN NOW.

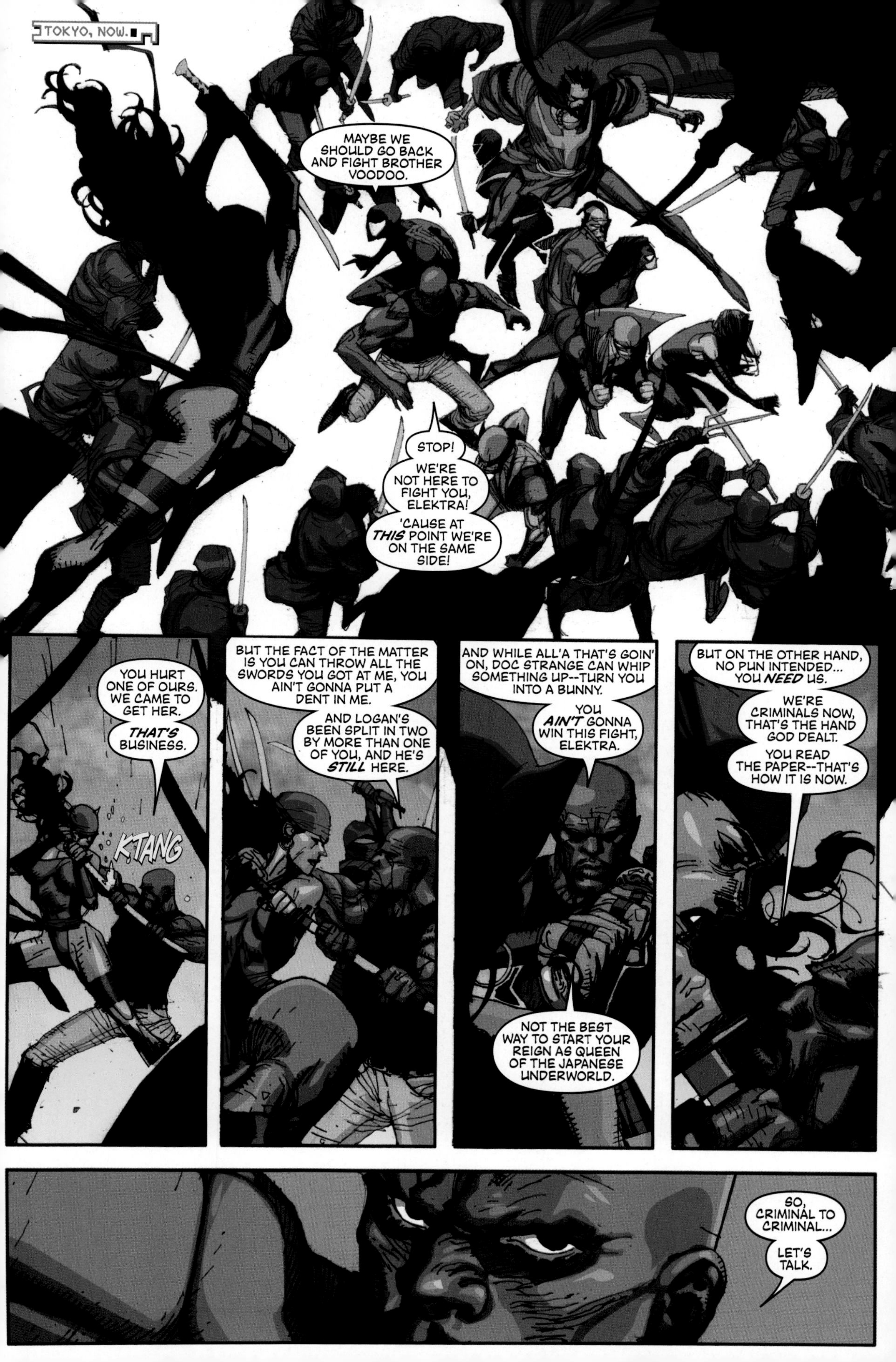
TOKYO, NOW.
MAYBE WE SHOULD GO BACK AND FIGHT BROTHER VOODOO.
STOP! WE'RE NOT HERE TO FIGHT YOU, ELEKTRA!
'CAUSE AT THIS POINT WE'RE ON THE SAME SIDE!
YOU HURT ONE OF OURS. WE CAME TO GET HER.
THAT'S BUSINESS.
KTANG
BUT THE FACT OF THE MATTER IS YOU CAN THROW ALL THE SWORDS YOU GOT AT ME, YOU AIN'T GONNA PUT A DENT IN ME.
AND LOGAN'S BEEN SPLIT IN TWO BY MORE THAN ONE OF YOU, AND HE'S STILL HERE.
AND WHILE ALL'A THAT'S GOIN' ON, DOC STRANGE CAN WHIP SOMETHING UP--TURN YOU INTO A BUNNY.
YOU AIN'T GONNA WIN THIS FIGHT, ELEKTRA.
NOT THE BEST WAY TO START YOUR REIGN AS QUEEN OF THE JAPANESE UNDERWORLD.
BUT ON THE OTHER HAND, NO PUN INTENDED... YOU NEED US.
WE'RE CRIMINALS NOW, THAT'S THE HAND GOD DEALT.
YOU READ THE PAPER--THAT'S HOW IT IS NOW.
SO, CRIMINAL TO CRIMINAL...
LET'S TALK.

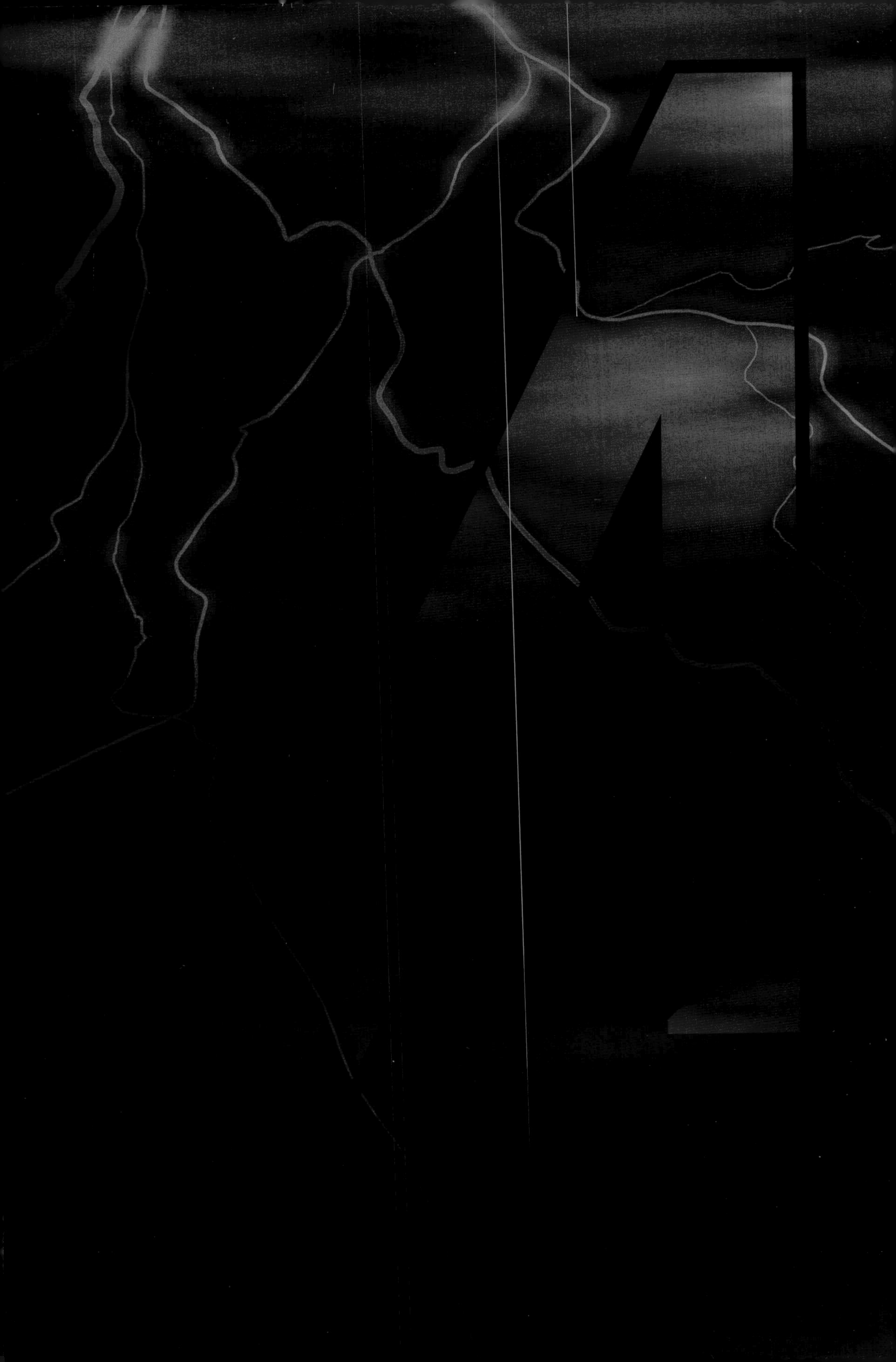
4

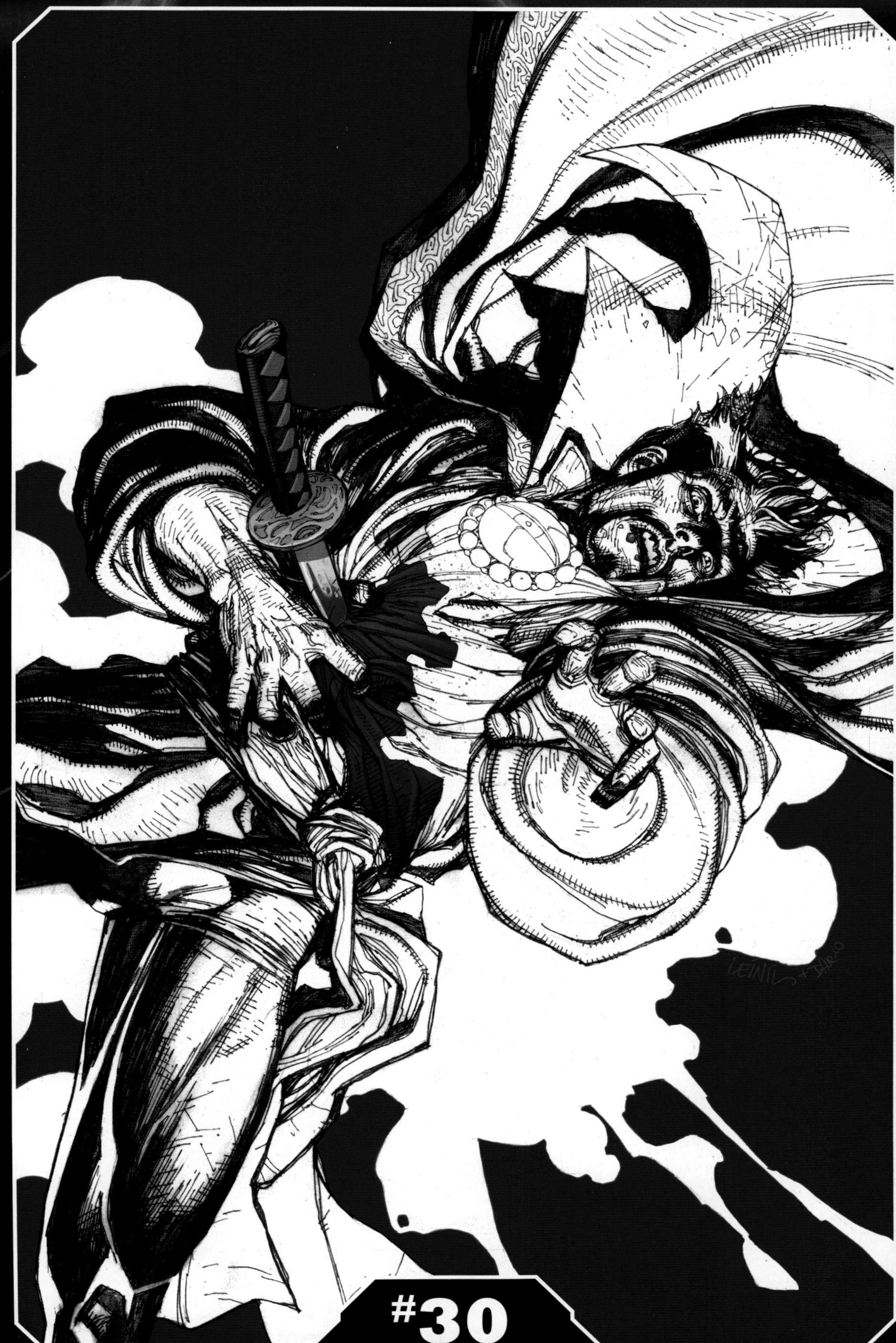
#30

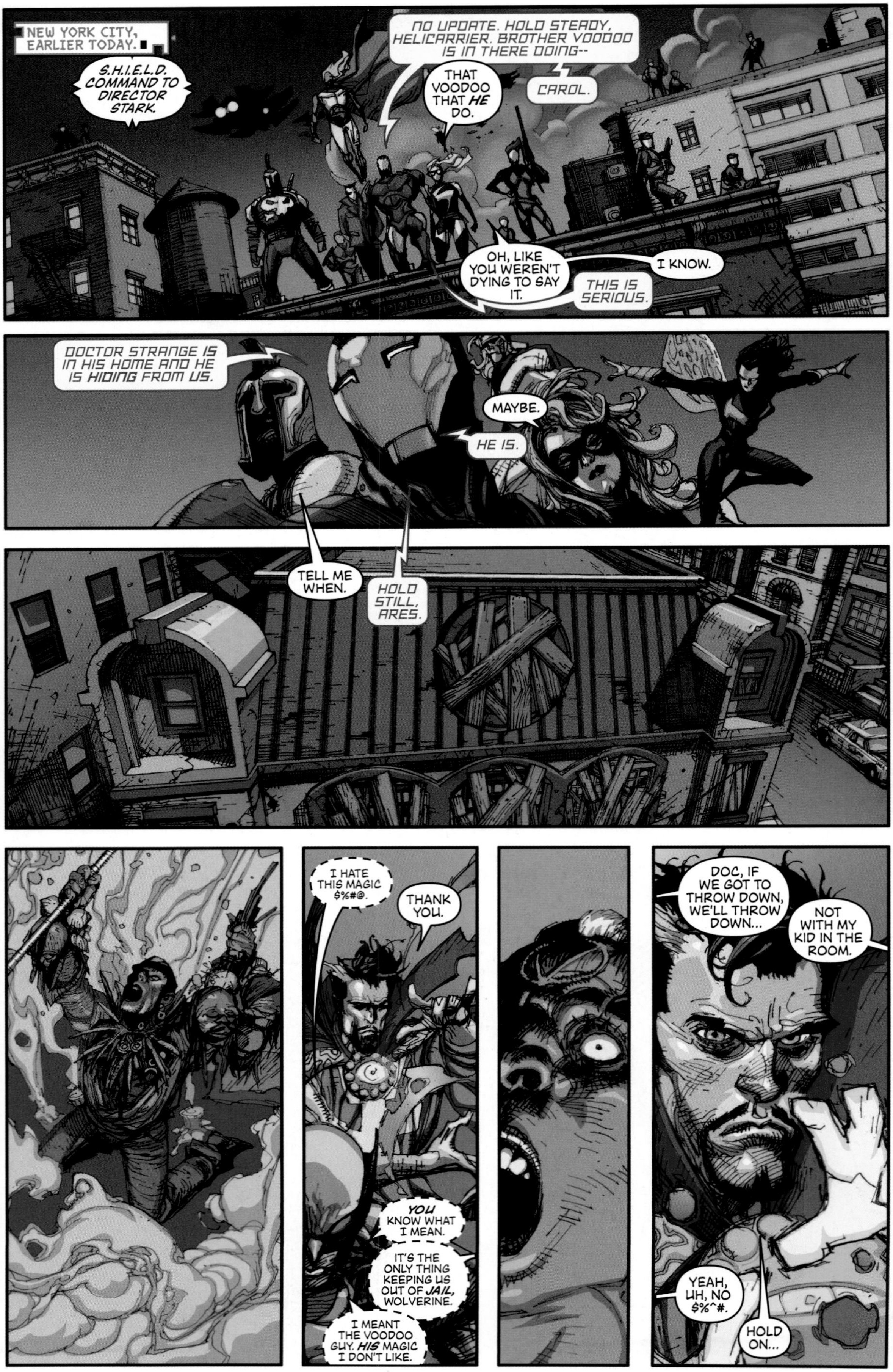

NEW YORK CITY, EARLIER TODAY.
S.H.I.E.L.D. COMMAND TO DIRECTOR STARK.
NO UPDATE. HOLD STEADY, HELICARRIER. BROTHER VOODOO IS IN THERE DOING--
THAT VOODOO THAT HE DO.
CAROL.
OH, LIKE YOU WEREN'T DYING TO SAY IT.
I KNOW.
THIS IS SERIOUS.
DOCTOR STRANGE IS IN HIS HOME AND HE IS HIDING FROM US.
MAYBE.
HE IS.
TELL ME WHEN.
HOLD STILL, ARES.
I HATE THIS MAGIC $%#@.
THANK YOU.
YOU KNOW WHAT I MEAN.
IT'S THE ONLY THING KEEPING US OUT OF JAIL, WOLVERINE.
I MEANT THE VOODOO GUY. HIS MAGIC I DON'T LIKE.
DOC, IF WE GOT TO THROW DOWN, WE'LL THROW DOWN...
NOT WITH MY KID IN THE ROOM.
YEAH, UH, NO $%^#.
HOLD ON...

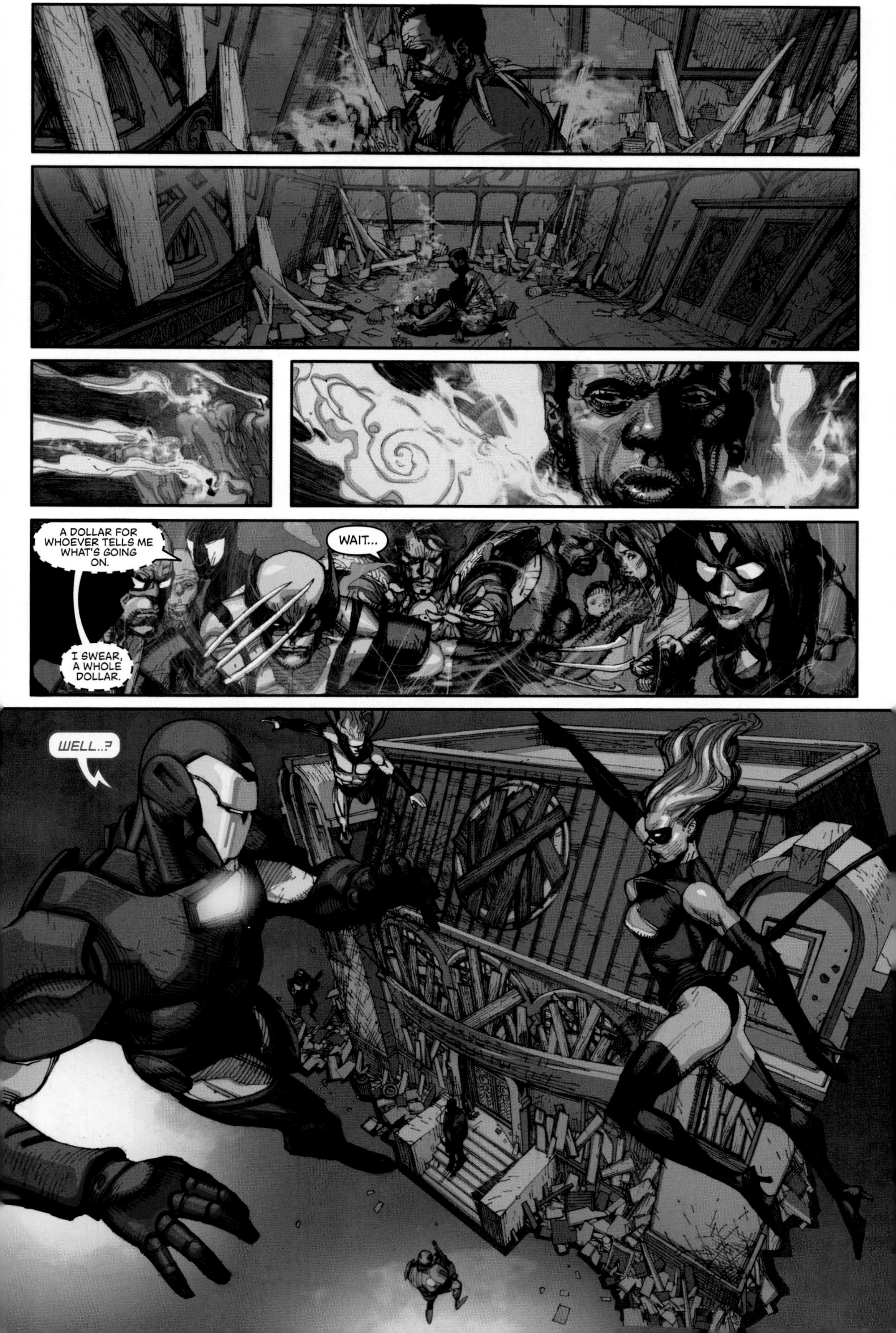
A DOLLAR FOR WHOEVER TELLS ME WHAT'S GOING ON.
WAIT...
I SWEAR, A WHOLE DOLLAR.
WELL..?

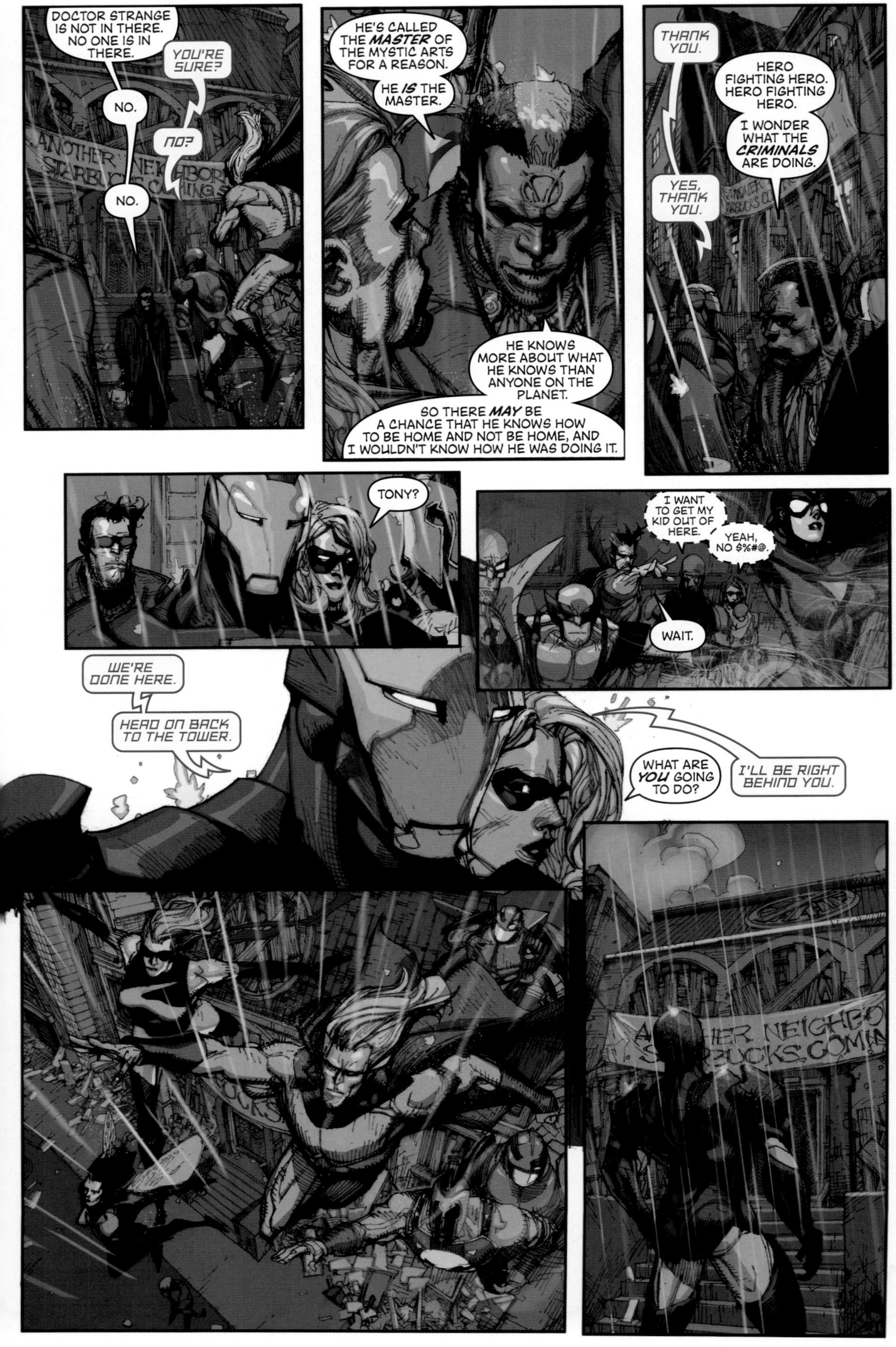
DOCTOR STRANGE IS NOT IN THERE. NO ONE IS IN THERE.
YOU'RE SURE?
NO.
NO?
NO.
ANOTHER NEIGHBOR STARBUCKS COMING
HE'S CALLED THE MASTER OF THE MYSTIC ARTS FOR A REASON.
HE IS THE MASTER.
HE KNOWS MORE ABOUT WHAT HE KNOWS THAN ANYONE ON THE PLANET.
SO THERE MAY BE A CHANCE THAT HE KNOWS HOW TO BE HOME AND NOT BE HOME, AND I WOULDN'T KNOW HOW HE WAS DOING IT.
THANK YOU.
HERO FIGHTING HERO. HERO FIGHTING HERO.
I WONDER WHAT THE CRIMINALS ARE DOING.
YES, THANK YOU.
TONY?
I WANT TO GET MY KID OUT OF HERE.
YEAH, NO $%#@.
WAIT.
WE'RE DONE HERE.
HEAD ON BACK TO THE TOWER.
WHAT ARE YOU GOING TO DO?
I'LL BE RIGHT BEHIND YOU.

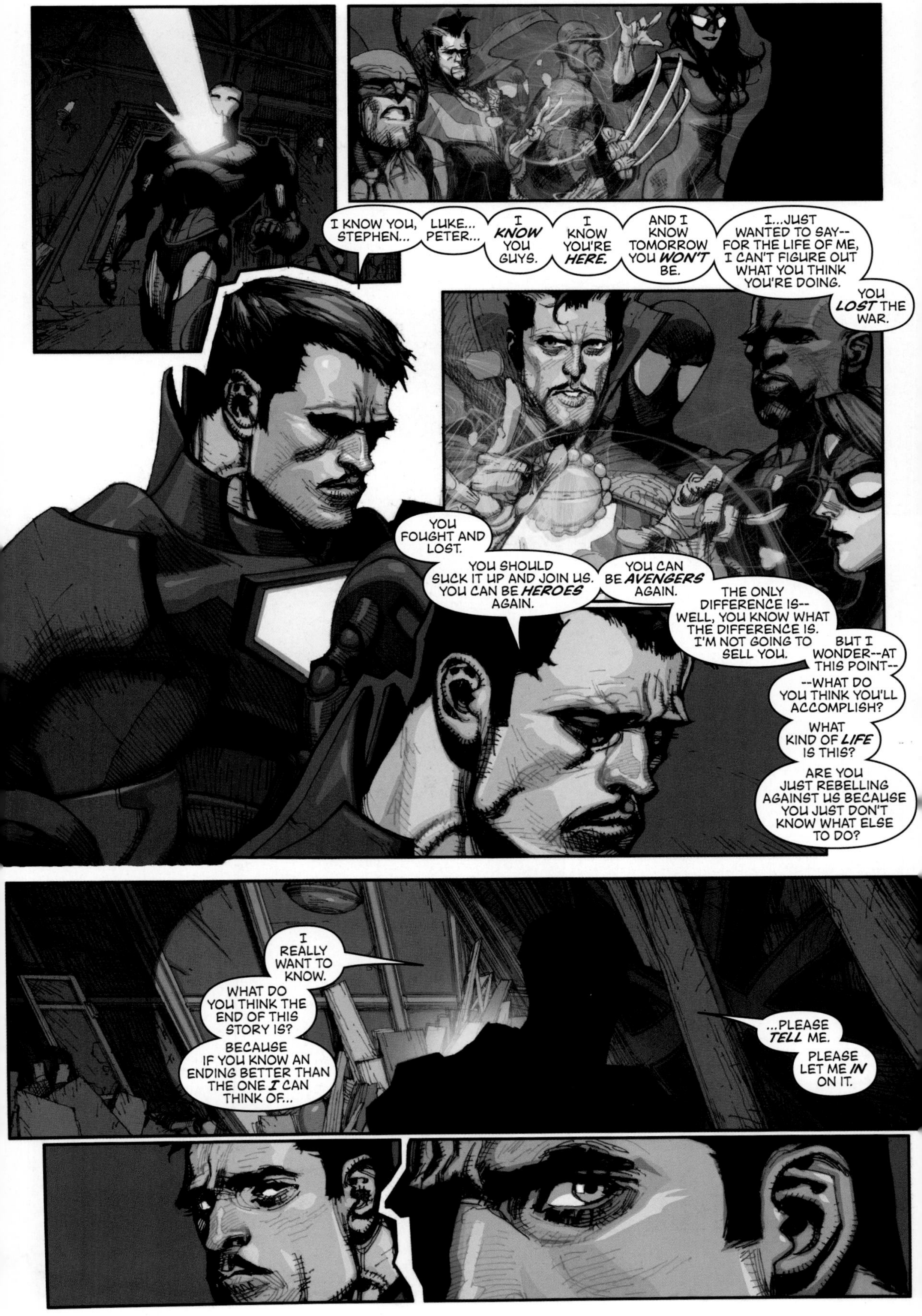
I KNOW YOU, STEPHEN...
LUKE... PETER...
I KNOW YOU GUYS.
I KNOW YOU'RE HERE.
AND I KNOW TOMORROW YOU WON'T BE.
I...JUST WANTED TO SAY-- FOR THE LIFE OF ME, I CAN'T FIGURE OUT WHAT YOU THINK YOU'RE DOING.
YOU LOST THE WAR.
YOU FOUGHT AND LOST.
YOU SHOULD SUCK IT UP AND JOIN US. YOU CAN BE HEROES AGAIN.
YOU CAN BE AVENGERS AGAIN.
THE ONLY DIFFERENCE IS-- WELL, YOU KNOW WHAT THE DIFFERENCE IS. I'M NOT GOING TO SELL YOU.
BUT I WONDER--AT THIS POINT--
--WHAT DO YOU THINK YOU'LL ACCOMPLISH?
WHAT KIND OF LIFE IS THIS?
ARE YOU JUST REBELLING AGAINST US BECAUSE YOU JUST DON'T KNOW WHAT ELSE TO DO?
I REALLY WANT TO KNOW.
WHAT DO YOU THINK THE END OF THIS STORY IS?
BECAUSE IF YOU KNOW AN ENDING BETTER THAN THE ONE I CAN THINK OF...
...PLEASE TELL ME.
PLEASE LET ME IN ON IT.

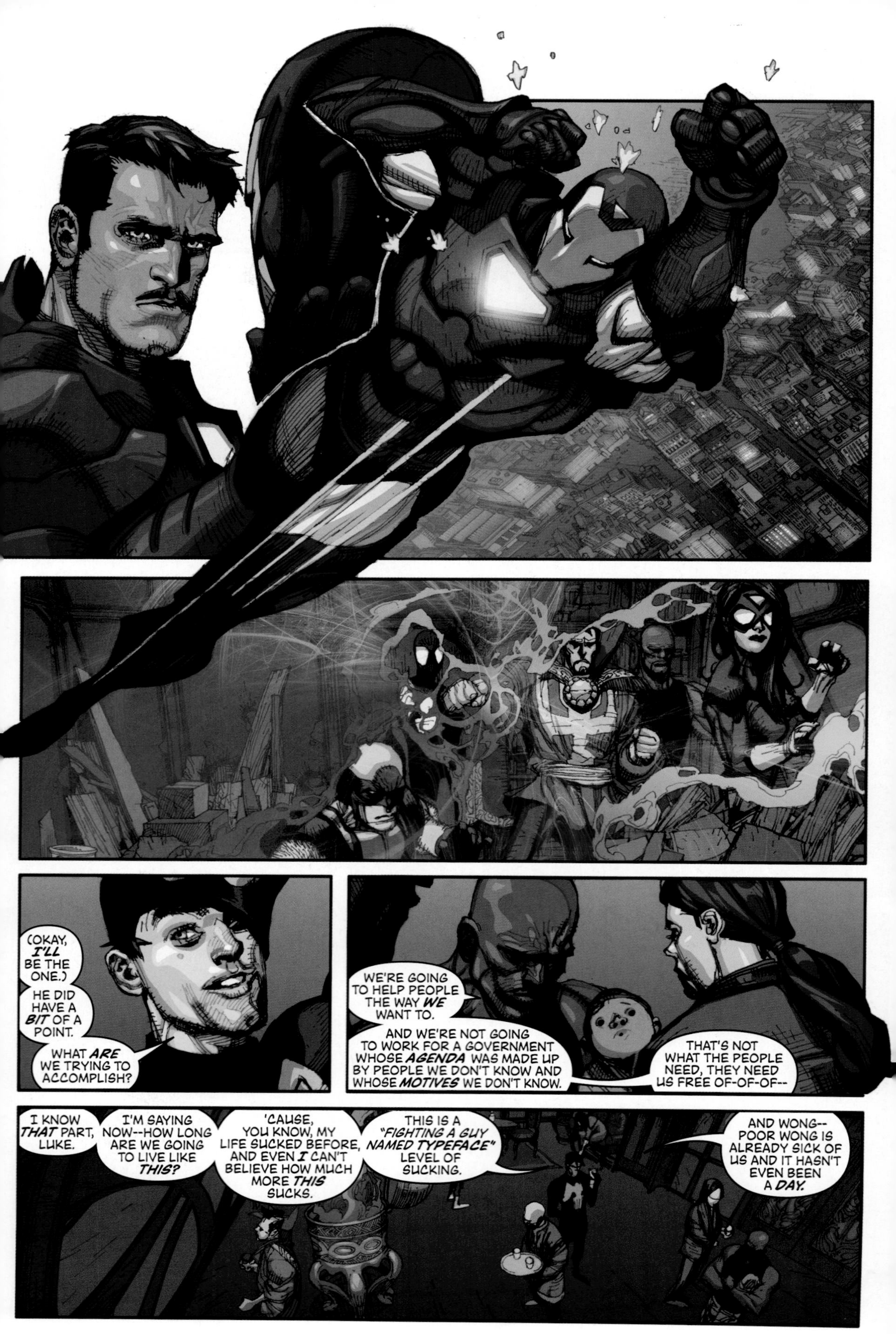

(OKAY, I'LL BE THE ONE.)
HE DID HAVE A BIT OF A POINT.
WHAT ARE WE TRYING TO ACCOMPLISH?
WE'RE GOING TO HELP PEOPLE THE WAY WE WANT TO.
AND WE'RE NOT GOING TO WORK FOR A GOVERNMENT WHOSE AGENDA WAS MADE UP BY PEOPLE WE DON'T KNOW AND WHOSE MOTIVES WE DON'T KNOW.
THAT'S NOT WHAT THE PEOPLE NEED, THEY NEED US FREE OF-OF-OF--
I KNOW THAT PART, LUKE.
I'M SAYING NOW--HOW LONG ARE WE GOING TO LIVE LIKE THIS?
'CAUSE, YOU KNOW, MY LIFE SUCKED BEFORE, AND EVEN I CAN'T BELIEVE HOW MUCH MORE THIS SUCKS.
THIS IS A "FIGHTING A GUY NAMED TYPEFACE" LEVEL OF SUCKING.
AND WONG-- POOR WONG IS ALREADY SICK OF US AND IT HASN'T EVEN BEEN A DAY.

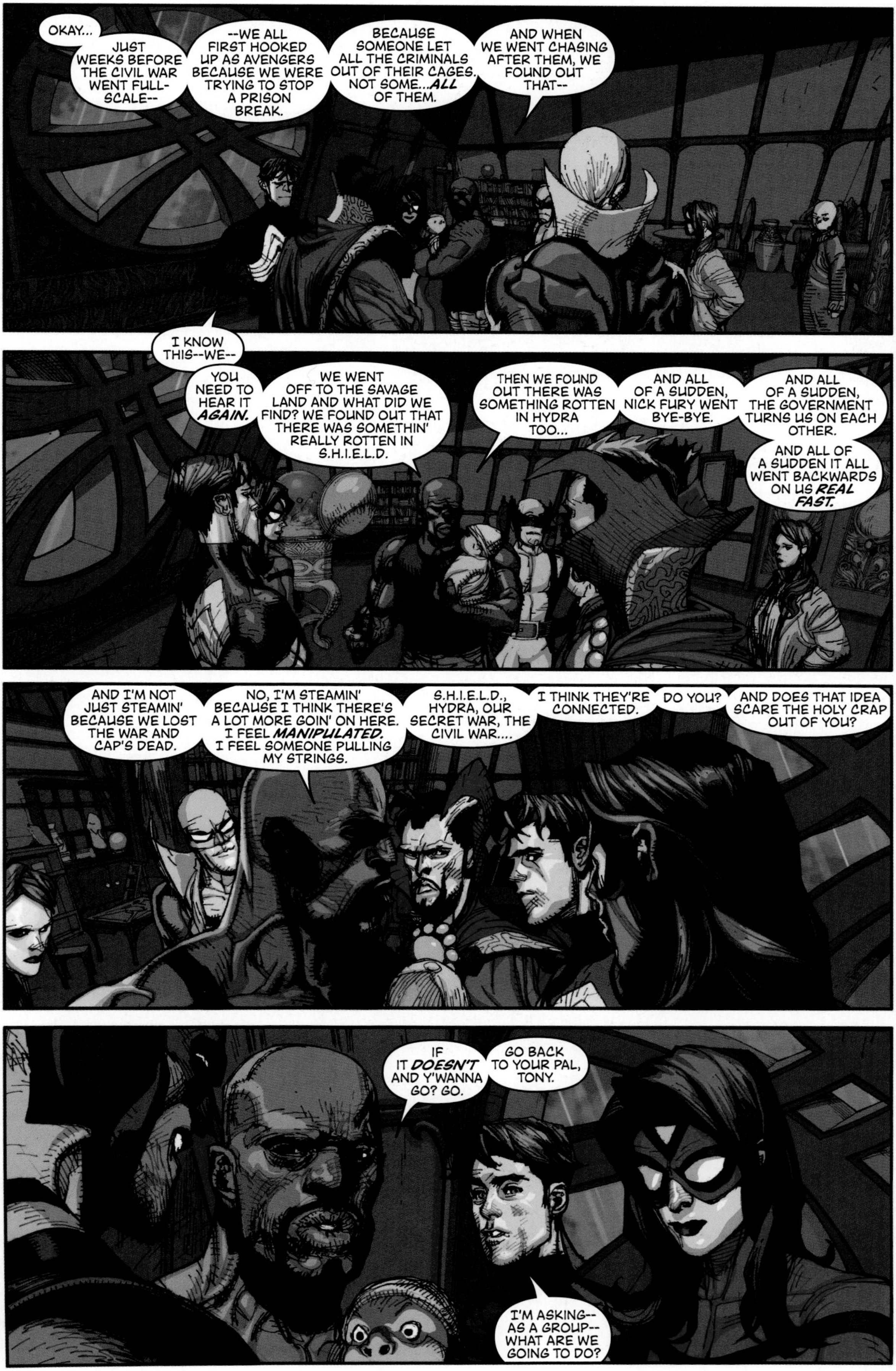
OKAY...
JUST WEEKS BEFORE THE CIVIL WAR WENT FULL-SCALE--
--WE ALL FIRST HOOKED UP AS AVENGERS BECAUSE WE WERE TRYING TO STOP A PRISON BREAK.
BECAUSE SOMEONE LET ALL THE CRIMINALS OUT OF THEIR CAGES. NOT SOME... ***ALL*** OF THEM.
AND WHEN WE WENT CHASING AFTER THEM, WE FOUND OUT THAT--
I KNOW THIS--WE--
YOU NEED TO HEAR IT ***AGAIN.***
WE WENT OFF TO THE SAVAGE LAND AND WHAT DID WE FIND? WE FOUND OUT THAT THERE WAS SOMETHIN' REALLY ROTTEN IN S.H.I.E.L.D.
THEN WE FOUND OUT THERE WAS SOMETHING ROTTEN IN HYDRA TOO...
AND ALL OF A SUDDEN, NICK FURY WENT BYE-BYE.
AND ALL OF A SUDDEN, THE GOVERNMENT TURNS US ON EACH OTHER.
AND ALL OF A SUDDEN IT ALL WENT BACKWARDS ON US ***REAL FAST.***
AND I'M NOT JUST STEAMIN' BECAUSE WE LOST THE WAR AND CAP'S DEAD.
NO, I'M STEAMIN' BECAUSE I THINK THERE'S A LOT MORE GOIN' ON HERE. I FEEL ***MANIPULATED.*** I FEEL SOMEONE PULLING MY STRINGS.
S.H.I.E.L.D., HYDRA, OUR SECRET WAR, THE CIVIL WAR....
I THINK THEY'RE CONNECTED.
DO YOU?
AND DOES THAT IDEA SCARE THE HOLY CRAP OUT OF YOU?
IF IT ***DOESN'T*** AND Y'WANNA GO? GO.
GO BACK TO YOUR PAL, TONY.
I'M ASKING-- AS A GROUP-- WHAT ARE WE GOING TO DO?

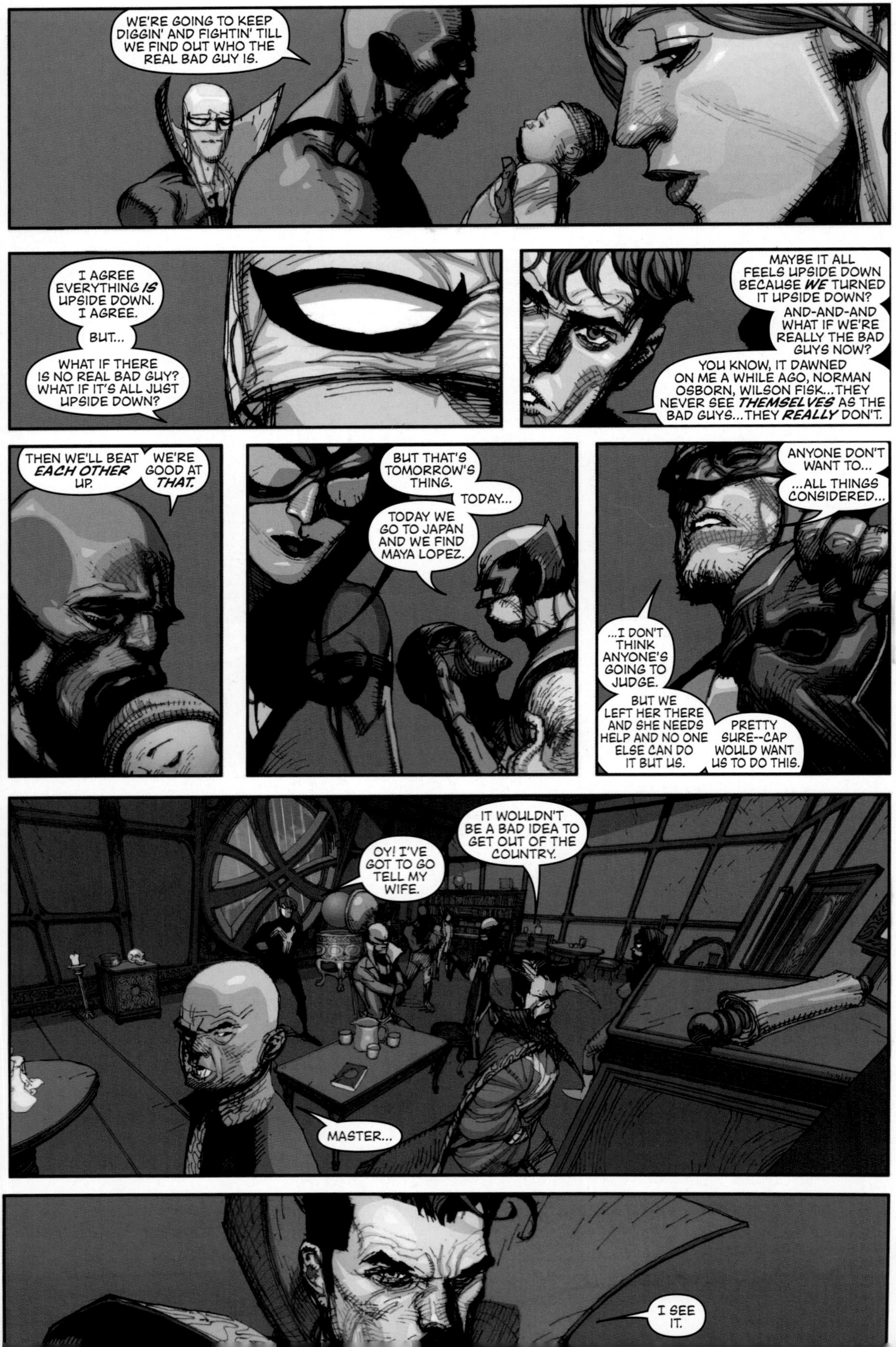
WE'RE GOING TO KEEP DIGGIN' AND FIGHTIN' TILL WE FIND OUT WHO THE REAL BAD GUY IS.
I AGREE EVERYTHING *IS* UPSIDE DOWN. I AGREE.
BUT...
WHAT IF THERE IS NO REAL BAD GUY? WHAT IF IT'S ALL JUST UPSIDE DOWN?
MAYBE IT ALL FEELS UPSIDE DOWN BECAUSE *WE* TURNED IT UPSIDE DOWN?
AND-AND-AND WHAT IF WE'RE REALLY THE BAD GUYS NOW?
YOU KNOW, IT DAWNED ON ME A WHILE AGO, NORMAN OSBORN, WILSON FISK...THEY NEVER SEE *THEMSELVES* AS THE BAD GUYS...THEY *REALLY* DON'T.
THEN WE'LL BEAT *EACH OTHER* UP.
WE'RE GOOD AT *THAT.*
BUT THAT'S TOMORROW'S THING.
TODAY...
TODAY WE GO TO JAPAN AND WE FIND MAYA LOPEZ.
ANYONE DON'T WANT TO...
...ALL THINGS CONSIDERED...
...I DON'T THINK ANYONE'S GOING TO JUDGE.
BUT WE LEFT HER THERE AND SHE NEEDS HELP AND NO ONE ELSE CAN DO IT BUT US.
PRETTY SURE--CAP WOULD WANT US TO DO THIS.
OY! I'VE GOT TO GO TELL MY WIFE.
IT WOULDN'T BE A BAD IDEA TO GET OUT OF THE COUNTRY.
MASTER...
I SEE IT.

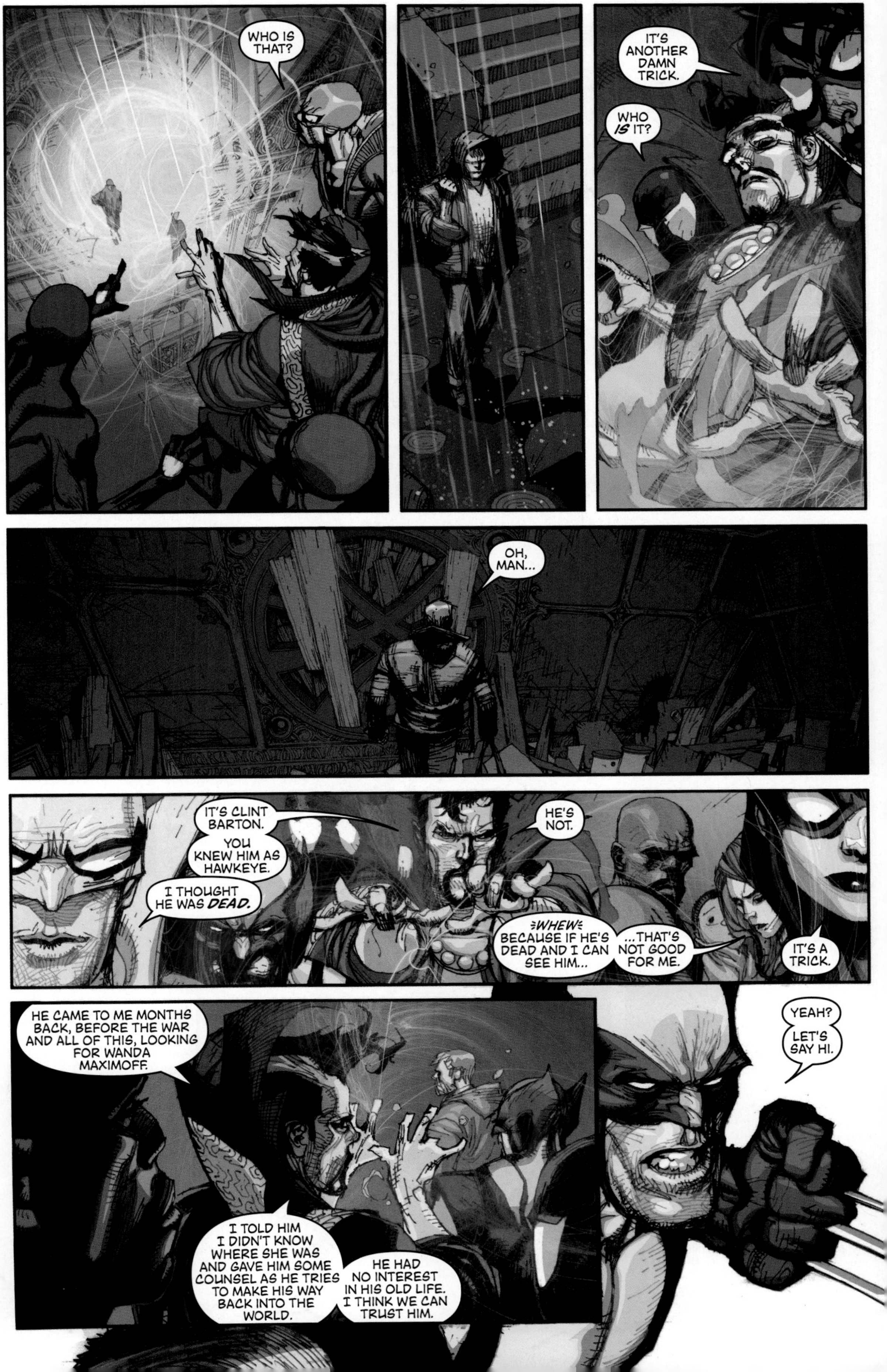
WHO IS THAT?
IT'S ANOTHER DAMN TRICK.
WHO *IS* IT?
OH, MAN...
IT'S CLINT BARTON.
YOU KNEW HIM AS HAWKEYE.
I THOUGHT HE WAS *DEAD.*
HE'S NOT.
WHEW BECAUSE IF HE'S DEAD AND I CAN SEE HIM...
...THAT'S NOT GOOD FOR ME.
IT'S A TRICK.
HE CAME TO ME MONTHS BACK, BEFORE THE WAR AND ALL OF THIS, LOOKING FOR WANDA MAXIMOFF.
I TOLD HIM I DIDN'T KNOW WHERE SHE WAS AND GAVE HIM SOME COUNSEL AS HE TRIES TO MAKE HIS WAY BACK INTO THE WORLD.
HE HAD NO INTEREST IN HIS OLD LIFE. I THINK WE CAN TRUST HIM.
YEAH?
LET'S SAY HI.

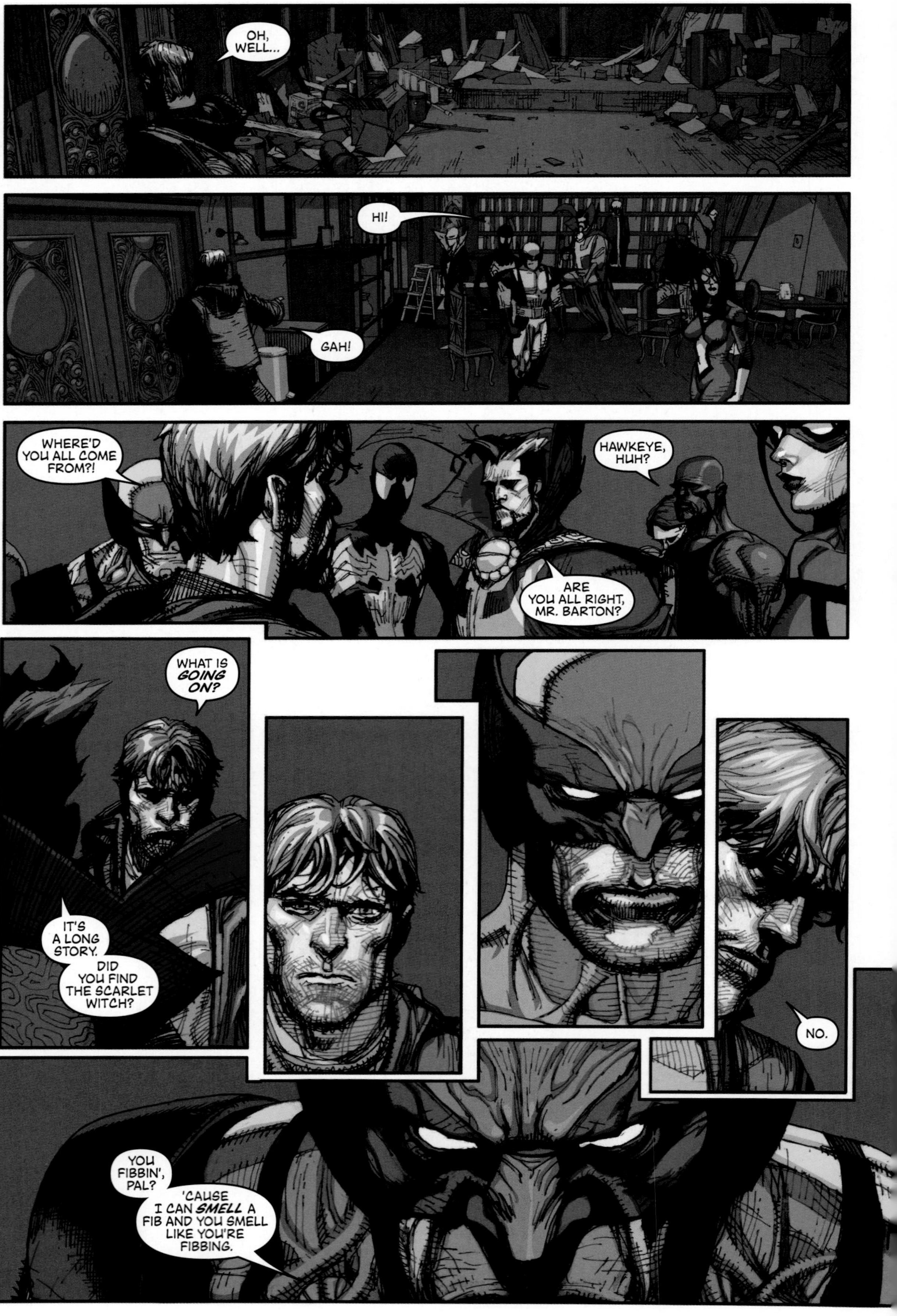
OH, WELL...
HI!
GAH!
WHERE'D YOU ALL COME FROM?!
HAWKEYE, HUH?
ARE YOU ALL RIGHT, MR. BARTON?
WHAT IS *GOING ON?*
IT'S A LONG STORY.
DID YOU FIND THE SCARLET WITCH?
NO.
YOU FIBBIN', PAL?
'CAUSE I CAN *SMELL* A FIB AND YOU SMELL LIKE YOU'RE FIBBING.

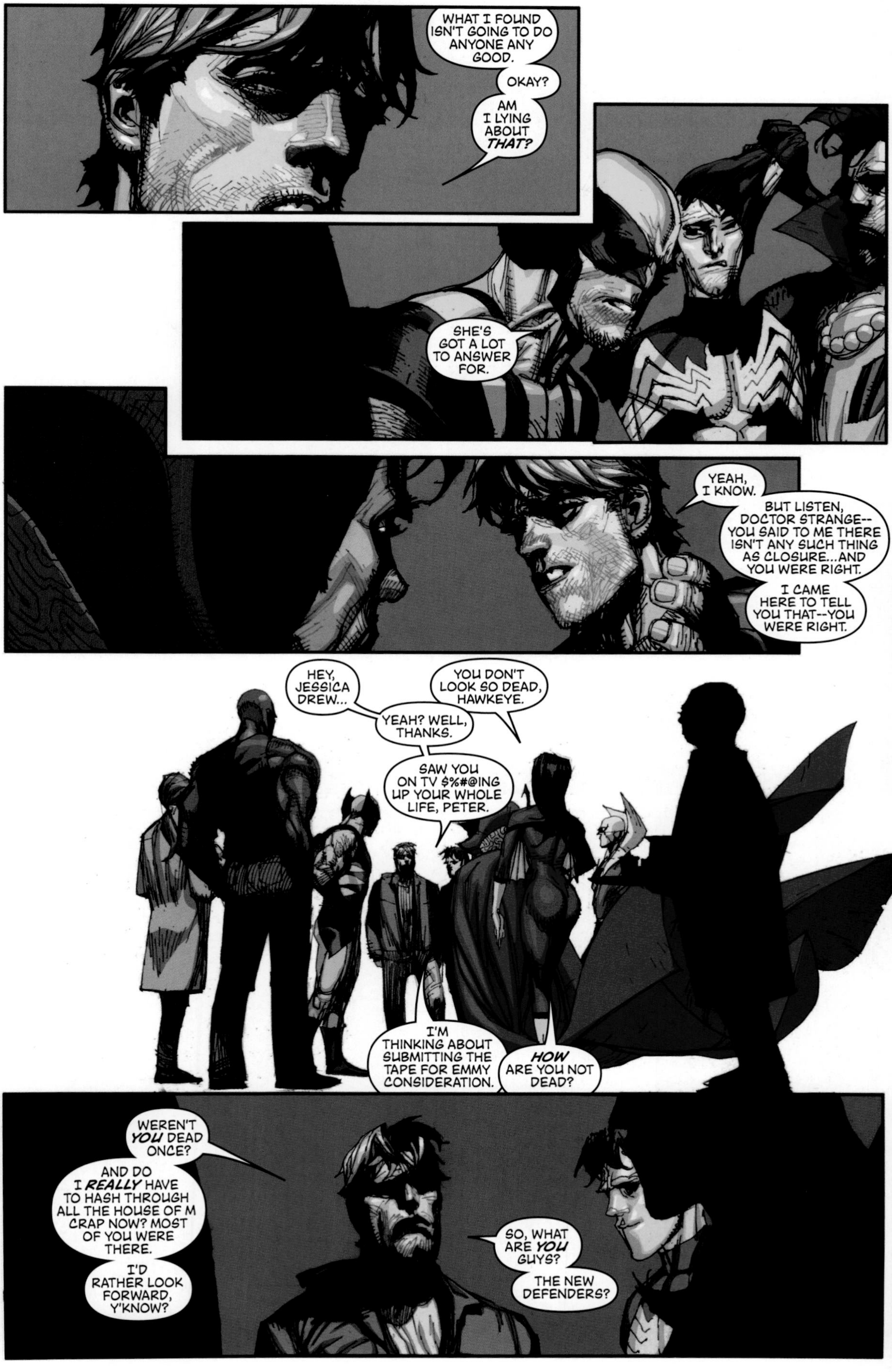
WHAT I FOUND ISN'T GOING TO DO ANYONE ANY GOOD.
OKAY?
AM I LYING ABOUT *THAT?*
SHE'S GOT A LOT TO ANSWER FOR.
YEAH, I KNOW.
BUT LISTEN, DOCTOR STRANGE-- YOU SAID TO ME THERE ISN'T ANY SUCH THING AS CLOSURE...AND YOU WERE RIGHT.
I CAME HERE TO TELL YOU THAT--YOU WERE RIGHT.
HEY, JESSICA DREW...
YOU DON'T LOOK SO DEAD, HAWKEYE.
YEAH? WELL, THANKS.
SAW YOU ON TV $%#@ING UP YOUR WHOLE LIFE, PETER.
I'M THINKING ABOUT SUBMITTING THE TAPE FOR EMMY CONSIDERATION.
HOW ARE YOU NOT DEAD?
WEREN'T *YOU* DEAD ONCE?
AND DO I *REALLY* HAVE TO HASH THROUGH ALL THE HOUSE OF M CRAP NOW? MOST OF YOU WERE THERE.
I'D RATHER LOOK FORWARD, Y'KNOW?
SO, WHAT ARE *YOU* GUYS?
THE NEW DEFENDERS?

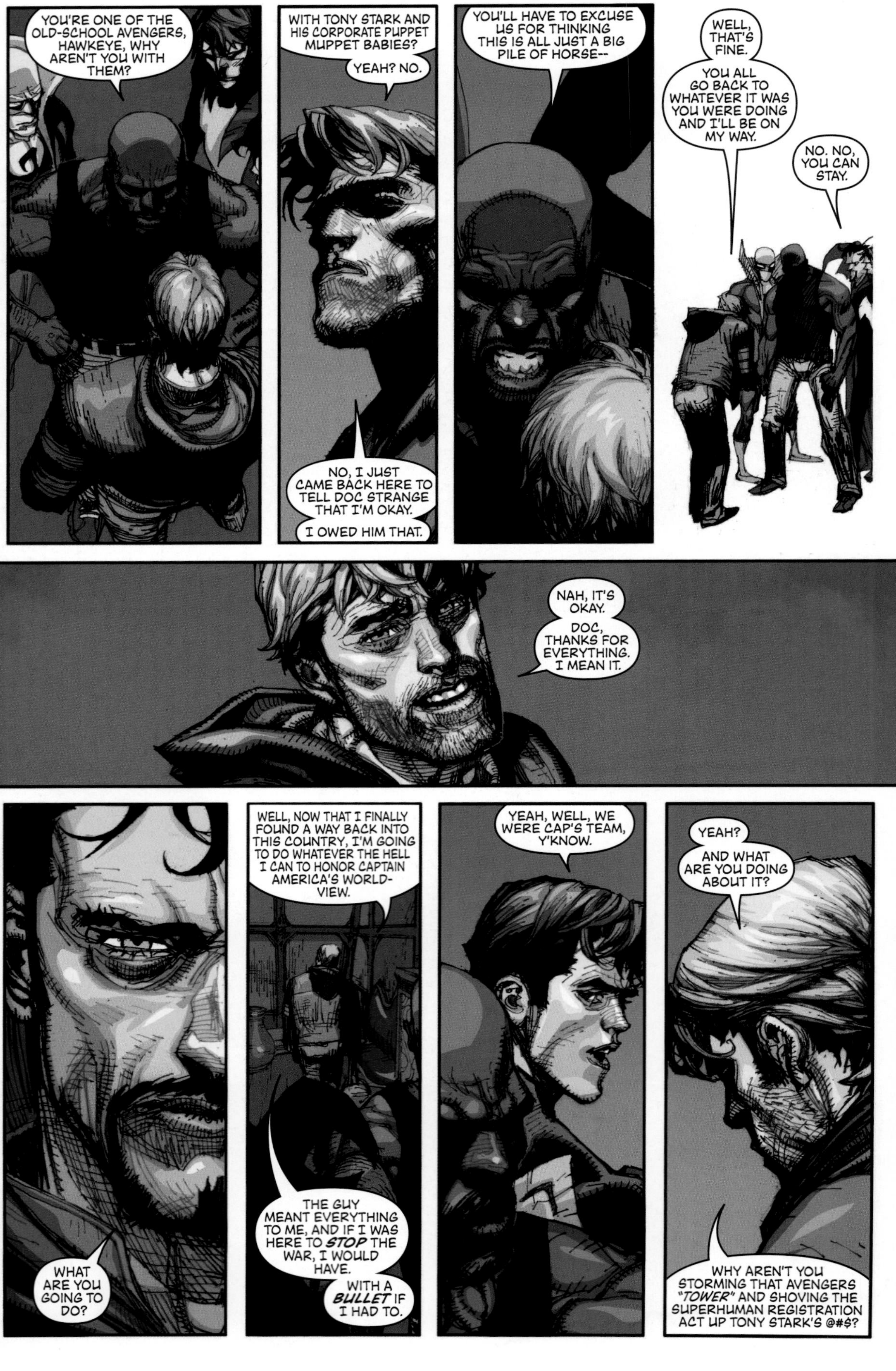
YOU'RE ONE OF THE OLD-SCHOOL AVENGERS, HAWKEYE, WHY AREN'T YOU WITH THEM?
WITH TONY STARK AND HIS CORPORATE PUPPET MUPPET BABIES?
YEAH? NO.
NO, I JUST CAME BACK HERE TO TELL DOC STRANGE THAT I'M OKAY.
I OWED HIM THAT.
YOU'LL HAVE TO EXCUSE US FOR THINKING THIS IS ALL JUST A BIG PILE OF HORSE--
WELL, THAT'S FINE.
YOU ALL GO BACK TO WHATEVER IT WAS YOU WERE DOING AND I'LL BE ON MY WAY.
NO. NO, YOU CAN STAY.
NAH, IT'S OKAY.
DOC, THANKS FOR EVERYTHING. I MEAN IT.
WHAT ARE YOU GOING TO DO?
WELL, NOW THAT I FINALLY FOUND A WAY BACK INTO THIS COUNTRY, I'M GOING TO DO WHATEVER THE HELL I CAN TO HONOR CAPTAIN AMERICA'S WORLD-VIEW.
THE GUY MEANT EVERYTHING TO ME, AND IF I WAS HERE TO *STOP* THE WAR, I WOULD HAVE.
WITH A ***BULLET*** IF I HAD TO.
YEAH, WELL, WE WERE CAP'S TEAM, Y'KNOW.
YEAH?
AND WHAT ARE YOU DOING ABOUT IT?
WHY AREN'T YOU STORMING THAT AVENGERS *"TOWER"* AND SHOVING THE SUPERHUMAN REGISTRATION ACT UP TONY STARK'S @#$?

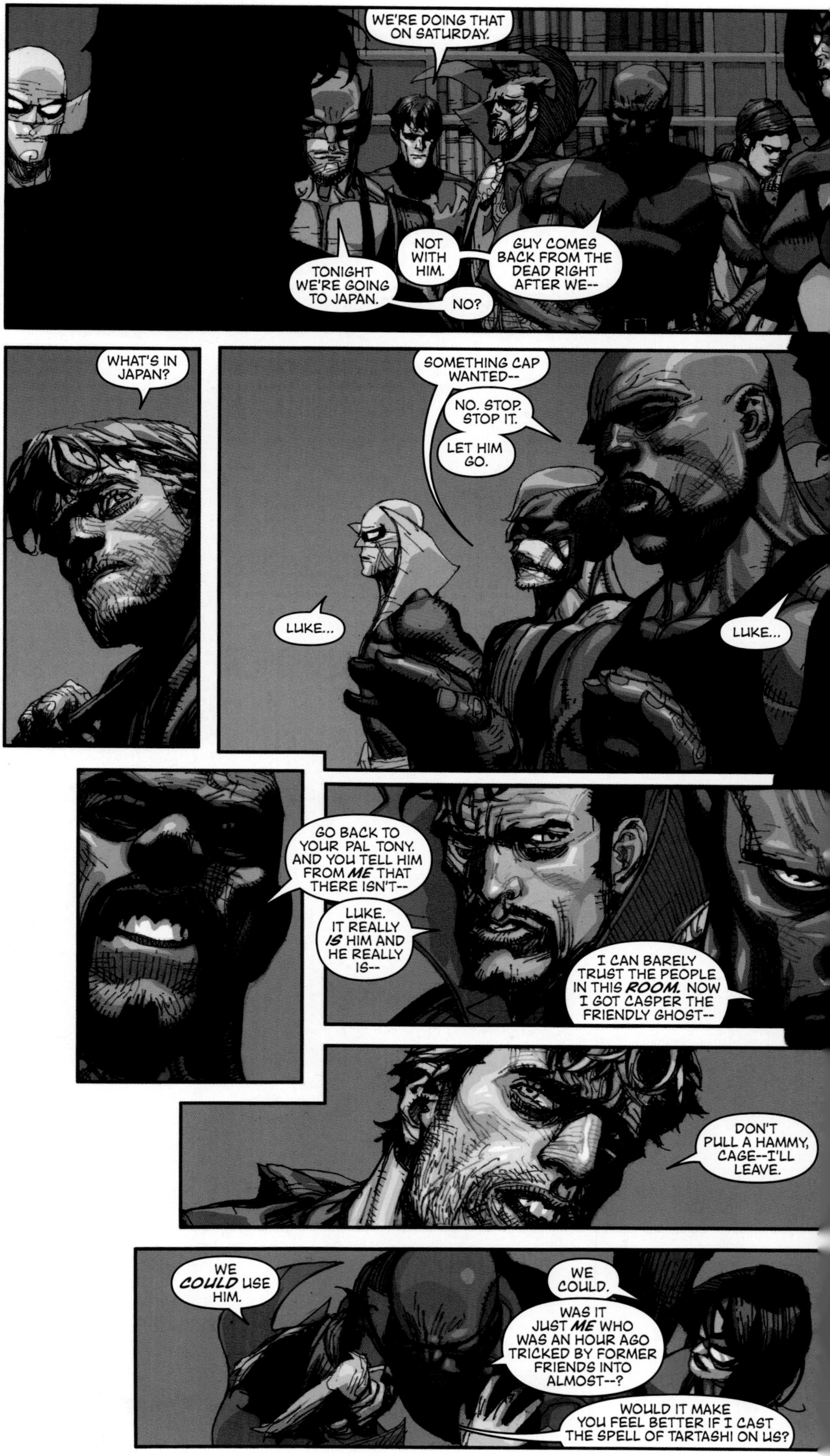

WE'RE DOING THAT ON SATURDAY.
TONIGHT WE'RE GOING TO JAPAN.
NOT WITH HIM.
GUY COMES BACK FROM THE DEAD RIGHT AFTER WE--
NO?
WHAT'S IN JAPAN?
SOMETHING CAP WANTED--
NO. STOP. STOP IT.
LET HIM GO.
LUKE...
LUKE...
GO BACK TO YOUR PAL TONY. AND YOU TELL HIM FROM ME THAT THERE ISN'T--
LUKE. IT REALLY IS HIM AND HE REALLY IS--
I CAN BARELY TRUST THE PEOPLE IN THIS ROOM. NOW I GOT CASPER THE FRIENDLY GHOST--
DON'T PULL A HAMMY, CAGE--I'LL LEAVE.
WE COULD USE HIM.
WE COULD.
WAS IT JUST ME WHO WAS AN HOUR AGO TRICKED BY FORMER FRIENDS INTO ALMOST--?
WOULD IT MAKE YOU FEEL BETTER IF I CAST THE SPELL OF TARTASHI ON US?

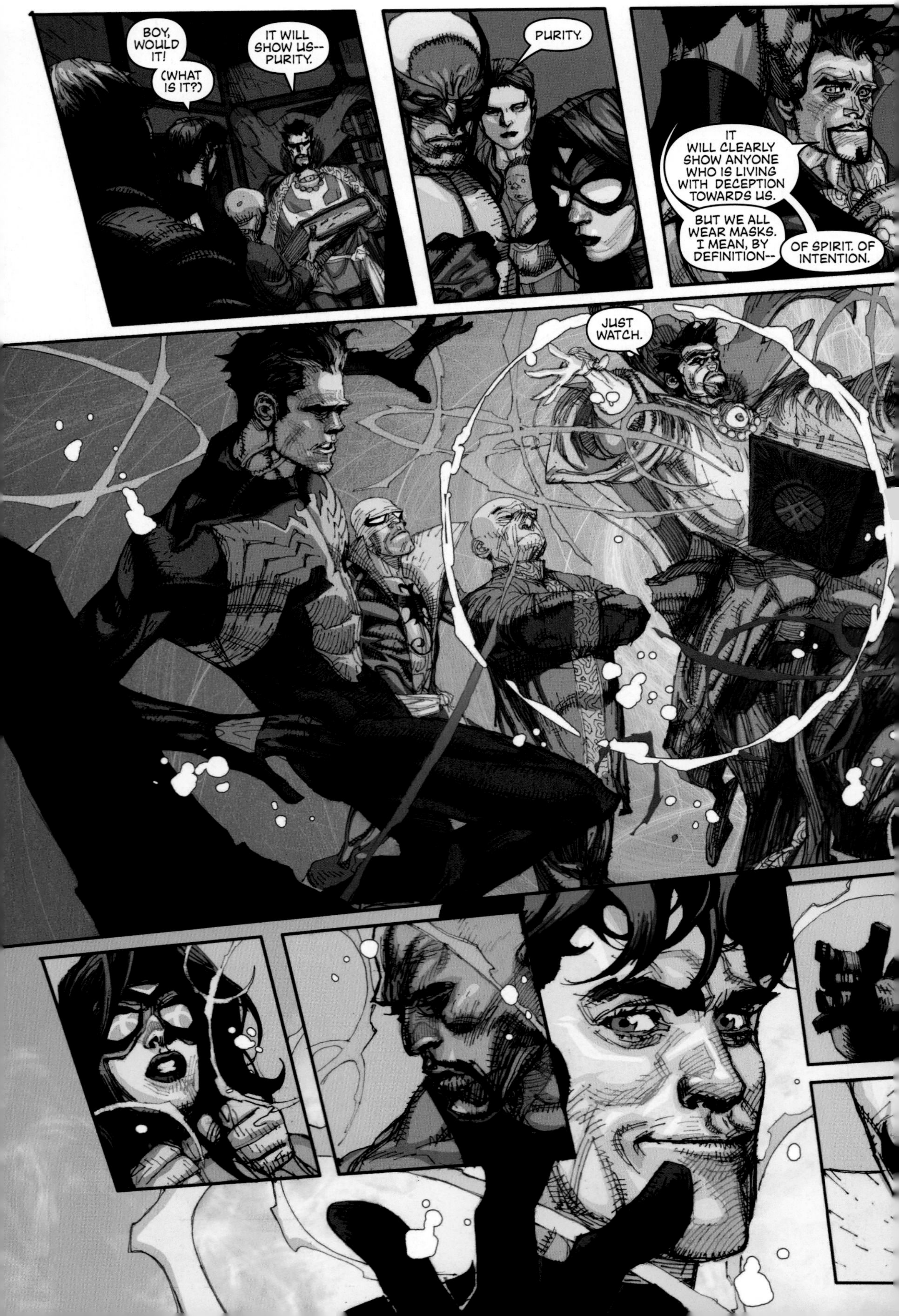
BOY, WOULD IT!
(WHAT IS IT?)
IT WILL SHOW US-- PURITY.
PURITY.
IT WILL CLEARLY SHOW ANYONE WHO IS LIVING WITH DECEPTION TOWARDS US.
BUT WE ALL WEAR MASKS. I MEAN, BY DEFINITION--
OF SPIRIT. OF INTENTION.
JUST WATCH.

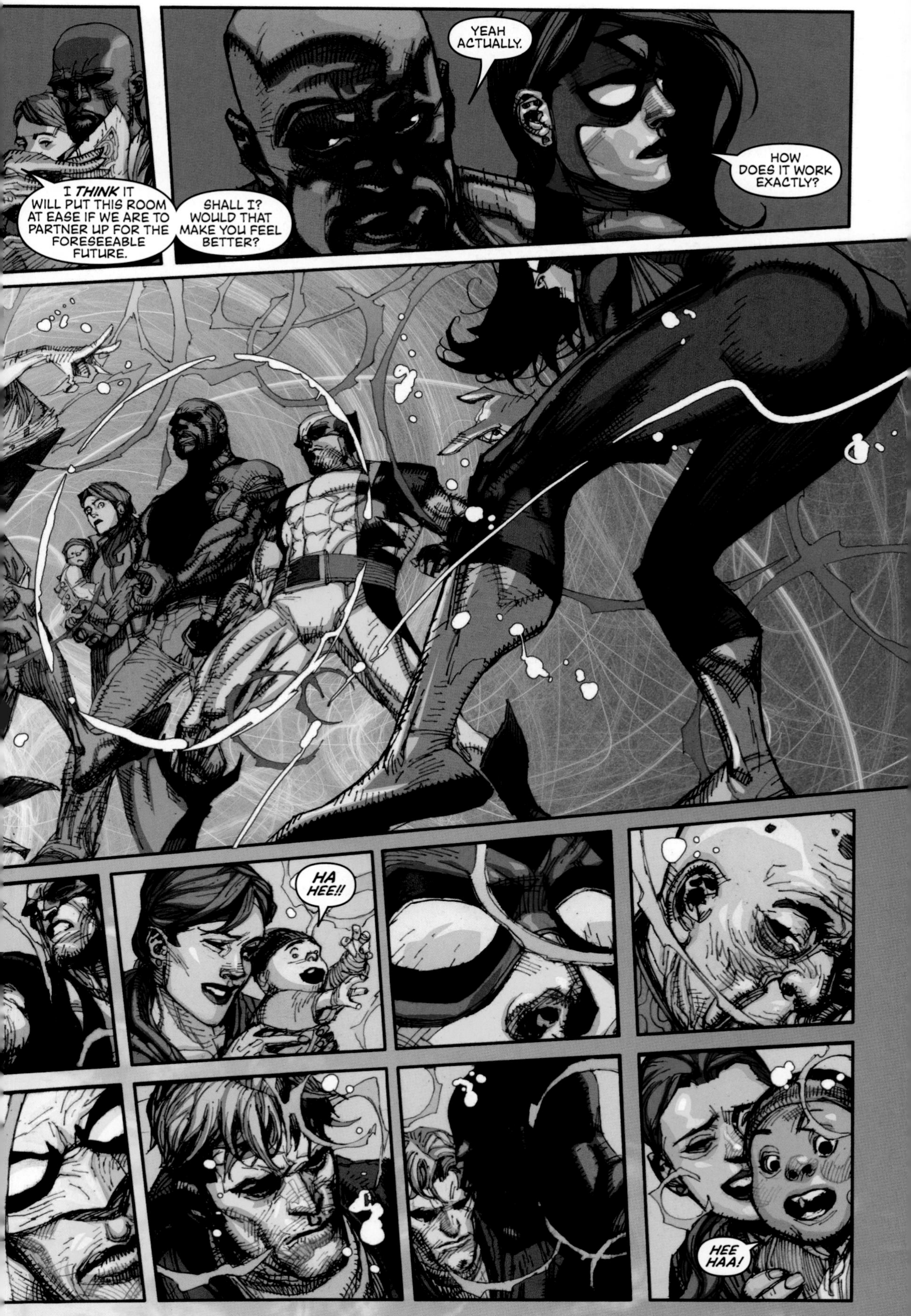
I *THINK* IT WILL PUT THIS ROOM AT EASE IF WE ARE TO PARTNER UP FOR THE FORESEEABLE FUTURE.
SHALL I? WOULD THAT MAKE YOU FEEL BETTER?
YEAH ACTUALLY.
HOW DOES IT WORK EXACTLY?
HA HEE!!
HEE HAA!

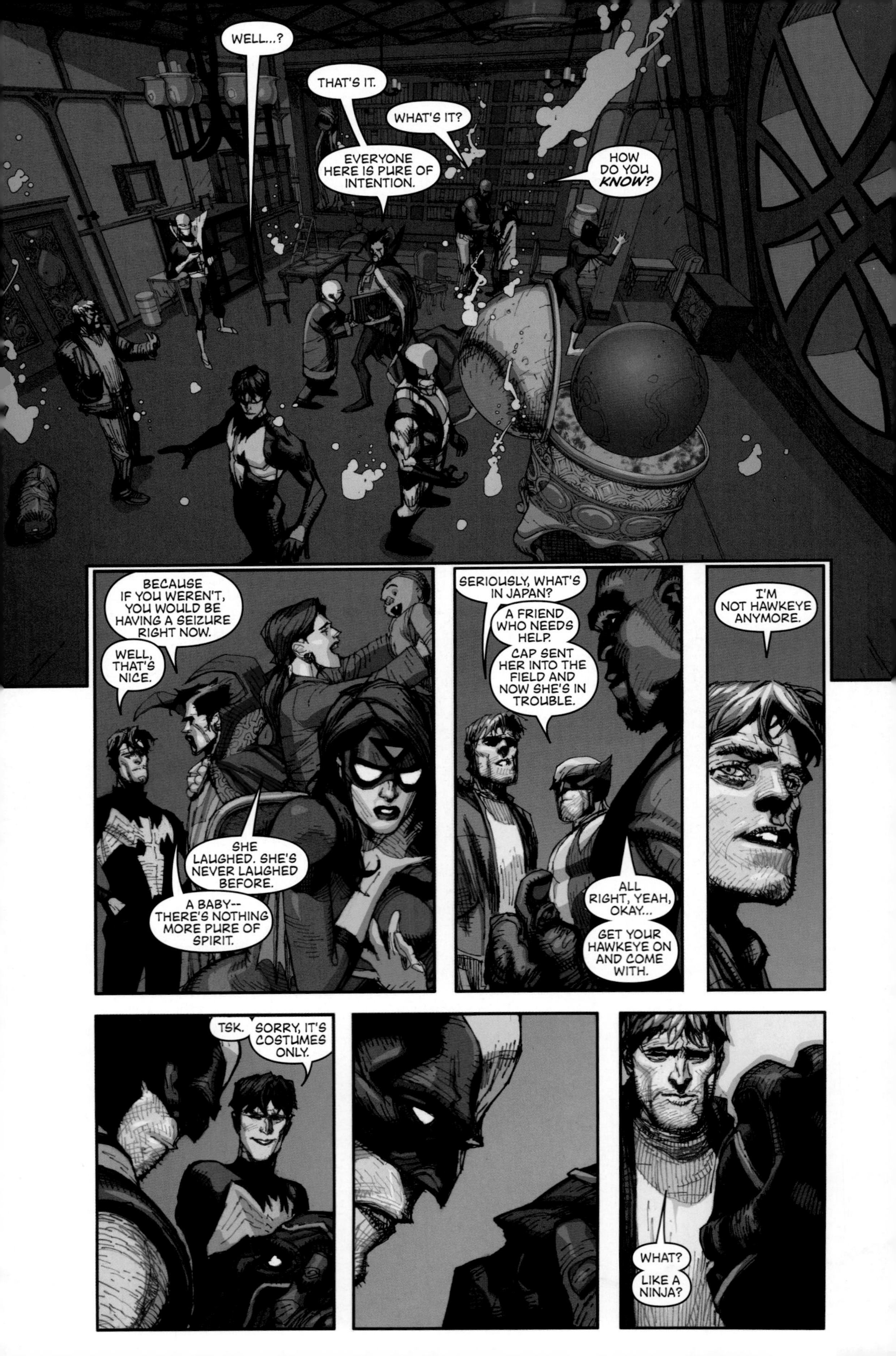
WELL...?
THAT'S IT.
WHAT'S IT?
EVERYONE HERE IS PURE OF INTENTION.
HOW DO YOU *KNOW?*
BECAUSE IF YOU WEREN'T, YOU WOULD BE HAVING A SEIZURE RIGHT NOW.
WELL, THAT'S NICE.
SHE LAUGHED. SHE'S NEVER LAUGHED BEFORE.
A BABY-- THERE'S NOTHING MORE PURE OF SPIRIT.
SERIOUSLY, WHAT'S IN JAPAN?
A FRIEND WHO NEEDS HELP.
CAP SENT HER INTO THE FIELD AND NOW SHE'S IN TROUBLE.
ALL RIGHT, YEAH, OKAY...
GET YOUR HAWKEYE ON AND COME WITH.
I'M NOT HAWKEYE ANYMORE.
TSK.
SORRY, IT'S COSTUMES ONLY.
WHAT?
LIKE A NINJA?

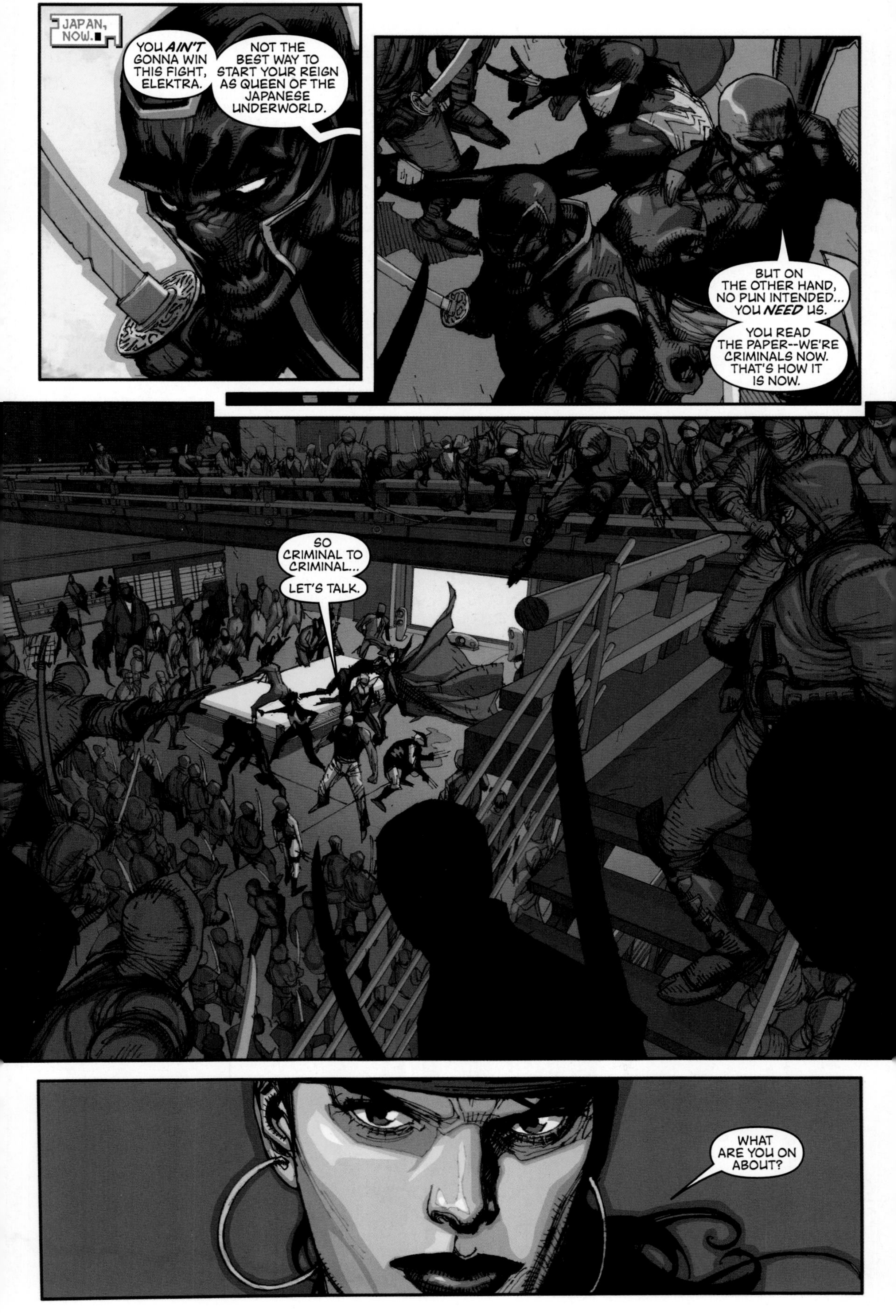
JAPAN, NOW.
YOU AIN'T GONNA WIN THIS FIGHT, ELEKTRA.
NOT THE BEST WAY TO START YOUR REIGN AS QUEEN OF THE JAPANESE UNDERWORLD.
BUT ON THE OTHER HAND, NO PUN INTENDED... YOU NEED US.
YOU READ THE PAPER--WE'RE CRIMINALS NOW. THAT'S HOW IT IS NOW.
SO CRIMINAL TO CRIMINAL...
LET'S TALK.
WHAT ARE YOU ON ABOUT?

WE HAVE NOTHING TO FIGHT OVER, YOU GUYS AND US.

WE *DON'T*?

WE *DON'T*!

(WOW, I COMPLETELY MISREAD THE ROOM.)

YOU'LL LIVE WITHOUT HER. IT'S NOT WORTH THE FIGHT.

IT'S JUST BAD BUSINESS.

YOU REALLY THINK SHE'S *WORTH* HOWEVER MANY MEN YOU'LL LOSE IF YOU COME AT US LIKE THIS?

I DON'T KNOW EVERYTHING ABOUT THE HAND, BUT AT SOME POINT, YOU *GOTTA* RUN OUT OF DUDES IN ROBES, RIGHT?

MEANWHILE, WE HAVE LARGER ITEMS ON THE AGENDA.

DO YOU KNOW WHY?

DO I KNOW WHY *WHAT*?

DO YOU KNOW WHY EVERYTHING IS UPSIDE DOWN?

CAGE... WHAT ARE YOU DOING?

NO, WE'RE GOING TO SETTLE THIS LIKE--

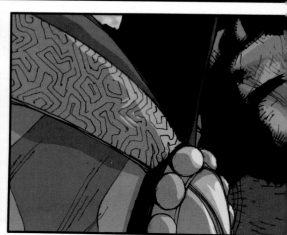

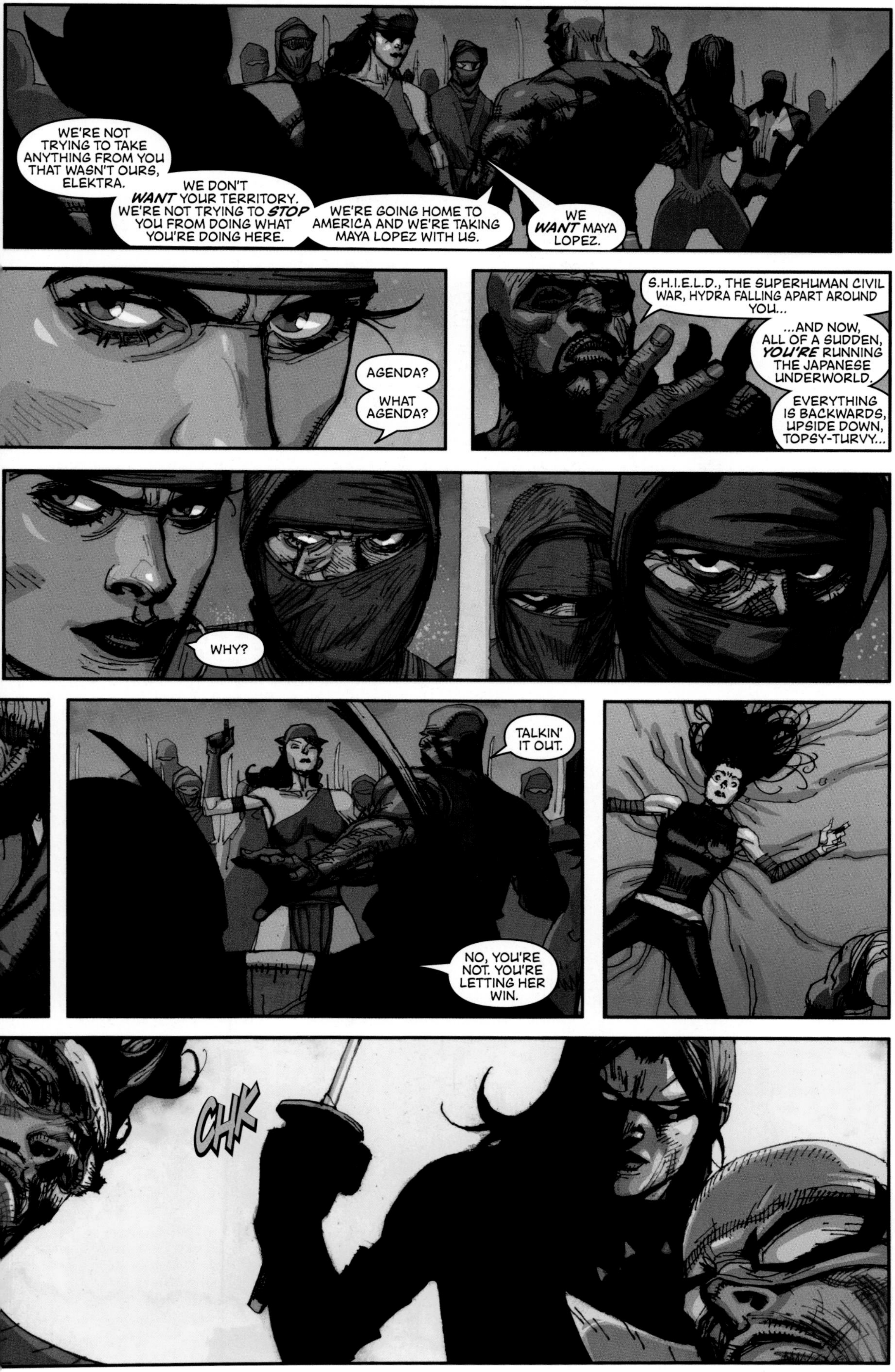
WE'RE NOT TRYING TO TAKE ANYTHING FROM YOU THAT WASN'T OURS, ELEKTRA.
WE DON'T *WANT* YOUR TERRITORY. WE'RE NOT TRYING TO *STOP* YOU FROM DOING WHAT YOU'RE DOING HERE.
WE'RE GOING HOME TO AMERICA AND WE'RE TAKING MAYA LOPEZ WITH US.
WE *WANT* MAYA LOPEZ.
AGENDA?
WHAT AGENDA?
S.H.I.E.L.D., THE SUPERHUMAN CIVIL WAR, HYDRA FALLING APART AROUND YOU...
...AND NOW, ALL OF A SUDDEN, *YOU'RE* RUNNING THE JAPANESE UNDERWORLD.
EVERYTHING IS BACKWARDS, UPSIDE DOWN, TOPSY-TURVY...
WHY?
TALKIN' IT OUT.
NO, YOU'RE NOT. YOU'RE LETTING HER WIN.
CHK

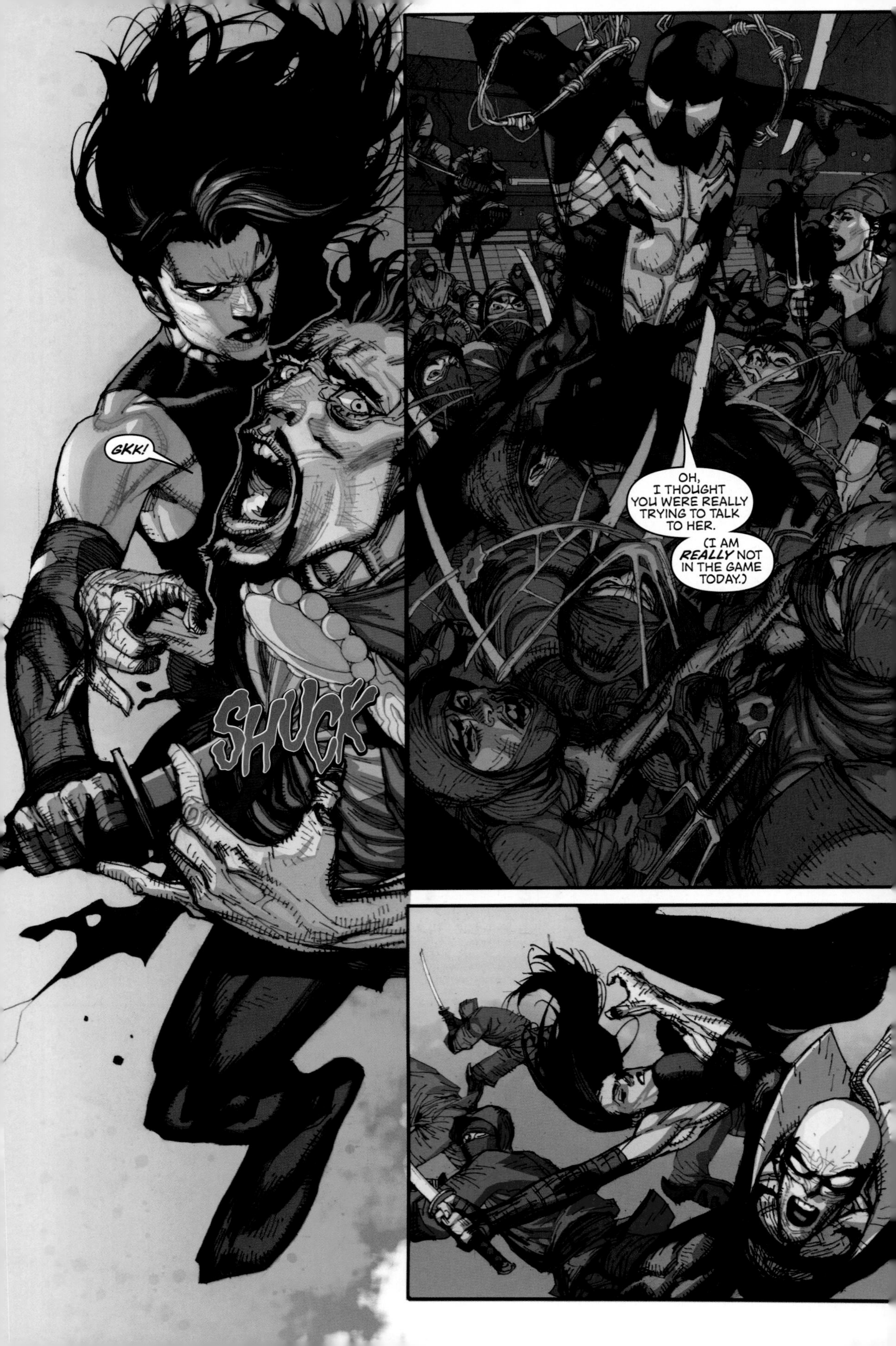
GKK!
SHUCK
OH, I THOUGHT YOU WERE REALLY TRYING TO TALK TO HER.
(I AM REALLY NOT IN THE GAME TODAY.)

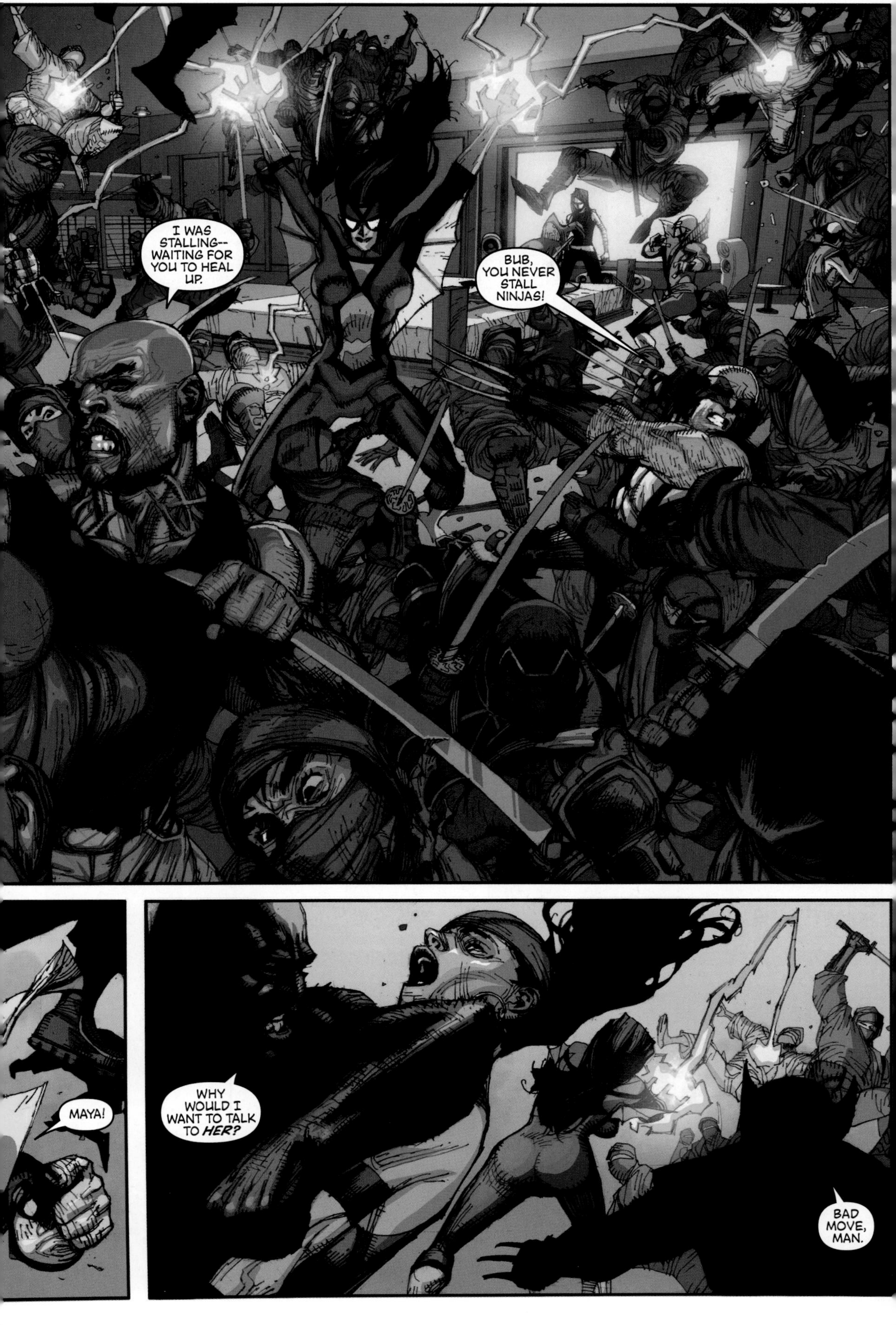
I WAS STALLING-- WAITING FOR YOU TO HEAL UP.
BUB, YOU NEVER STALL NINJAS!
MAYA!
WHY WOULD I WANT TO TALK TO *HER?*
BAD MOVE, MAN.

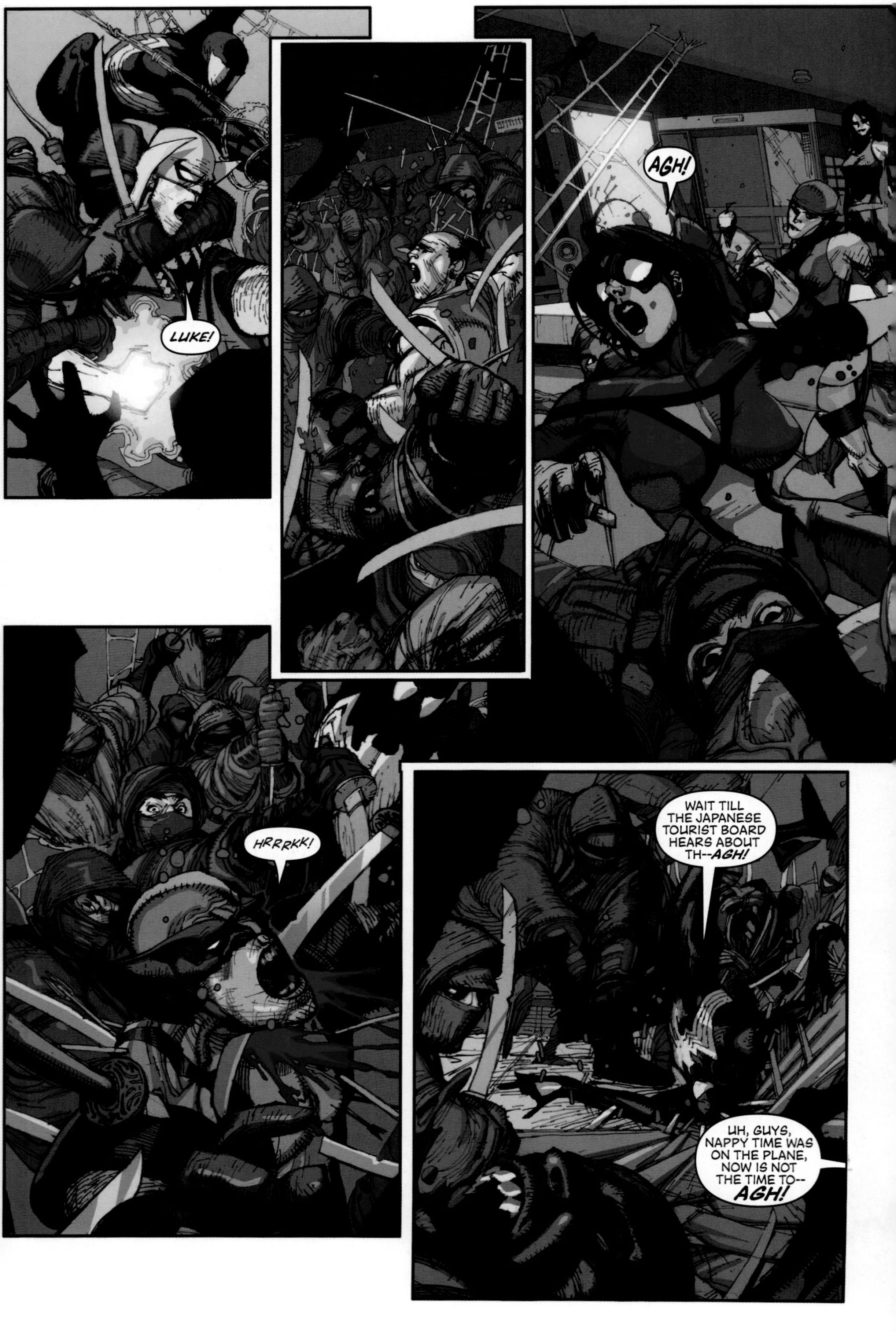
LUKE!
AGH!
HRRRKK!
WAIT TILL THE JAPANESE TOURIST BOARD HEARS ABOUT TH--AGH!
UH, GUYS, NAPPY TIME WAS ON THE PLANE, NOW IS NOT THE TIME TO-- AGH!

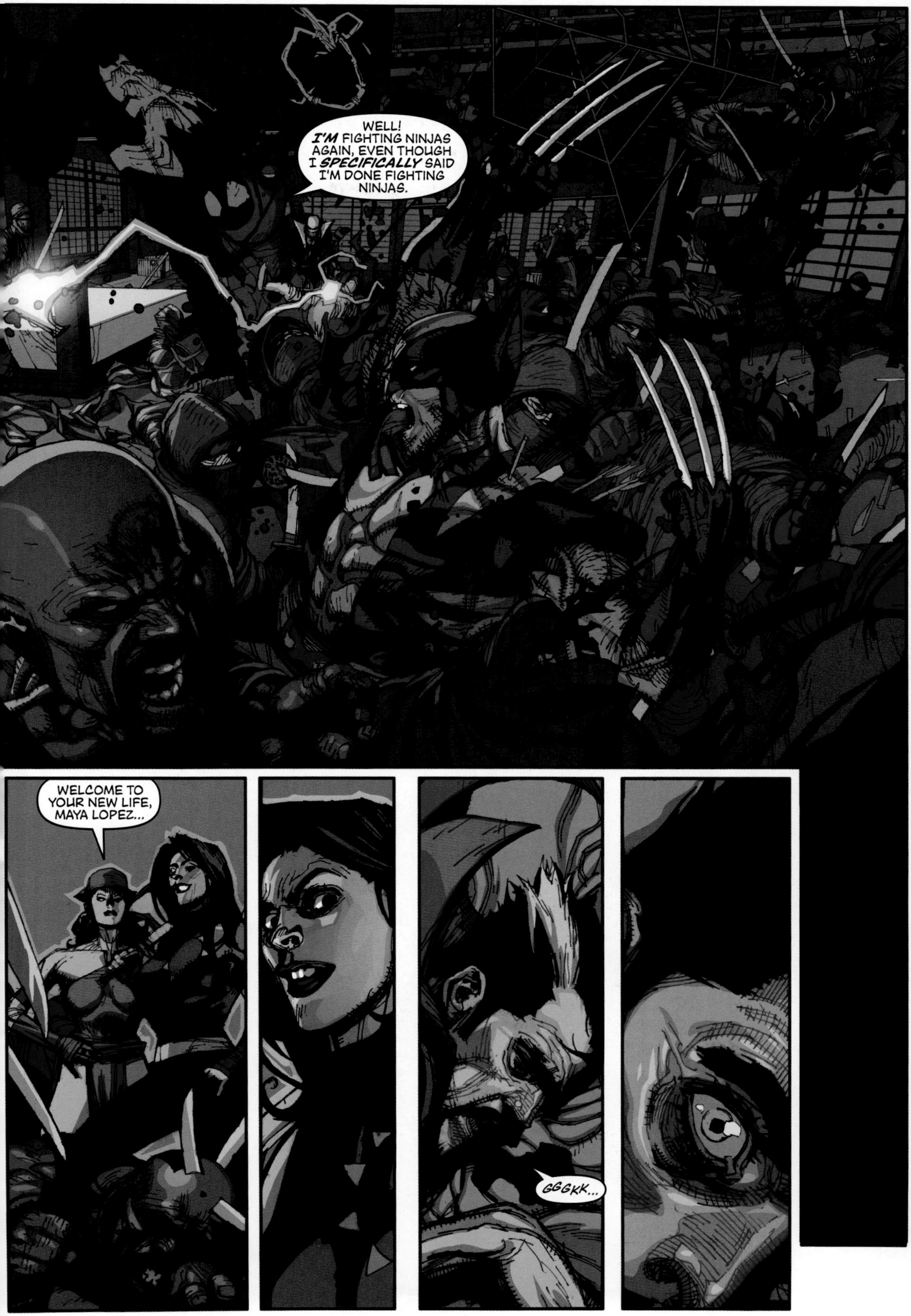
WELL! ***I'M*** FIGHTING NINJAS AGAIN, EVEN THOUGH I ***SPECIFICALLY*** SAID I'M DONE FIGHTING NINJAS.
WELCOME TO YOUR NEW LIFE, MAYA LOPEZ...
GGGKK...

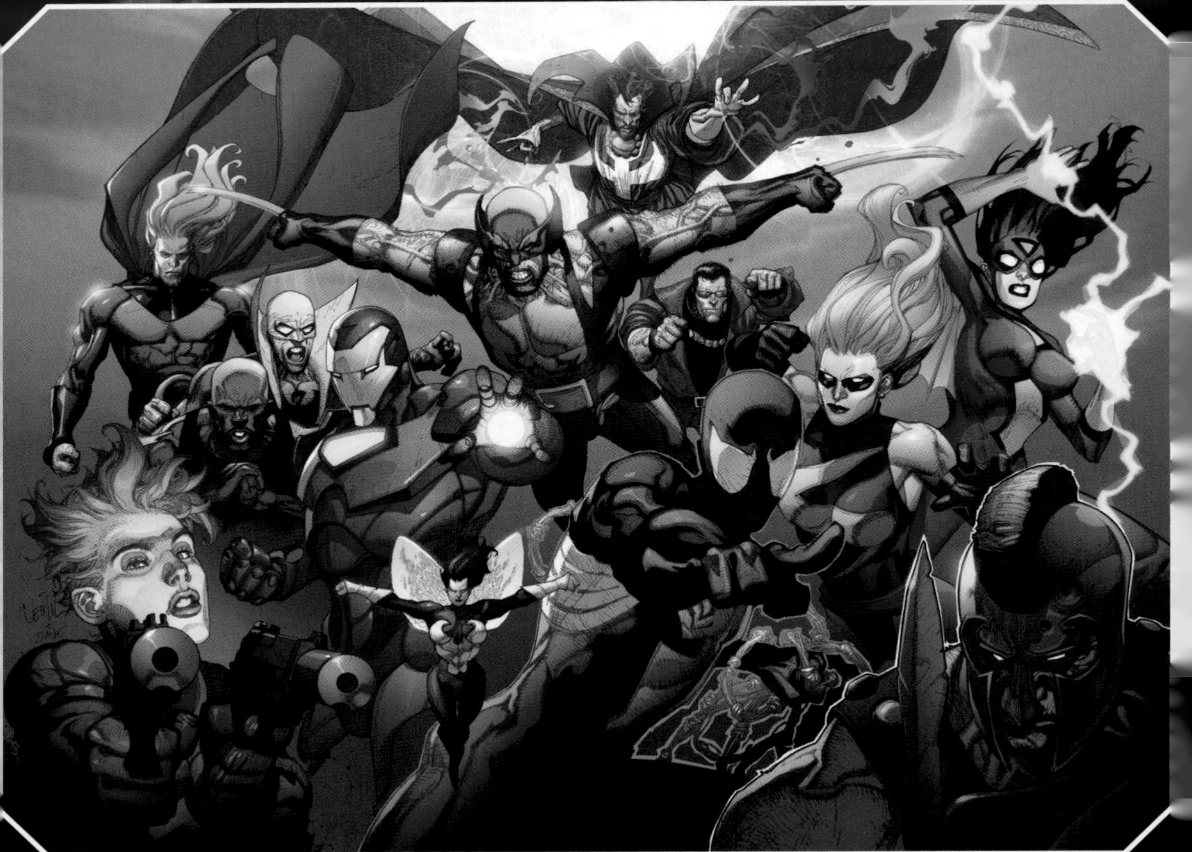

NEW AVENGERS #27 & MIGHTY AVENGERS #1 COMBINED VARIANTS BY LEINIL YU

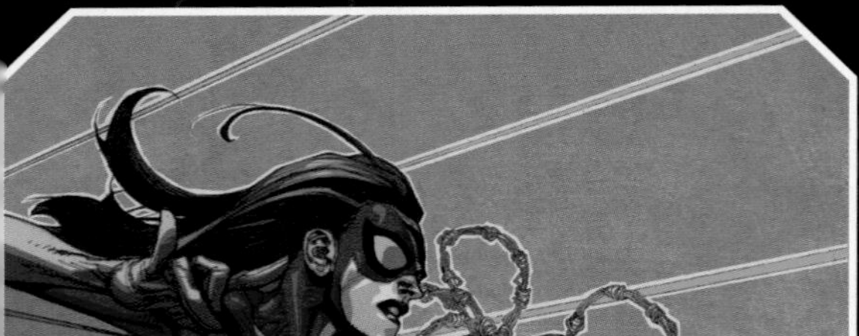

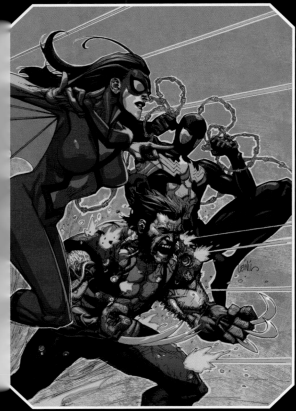

NEW AVENGERS #27 RETAILER VARIANT

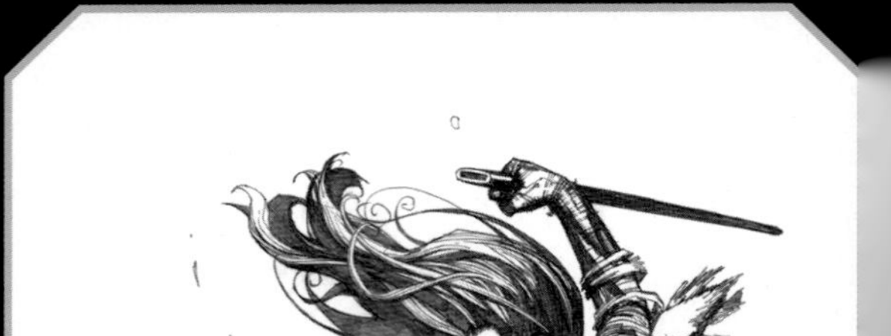

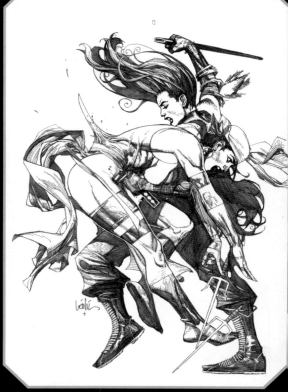

NEW AVENGERS #31 SKETCH VARIANT

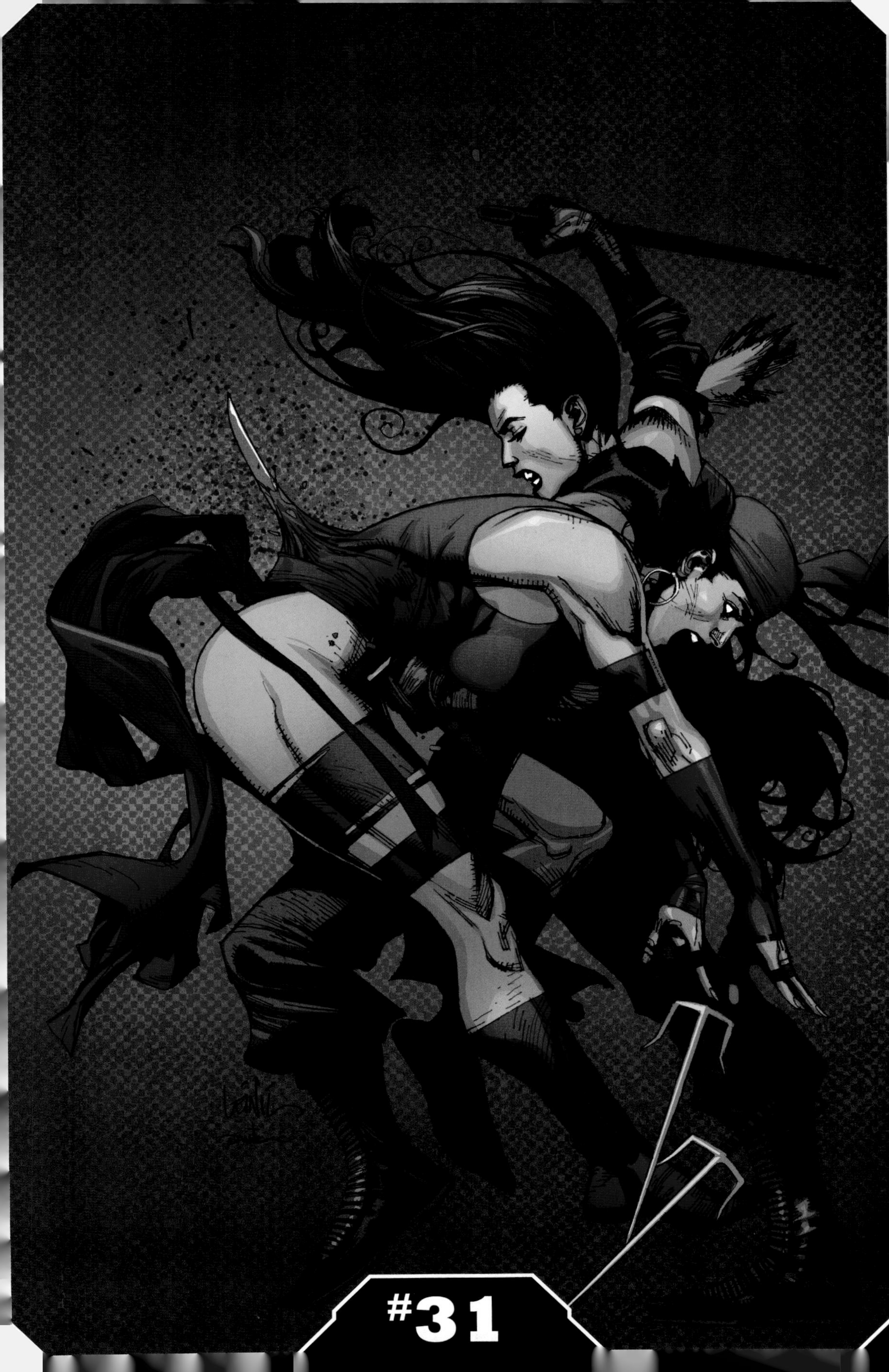
#31

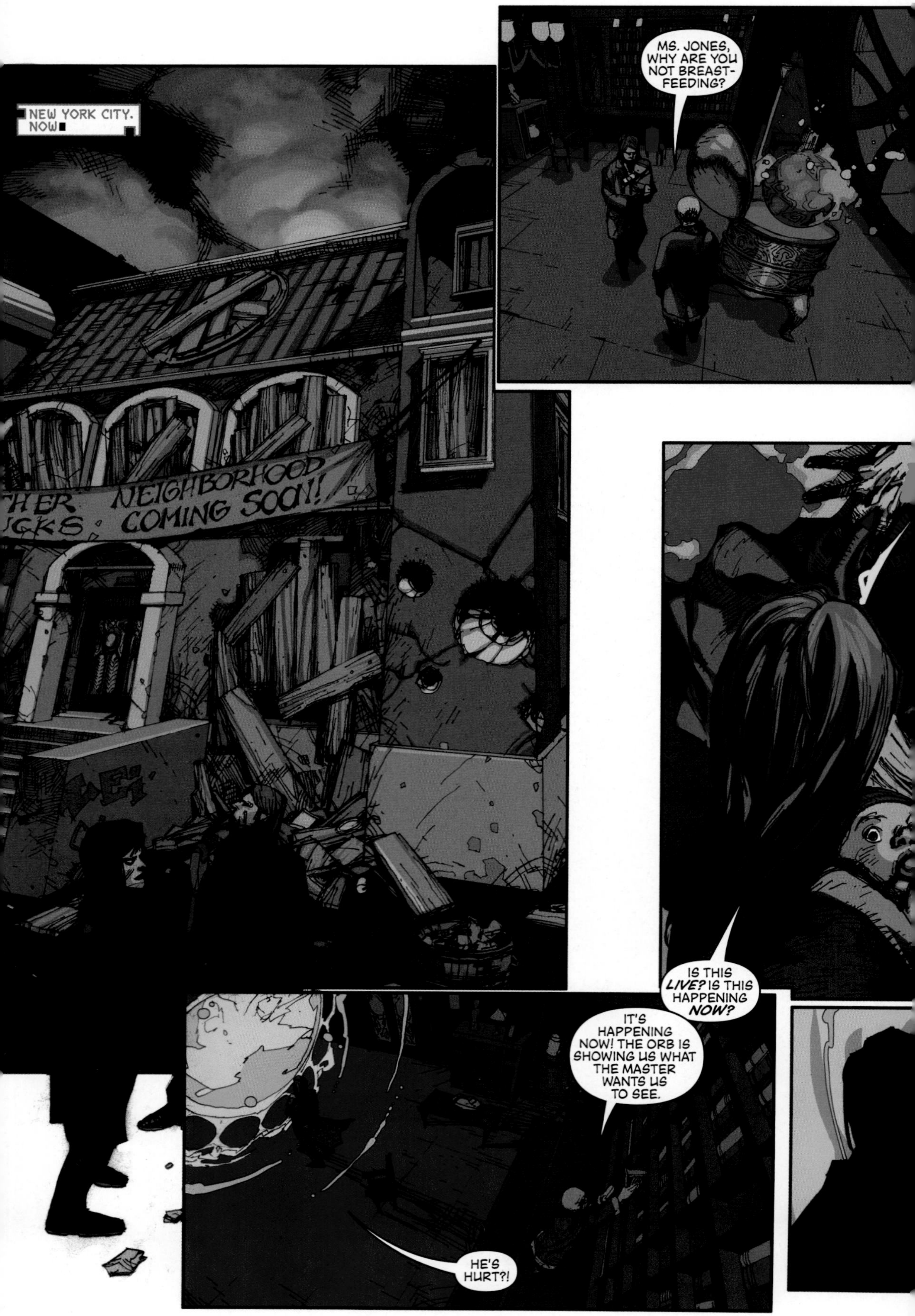

NEW YORK CITY. NOW
MS. JONES, WHY ARE YOU NOT BREAST-FEEDING?
NEIGHBORHOOD COMING SOON!!
IS THIS LIVE? IS THIS HAPPENING NOW?
IT'S HAPPENING NOW! THE ORB IS SHOWING US WHAT THE MASTER WANTS US TO SEE.
HE'S HURT?!

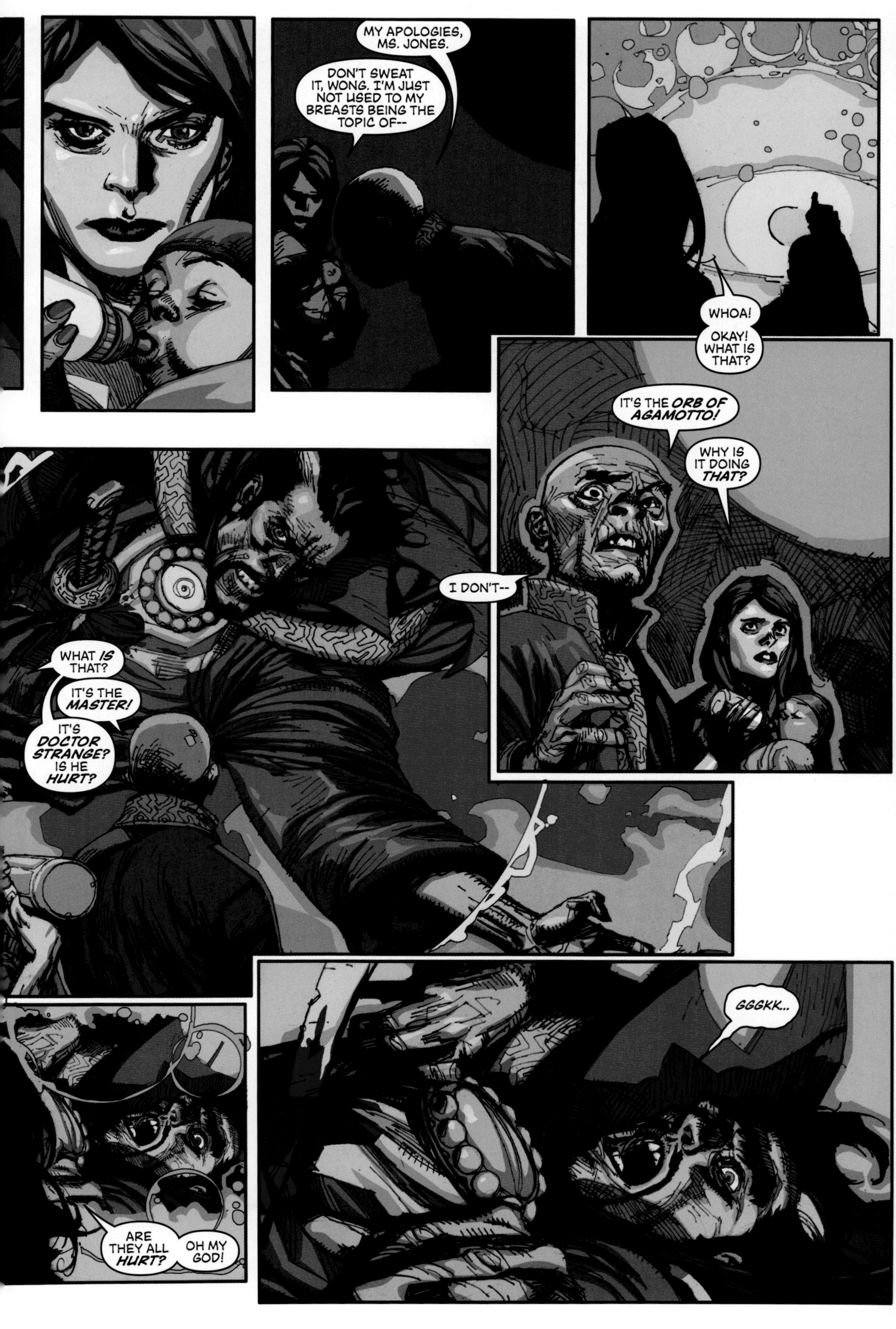

MY APOLOGIES, MS. JONES.
DON'T SWEAT IT, WONG. I'M JUST NOT USED TO MY BREASTS BEING THE TOPIC OF--
WHOA!
OKAY! WHAT IS THAT?
IT'S THE ORB OF AGAMOTTO!
WHY IS IT DOING THAT?
I DON'T--
WHAT IS THAT?
IT'S THE MASTER!
IT'S DOCTOR STRANGE? IS HE HURT?
ARE THEY ALL HURT?
OH MY GOD!
GGGKK...

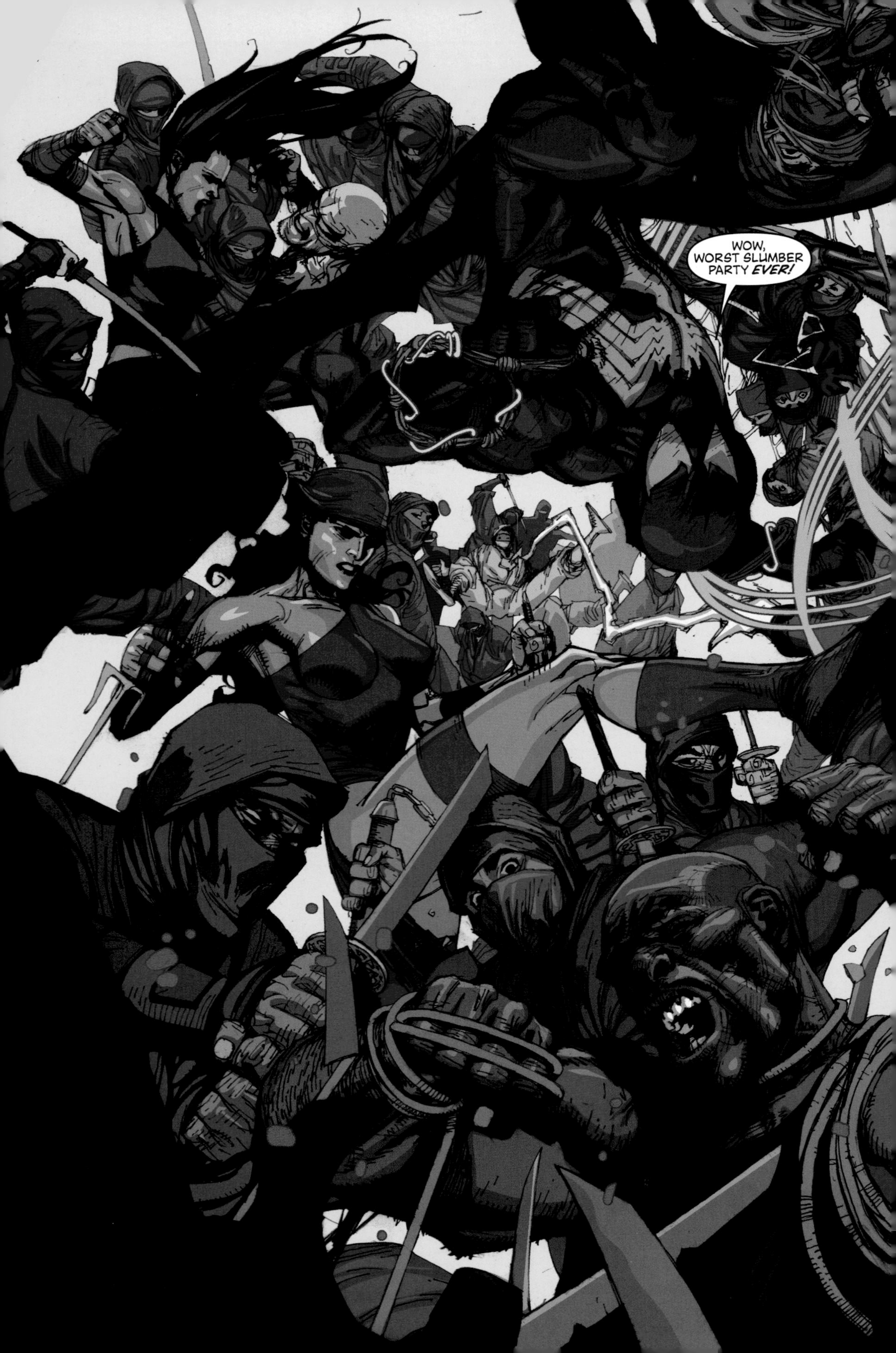
WOW, WORST SLUMBER PARTY *EVER!*

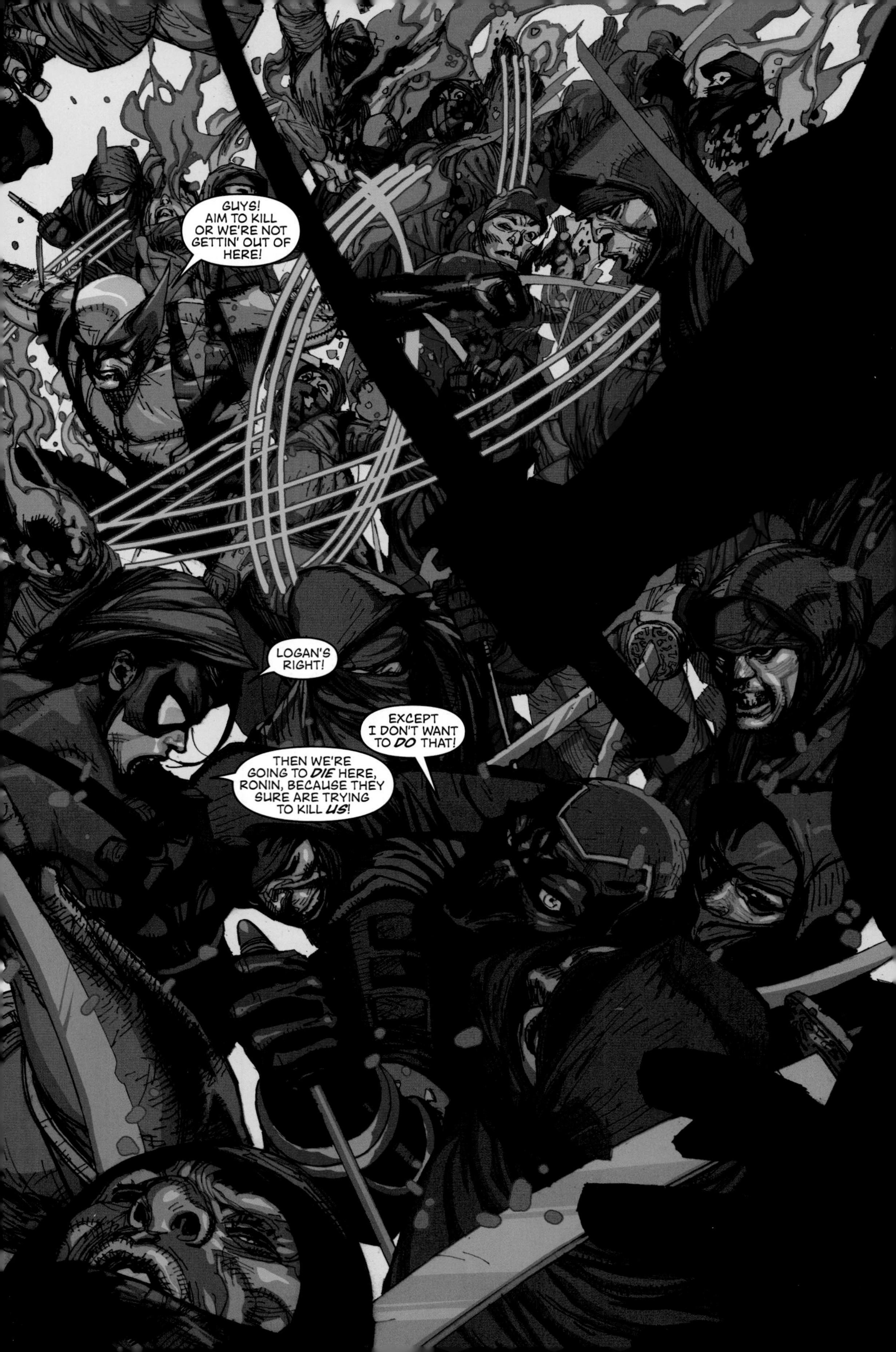
GUYS! AIM TO KILL OR WE'RE NOT GETTIN' OUT OF HERE!
LOGAN'S RIGHT!
EXCEPT I DON'T WANT TO DO THAT!
THEN WE'RE GOING TO DIE HERE, RONIN, BECAUSE THEY SURE ARE TRYING TO KILL US!

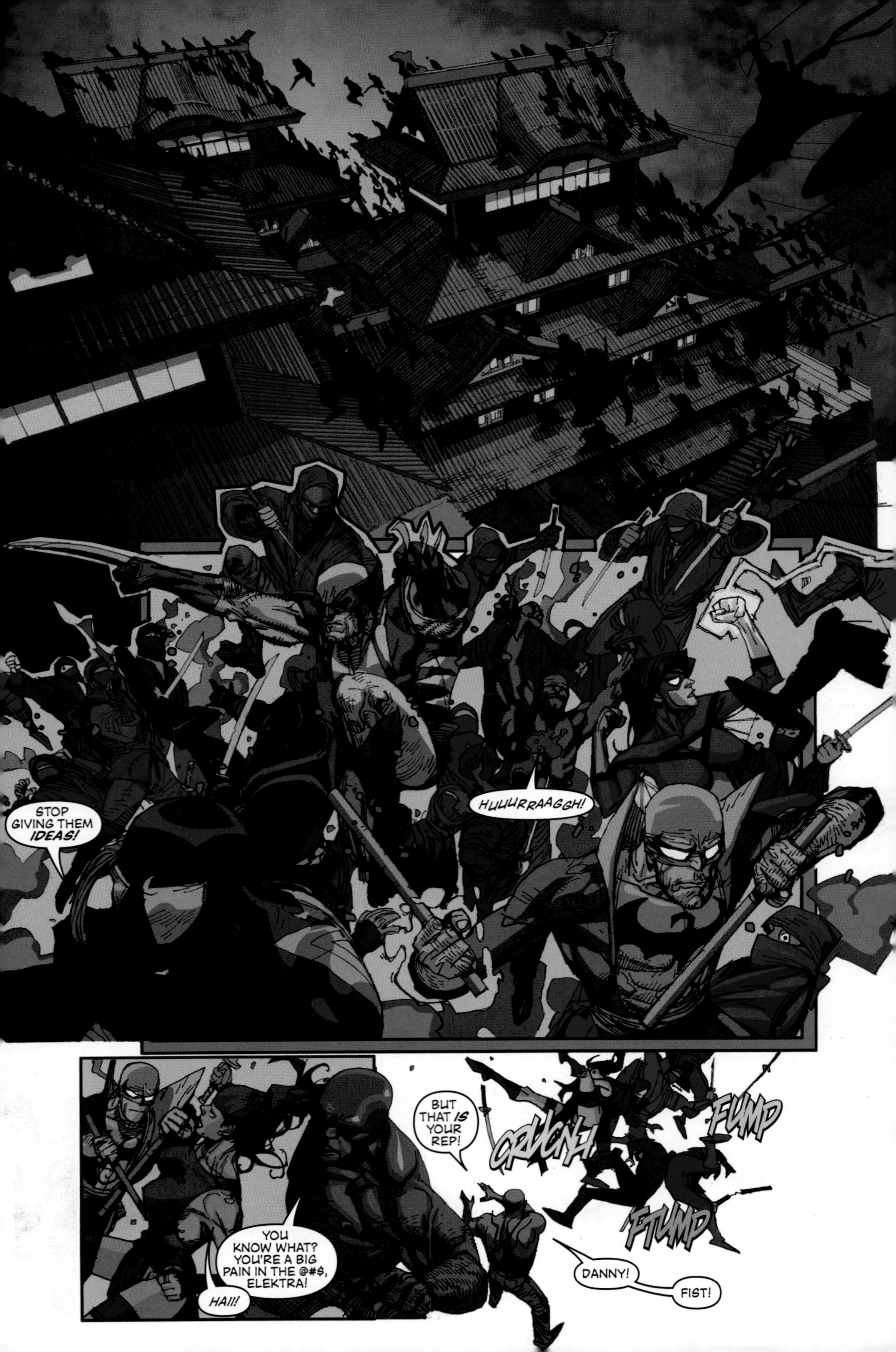
STOP GIVING THEM IDEAS!
HUUURRAAGGH!
BUT THAT IS YOUR REP!
CRUNCH
FUMP
FTUMP
YOU KNOW WHAT? YOU'RE A BIG PAIN IN THE @#$, ELEKTRA!
HAI!!
DANNY!
FIST!

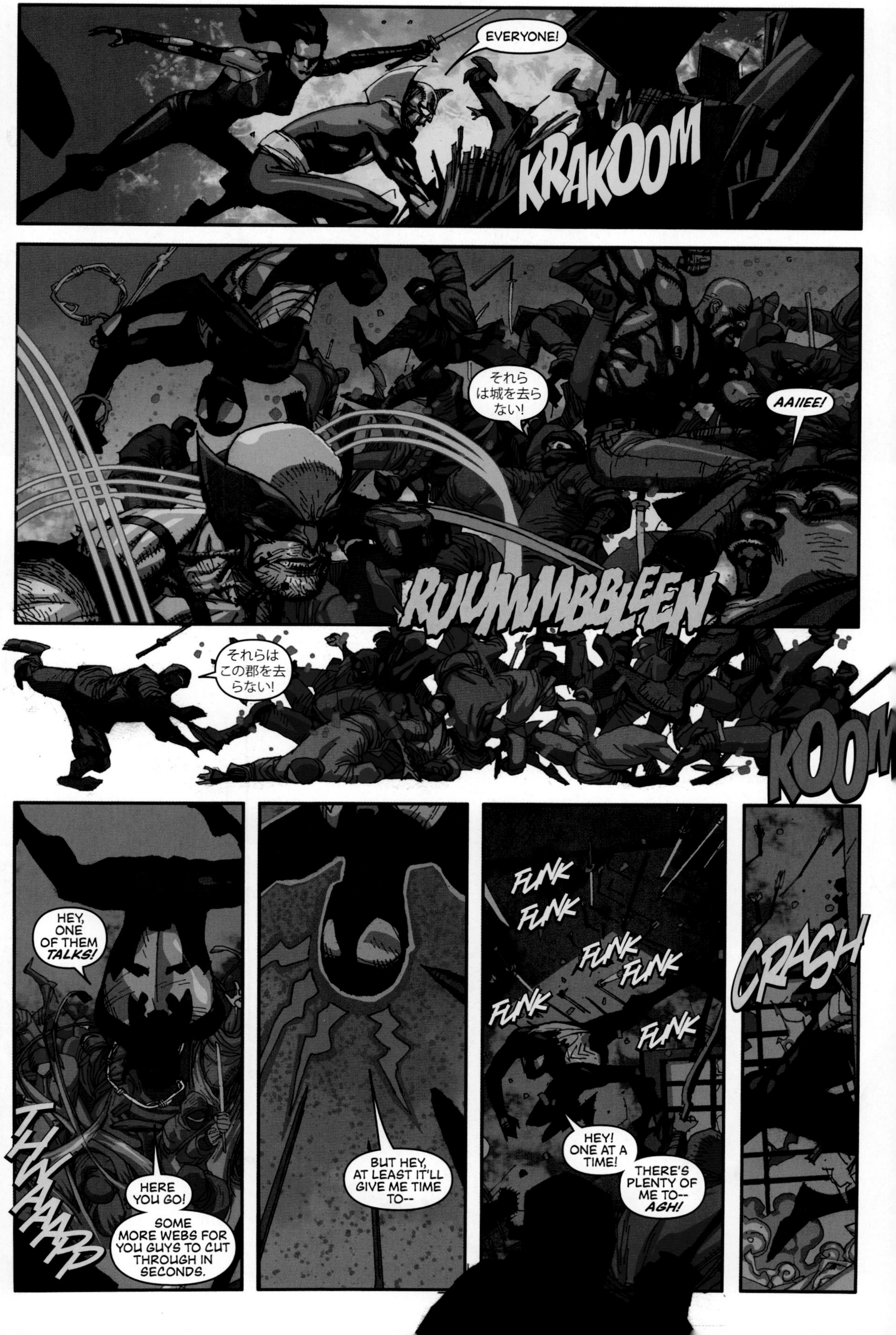
EVERYONE!
KRAKOOM
それらは城を去らない!
AAIIEE!
RUUMMBBLEEN
それらはこの郡を去らない!
KOOM
HEY, ONE OF THEM *TALKS!*
THWAAAPP
HERE YOU GO!
SOME MORE WEBS FOR YOU GUYS TO CUT THROUGH IN SECONDS.
BUT HEY, AT LEAST IT'LL GIVE ME TIME TO--
FUNK
FUNK
FUNK
FUNK
FUNK
FUNK
HEY! ONE AT A TIME!
THERE'S PLENTY OF ME TO-- *AGH!*
CRASH

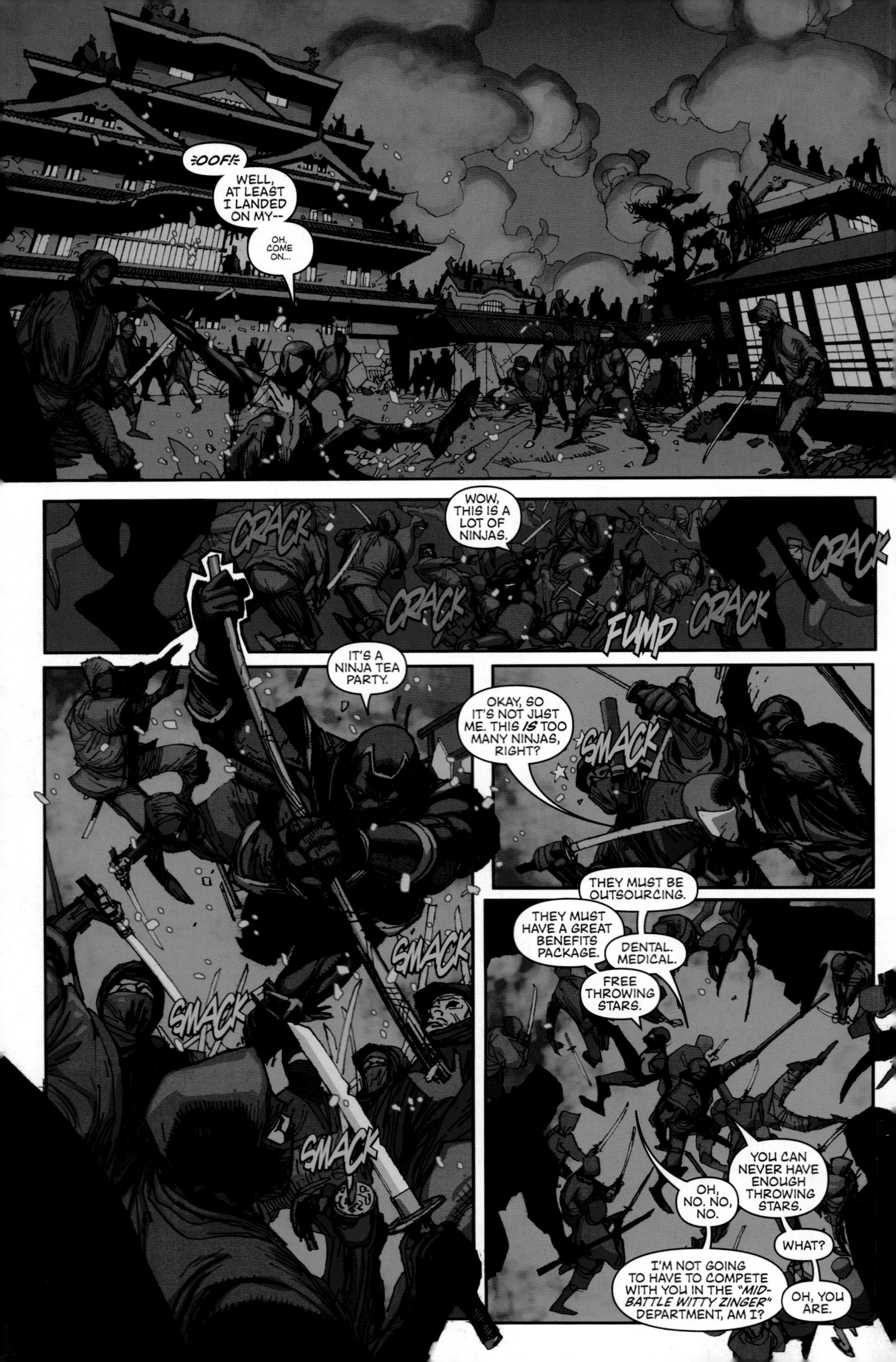
OOF!
WELL, AT LEAST I LANDED ON MY--
OH, COME ON...
CRACK
WOW, THIS IS A LOT OF NINJAS.
CRACK
FUMP
CRACK
CRACK
IT'S A NINJA TEA PARTY.
SMACK
SMACK
SMACK
OKAY, SO IT'S NOT JUST ME. THIS *IS* TOO MANY NINJAS, RIGHT?
SMACK
THEY MUST BE OUTSOURCING.
THEY MUST HAVE A GREAT BENEFITS PACKAGE.
DENTAL. MEDICAL.
FREE THROWING STARS.
YOU CAN NEVER HAVE ENOUGH THROWING STARS.
OH, NO. NO, NO.
I'M NOT GOING TO HAVE TO COMPETE WITH YOU IN THE *"MID-BATTLE WITTY ZINGER"* DEPARTMENT, AM I?
WHAT?
OH, YOU ARE.

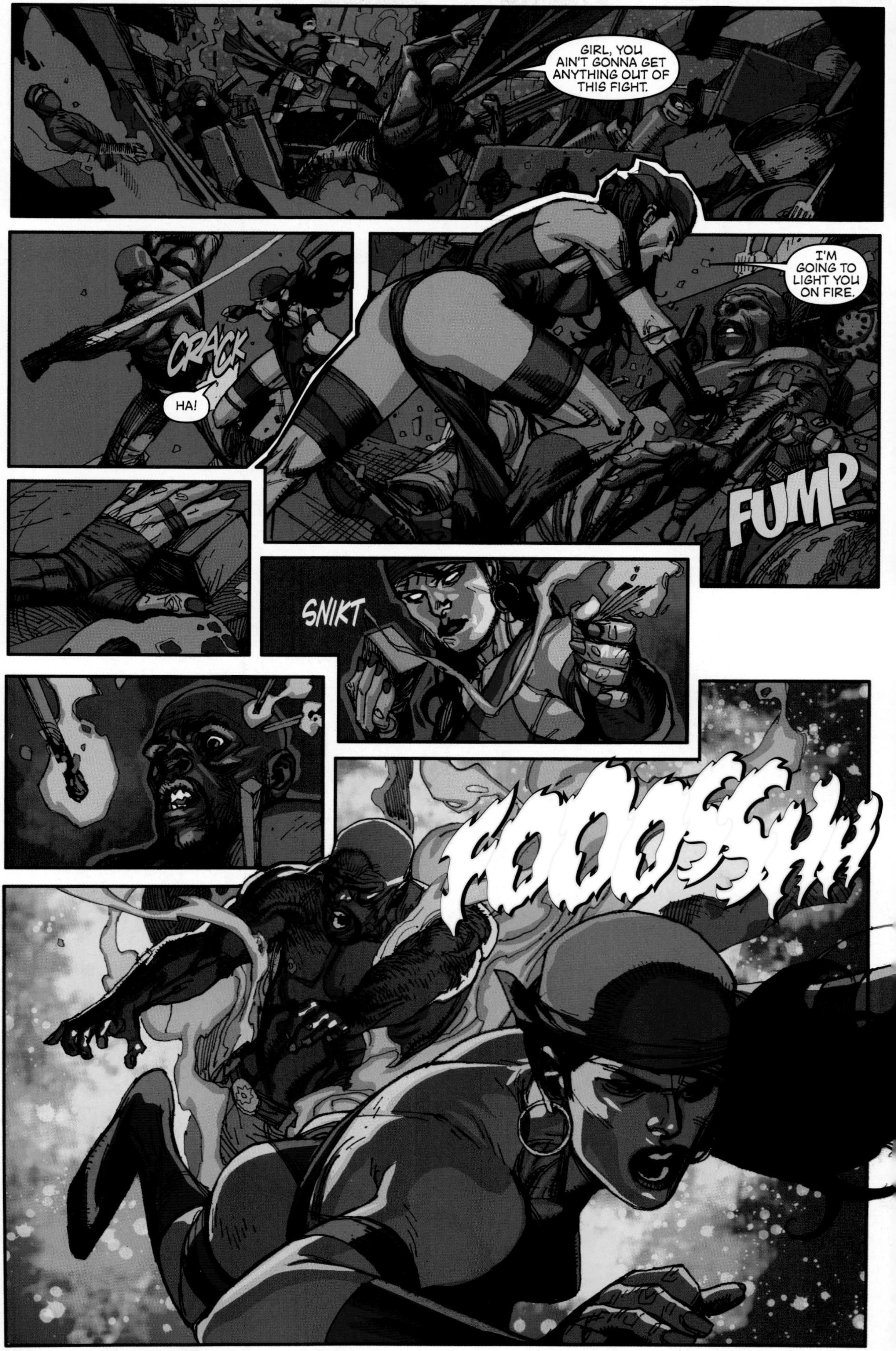

GIRL, YOU AIN'T GONNA GET ANYTHING OUT OF THIS FIGHT.
CRACK
HA!
I'M GOING TO LIGHT YOU ON FIRE.
FUMP
SNIKT
FOOOSH

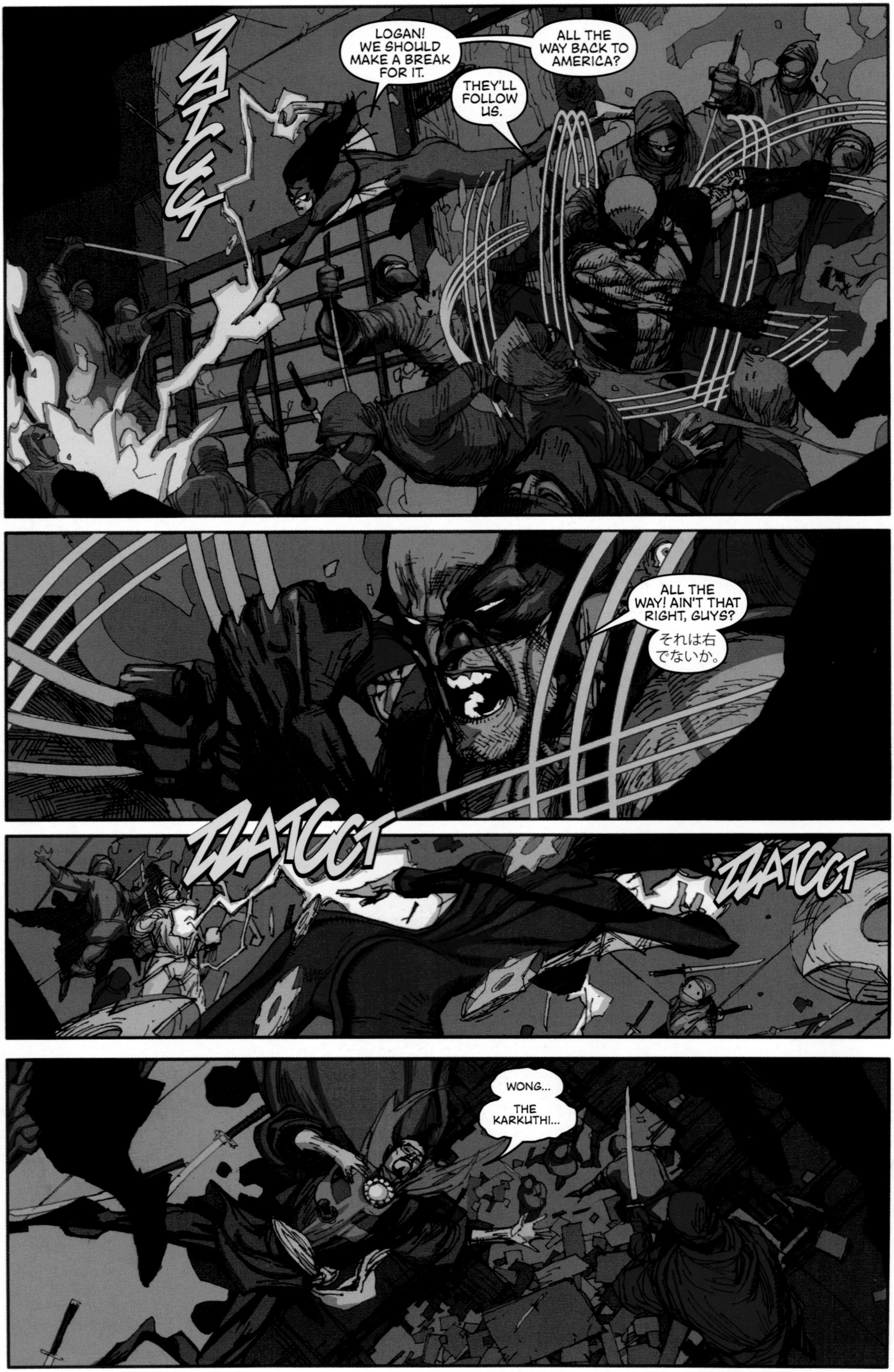
LOGAN! WE SHOULD MAKE A BREAK FOR IT.
ALL THE WAY BACK TO AMERICA?
THEY'LL FOLLOW US.
ALL THE WAY! AIN'T THAT RIGHT, GUYS?
それは右でないか。
ZZATCCT
ZZATCCT
WONG...
THE KARKUTHI...

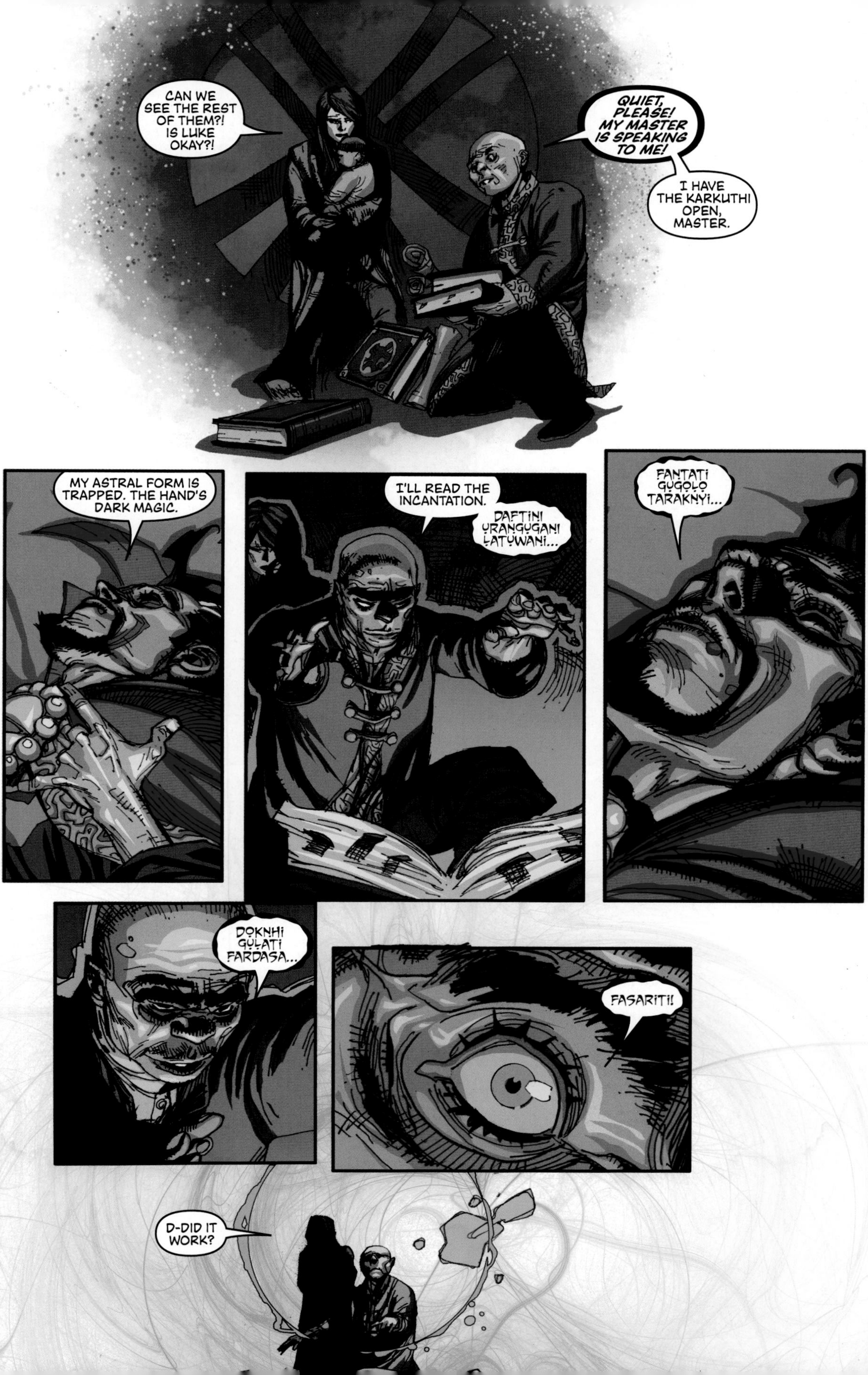
CAN WE SEE THE REST OF THEM?! IS LUKE OKAY?!
QUIET, PLEASE! MY MASTER IS SPEAKING TO ME!
I HAVE THE KARKUTHI OPEN, MASTER.
MY ASTRAL FORM IS TRAPPED. THE HAND'S DARK MAGIC.
I'LL READ THE INCANTATION.
DAFTINI URANGUGANI LATUWANI...
FANTATI GUGOLO TARAKNYI...
DOKNHI GULATI FARDASA...
FASARITI!
D-DID IT WORK?

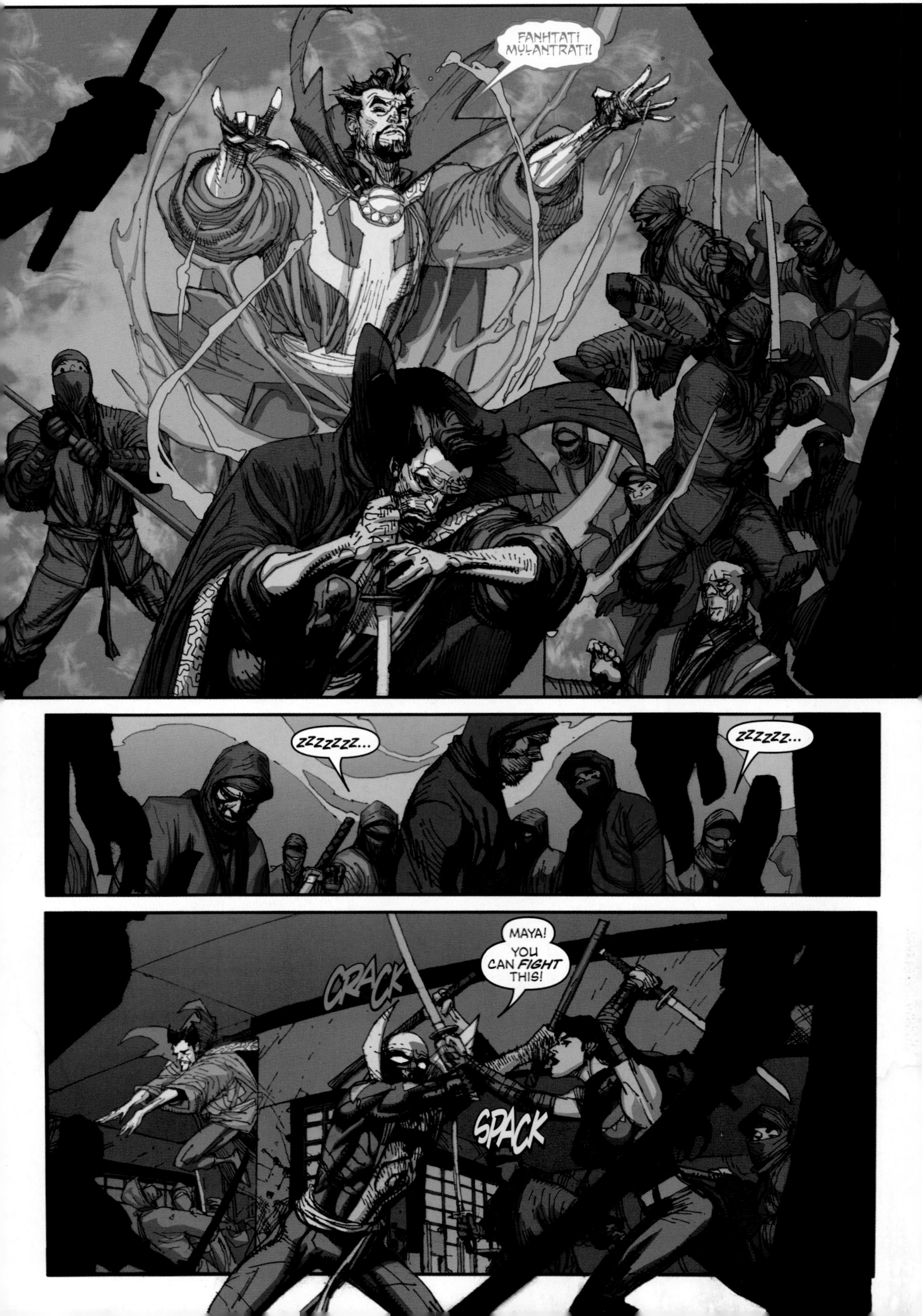
FANHTATI MULANTRATI!
ZZZZZZZ...
ZZZZZZ...
CRACK
MAYA! YOU CAN *FIGHT* THIS!
SPACK

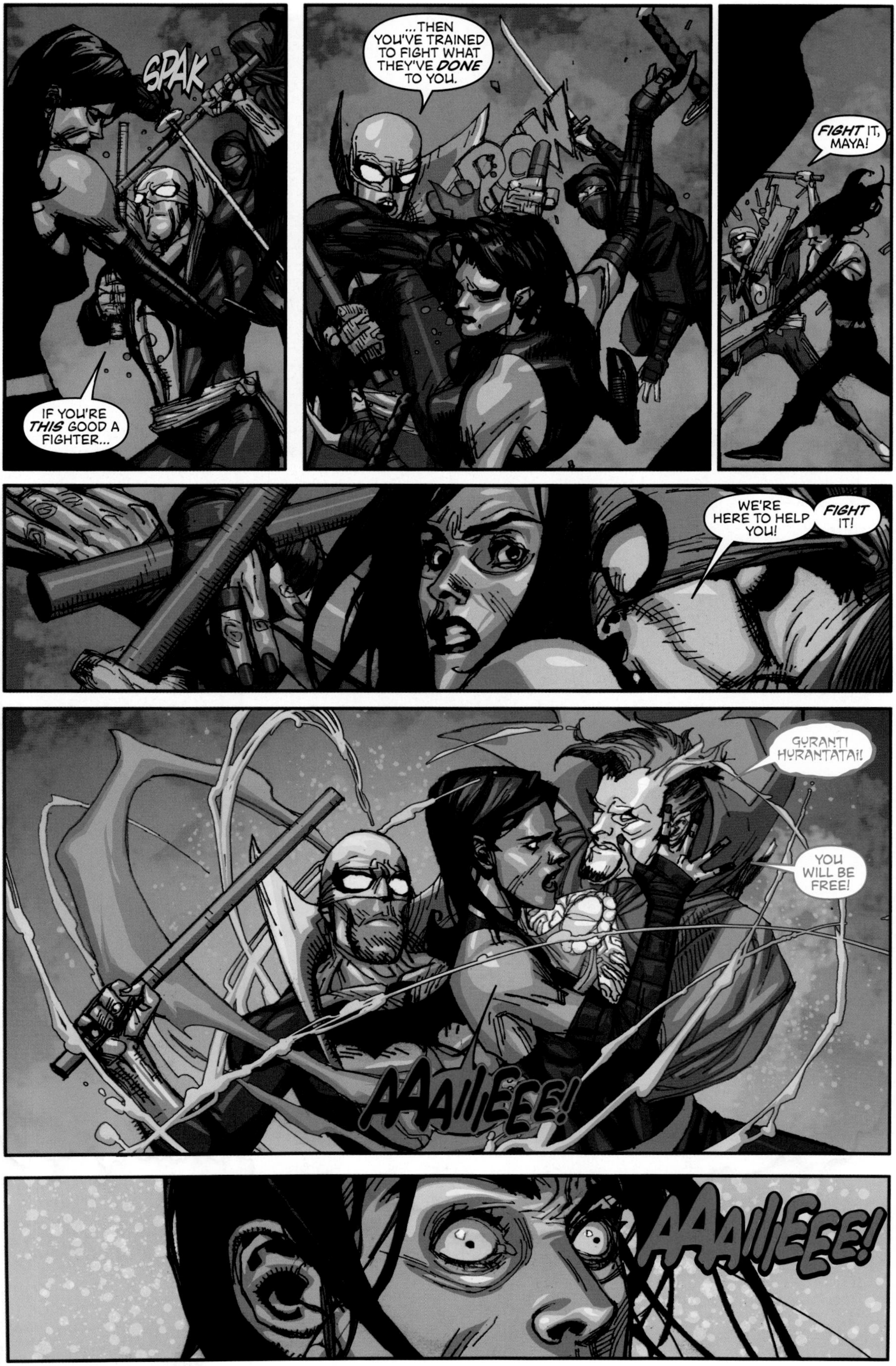
SPAK
IF YOU'RE THIS GOOD A FIGHTER...
...THEN YOU'VE TRAINED TO FIGHT WHAT THEY'VE DONE TO YOU.
FIGHT IT, MAYA!
WE'RE HERE TO HELP YOU!
FIGHT IT!
GURANTI HURANTATAI!
YOU WILL BE FREE!
AAAIIIEEE!
AAAIIIEEE!

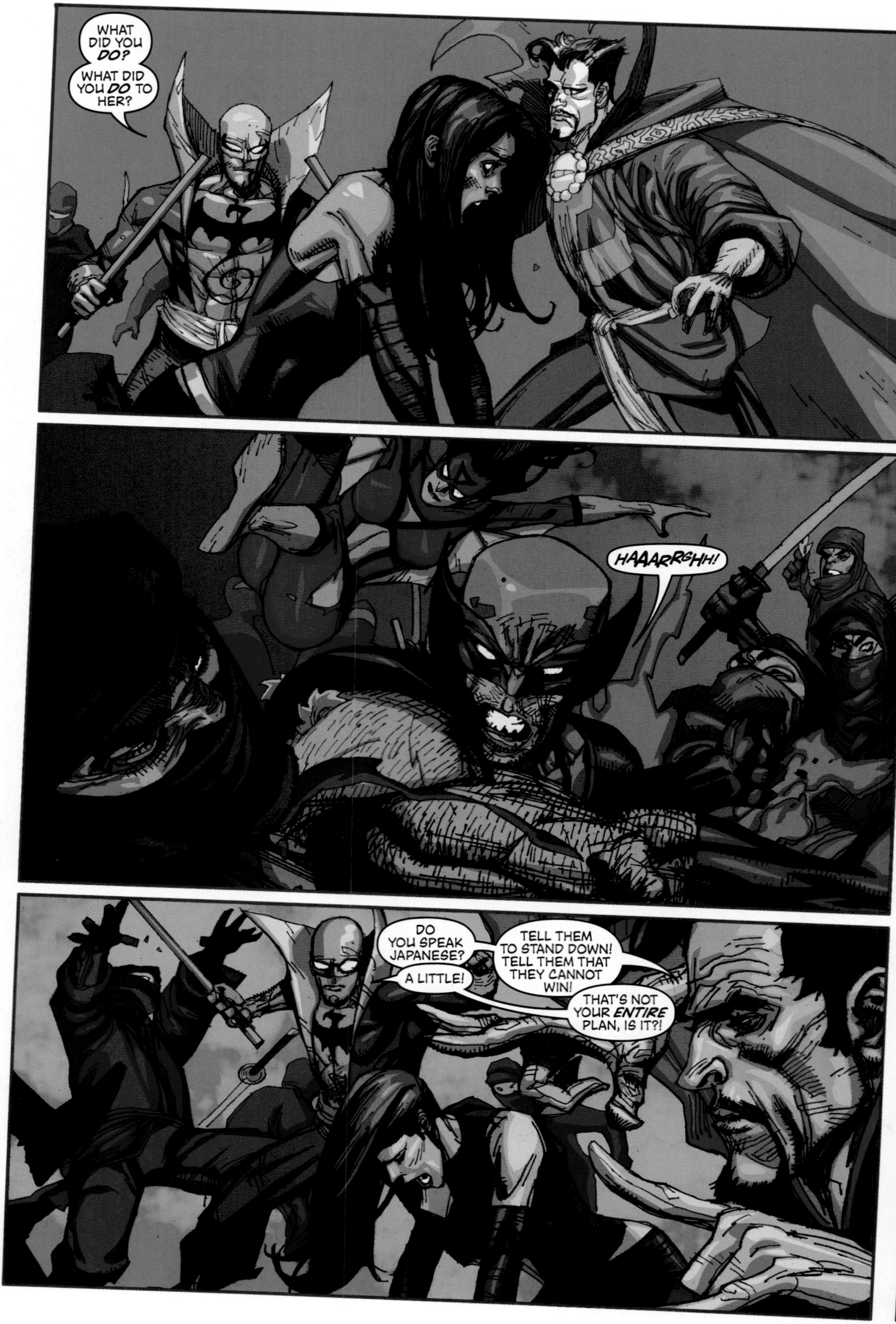
WHAT DID YOU *DO*? WHAT DID YOU *DO* TO HER?
HAAARRGHH!
DO YOU SPEAK JAPANESE?
A LITTLE!
TELL THEM TO STAND DOWN! TELL THEM THAT THEY CANNOT WIN!
THAT'S NOT YOUR *ENTIRE* PLAN, IS IT?!

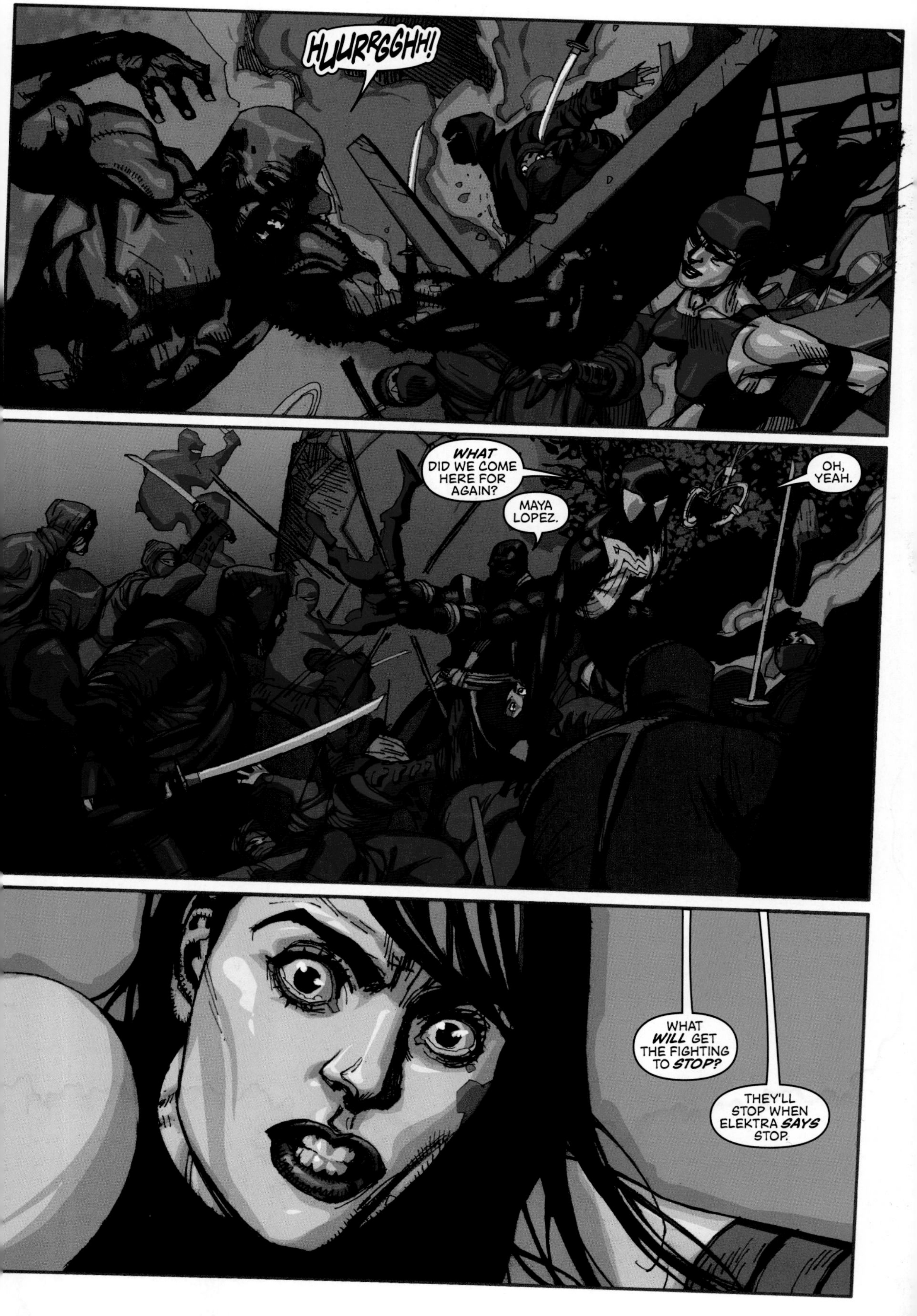
HUURRGGHH!
WHAT DID WE COME HERE FOR AGAIN?
MAYA LOPEZ.
OH, YEAH.
WHAT WILL GET THE FIGHTING TO STOP?
THEY'LL STOP WHEN ELEKTRA SAYS STOP.

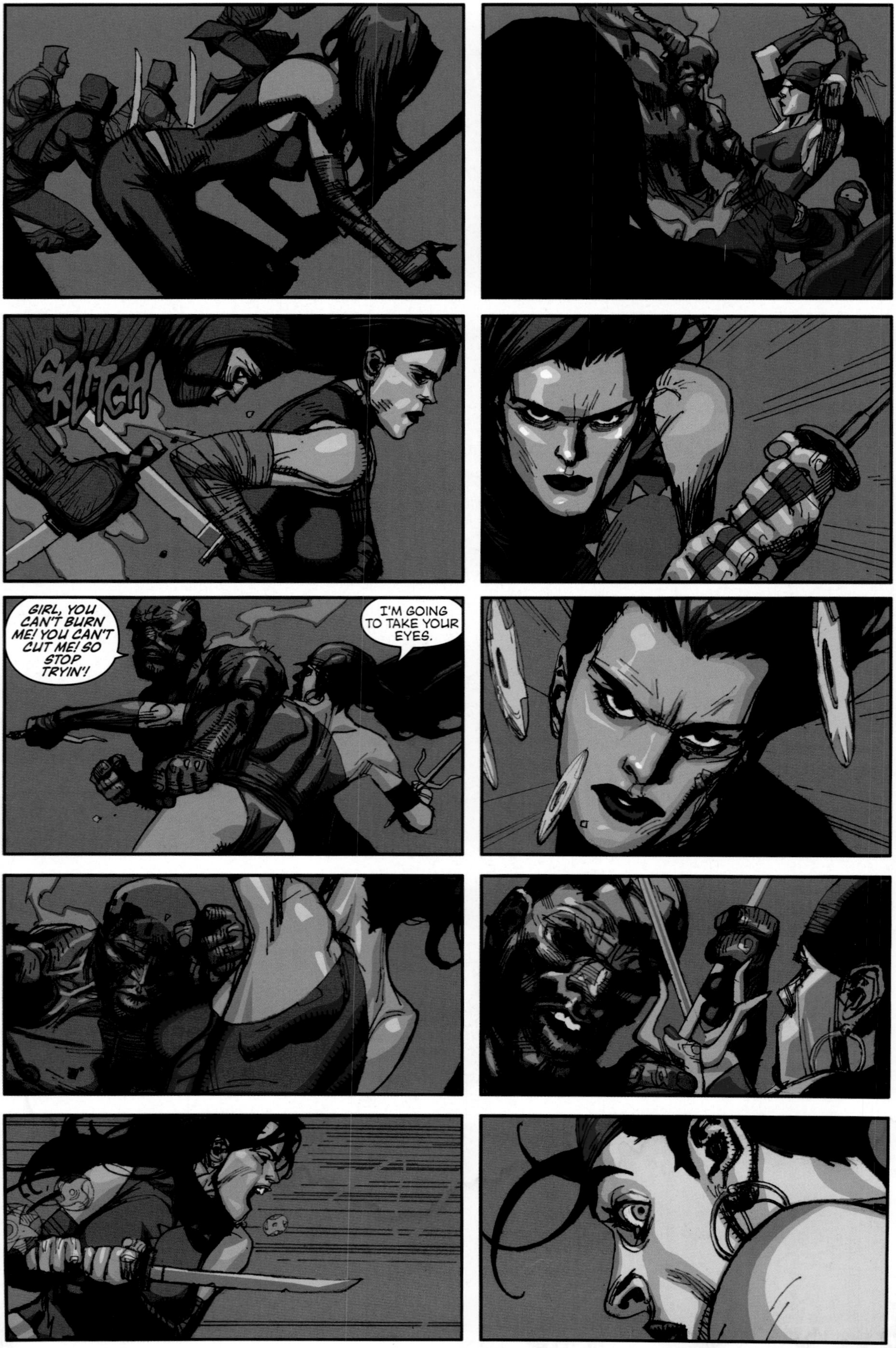
SKLITCH
GIRL, YOU CAN'T BURN ME! YOU CAN'T CUT ME! SO STOP TRYIN'!
I'M GOING TO TAKE YOUR EYES.

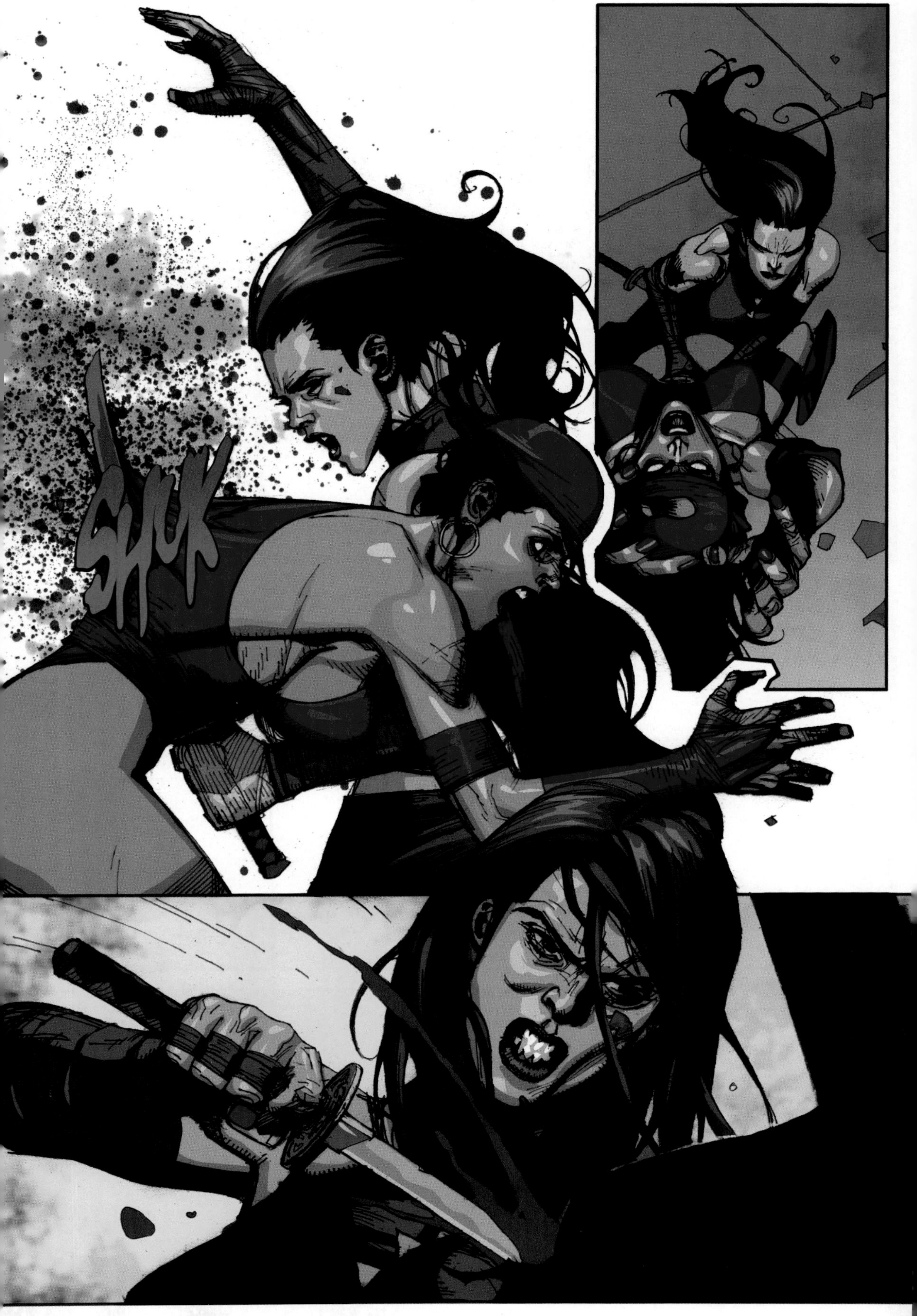
SHUK

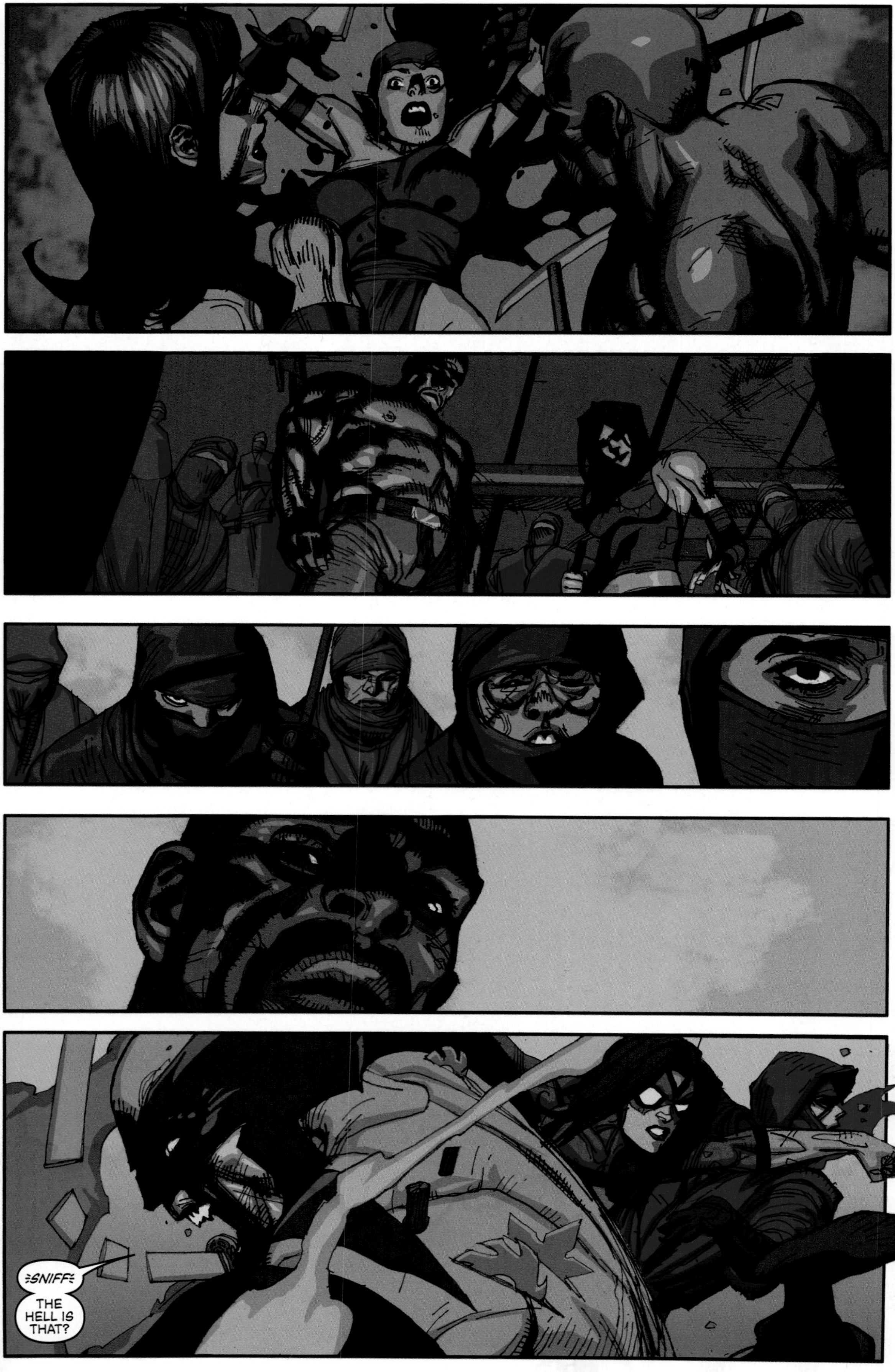
SNIFF
THE HELL IS THAT?

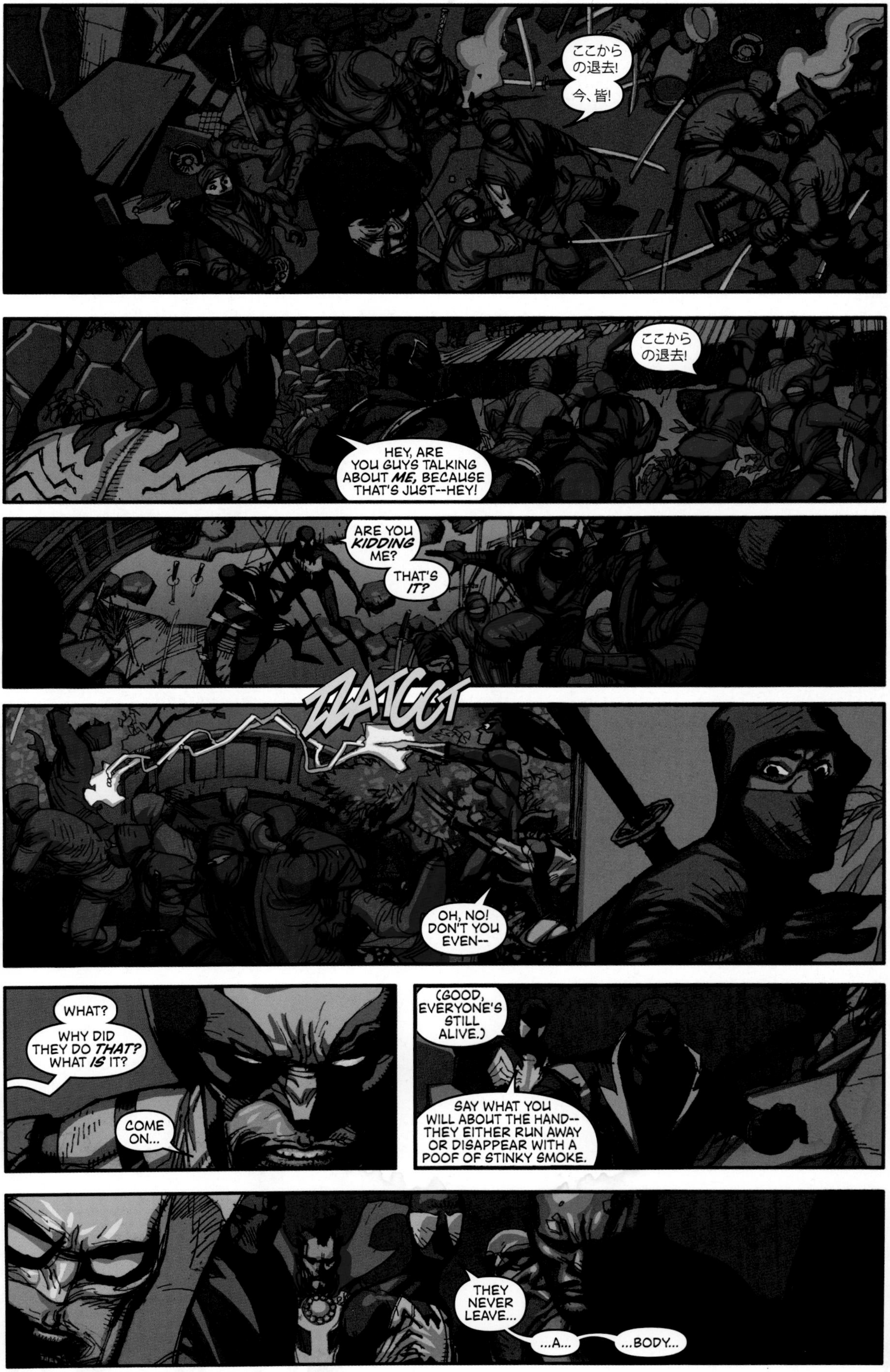
ここから
の退去!
今、皆!
ここから
の退去!
HEY, ARE YOU GUYS TALKING ABOUT *ME,* BECAUSE THAT'S JUST--HEY!
ARE YOU *KIDDING* ME?
THAT'S *IT?*
TZZATCCT
OH, NO! DON'T YOU EVEN--
WHAT?
WHY DID THEY DO *THAT?* WHAT *IS* IT?
COME ON...
(GOOD, EVERYONE'S STILL ALIVE.)
SAY WHAT YOU WILL ABOUT THE HAND-- THEY EITHER RUN AWAY OR DISAPPEAR WITH A POOF OF STINKY SMOKE.
THEY NEVER LEAVE...
...A...
...BODY...

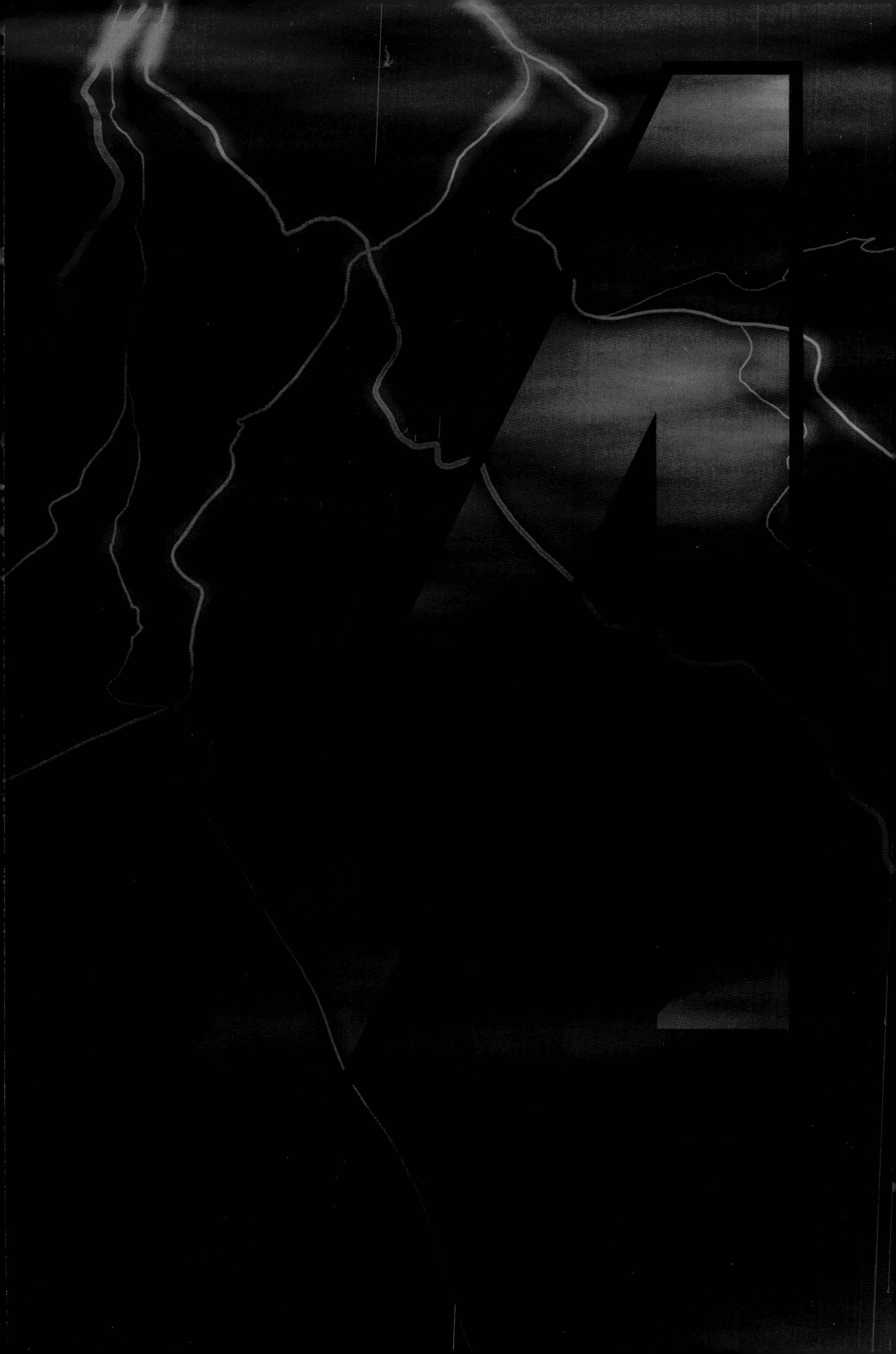

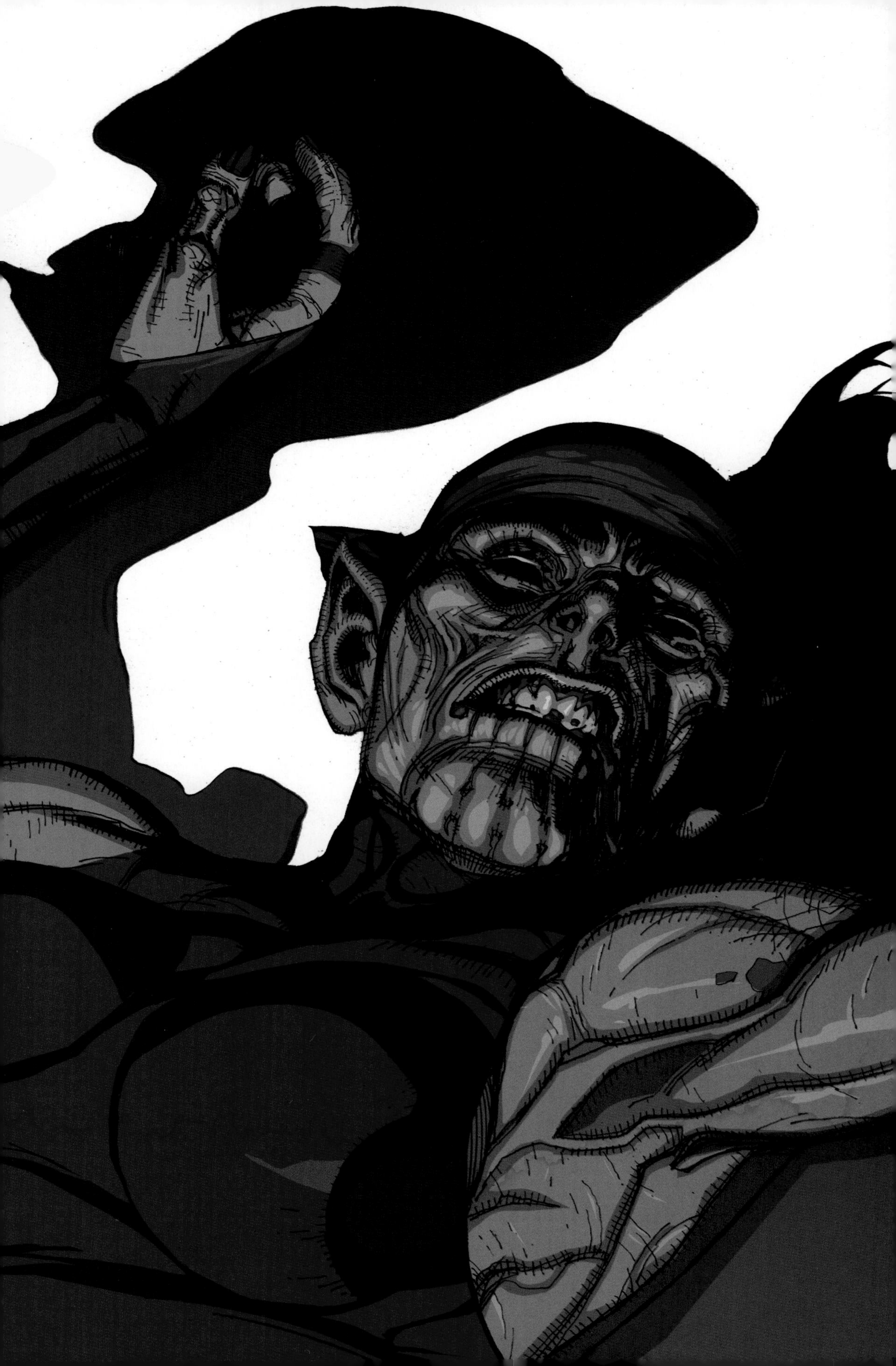

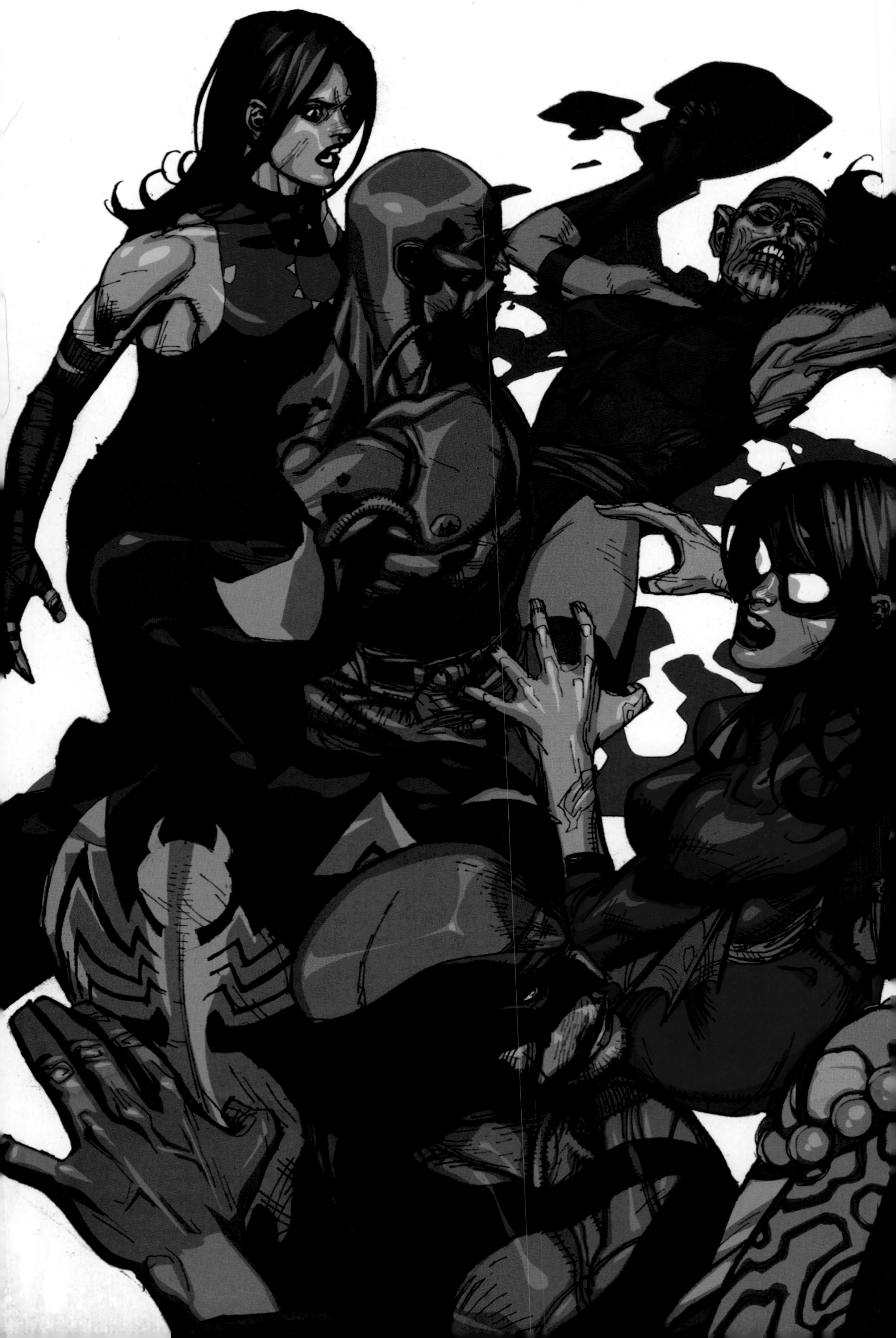

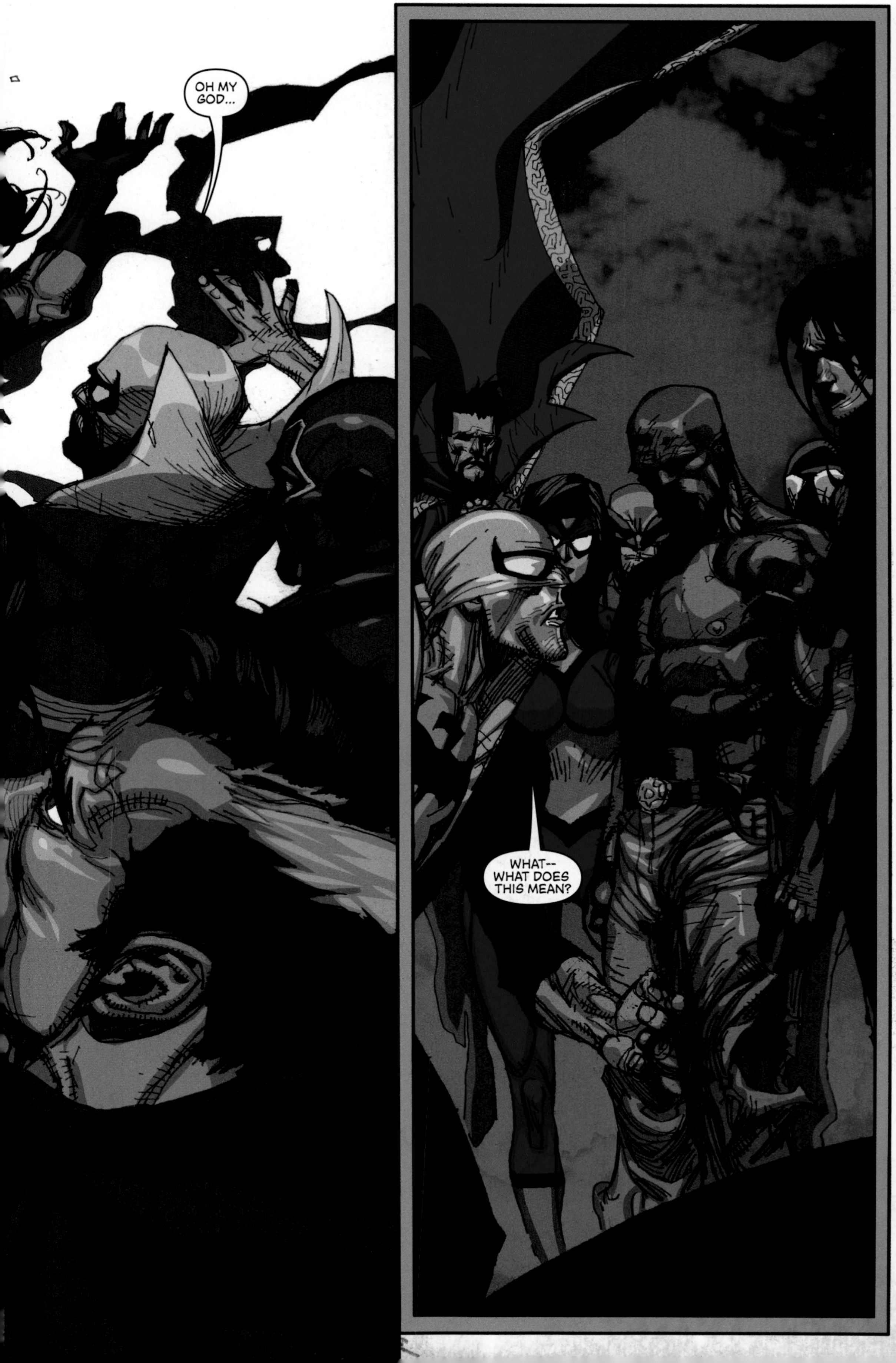
OH MY GOD...
WHAT-- WHAT DOES THIS MEAN?

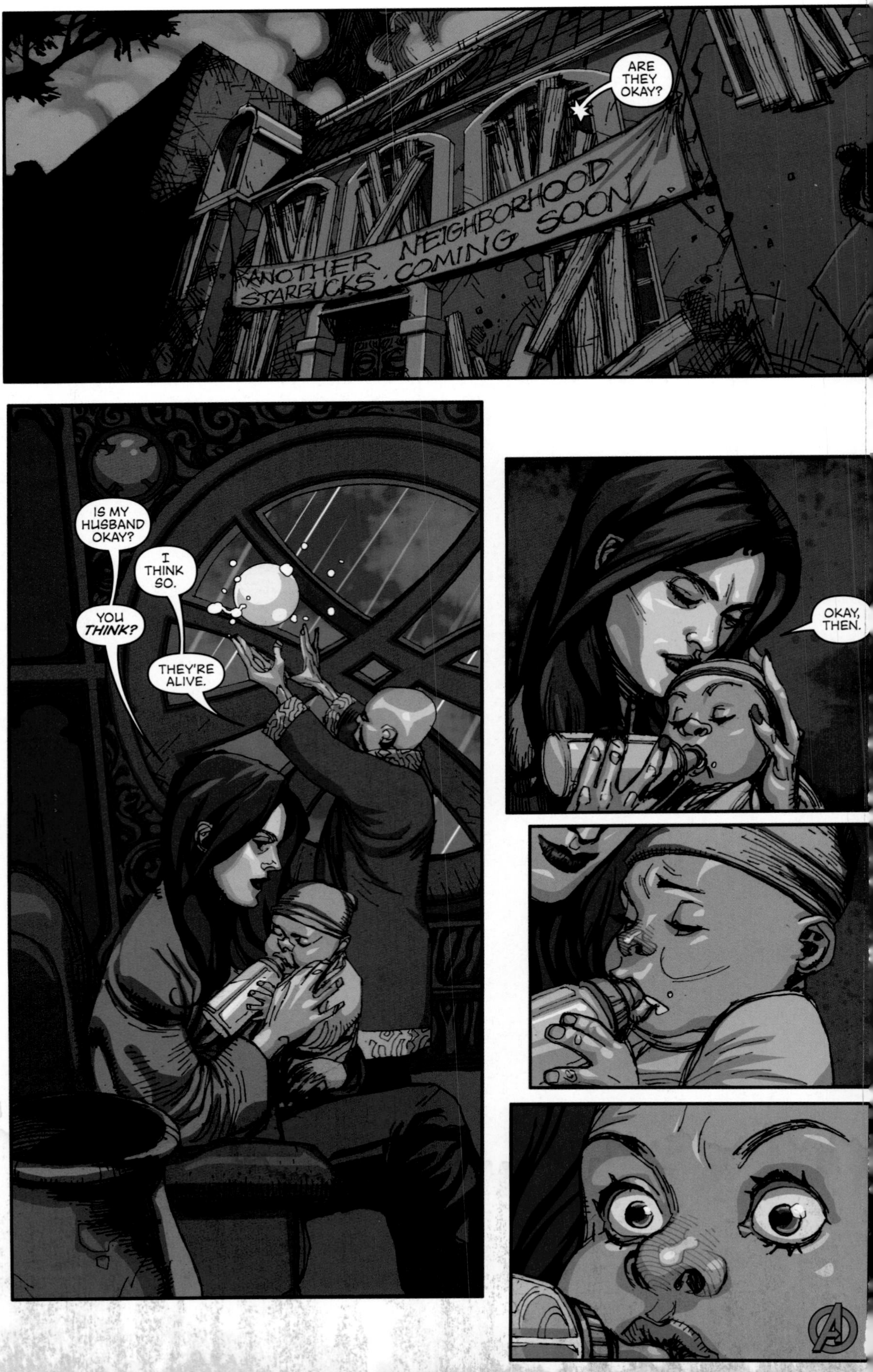
ARE THEY OKAY?
ANOTHER NEIGHBORHOOD STARBUCKS COMING SOON
IS MY HUSBAND OKAY?
I THINK SO.
YOU *THINK?*
THEY'RE ALIVE.
OKAY, THEN.